EAST
TO AMERICA

OTHER BOOKS BY ROBERT A. WILSON

Japan Journal, 1855–1861, by Henry Heusken
(edited and translated from the French)

Genesis of the Meiji Government in Japan, 1868–1871

OTHER BOOKS BY BILL HOSOKAWA

Thirty-five Years in the Frying Pan

Thunder in the Rockies

The Two Worlds of Jim Yoshida

Nisei

The Uranium Age

EAST
TO AMERICA

A History of the Japanese in the United States

by
Robert A. Wilson
and
Bill Hosokawa

QUILL

NEW YORK • 1982

Library of Congress Cataloging in Publication Data

Wilson, Robert Arden, 1910-
   East to America.

   Originally published: New York: Morrow, 1980

   Includes bibliographical references and index.
   1. Japanese Americans—History.   I. Hosokawa, Bill.
II. Title.
E184.J3W54   1982   973'.04956   82-5278
ISBN 0-688-03695-3   AACR2
ISBN 0-688-00745-7 (pbk.)

Printed in the United States of America

First Quill Edition

1 2 3 4 5 6 7 8 9 10

Book Design by Michael Mauceri

*This volume is dedicated
to all those splendid Americans
whose roots sprang from Japan*

☙ Contents

9

᭰ Foreword

No volunteer organization or program has an easy time. By their nature they must struggle along, depending on the dedication, energy, and hours that volunteer workers can spare from their other concerns and obligations. But somehow, if the project is a worthy one, the work is completed.

That, in a paragraph, is the story of the Japanese American Research Project (JARP), now winding down after two decades of effort. But perhaps the JARP story goes back even farther.

Long years ago, about the turn of the century, numbers of young Japanese immigrants began to arrive in the United States, drawn by the same kinds of dreams and hopes that attracted other immigrant groups. Yet, in many respects the Japanese American experience was unusual. They came primarily as temporary sojourners and not as immigrants cutting familial ties to sink their roots into the New World's fertile soil. However, as time passed, substantial numbers of them changed their goals for complex reasons examined in this volume.

If the experience of these Japanese had been unusual through the first third of this century, it was made unique by the savage attack on Pearl Harbor in 1941. That event fulfilled a prophecy of war between the two nations, which had been the shibboleth of two generations of politicians and an unfailing circulation stimulant for the yellow press.

Such constant dinning on the public consciousness had inevitable consequences. In February of 1942, two and a half months after the outbreak of war, the United States government ordered the summary imprisonment of some 70,000 American citizens and 40,000 resident aliens of Japanese blood as a "military necessity." By the stroke of President Franklin Delano Roosevelt's pen, the writ of habeas corpus and extensive constitutional safeguards of human rights were arbitrarily suspended with a minimum of public reaction. Thus, the United States, locked in a war against Fascist oppression, was involved in some rather peculiar and deplorable actions of its own.

After the war ended, it began to seem that the experience of the Japanese Americans, who had marched into U.S.-style concentration camps as their sacrifice to hasten victory, would become a buried chapter of the nation's history. That must not be.

This was when the long-nurtured idea of compiling a history of Japanese Americans was given impetus. The Japanese American Citizens League, a national civic organization with headquarters in San Francisco, had as one of its vague future projects a history of the Issei, meaning "first generation"—our immigrant forefathers.

I was national JACL president for the 1958–60 term when my board agreed that the feasibility of such a project, nebulous as it was, was worth further study. I was soon to discover the power of academia in enhancing such an idea.

Word came from Dr. T. Scott Miyakawa of Boston University that his colleagues—among them Oscar Handlin, Clyde Kluckhohn, Edwin O. Reischauer of Harvard, and Robert MacIver of Columbia University—were encouraging us to go ahead. They pointed out the crucial "gap" that needed to be filled in American education concerning the history and facts about immigrant groups from Asia, the Japanese in particular. A gap it was, indeed, through which racism, propelled by wartime hysteria, had scarred the Constitution and the conscience of the American people.

At the end of my term JACL's National Council mandated the history project. My successor, Frank Chuman of Los Angeles, appointed me to chair the effort. That was in 1960 at the national convention in Sacramento. I named my committee: Mike Masaoka of Washington, D.C.; Yone Satoda and Sim Togasaki of San Francisco; Masao Satow, national director of JACL; Akiji Yoshimura of Colusa, California; Bill Hosokawa of Denver; and Katsuma Mukaeda and Gongoro Nakamura, the Issei elder statesmen from Los Angeles.

For funds to support the project we turned to the entire Japanese American community. The response was gratifying. Many made contributions in memory of their immigrant parents. Responding to the need to record their story, the community contributed more than $200,000, an impressive sum in those times.

Our first meeting as a committee was held during a lunch break at the JACL convention in Seattle in 1962. We adjourned to a restaurant and, over coffee, Togasaki, JACL's venerable financial wizard chairing the fund drive, drafted a tentative budget on the back of an envelope. The project was beginning to take shape.

But we soon ran into problems in defining the scope of the project. The committee was agreed that it should chronicle the story of the Japanese Americans, but among those who had supported us there was no consensus about what that story was and how it should be told. My original concept was simply to commission a qualified writer to research the subject and produce a readable volume focusing on the drama, the struggles, and the tears and laughter in the experiences of a little-known American minority. Our friends in the academic community had in mind a vastly more ambitious program. They argued for a systematic study which would produce, in addition to the human materials we sought, the "hard" sociological and economic data necessary to measure progress and to put old myths to rest.

The "Outline of the Study" prepared at our request by Dr. Miyakawa listed three main objectives: (1) Conduct a sociological survey and research based on a national sampling of Issei and their Nisei descendants; (2) produce a definitive, scholarly volume on the history of the Japanese Americans; (3) assemble a documentary collection, including oral histories and memorabilia, which would be preserved at some university. There was no denying the importance of such a program, and the need to find an academic "home" for the study became obvious.

Because of the large numbers of Japanese Americans living in Southern California, the University of California at Los Angeles was a likely candidate. Frank Chuman approached UCLA, his alma mater, and through the good offices of Regent Ralph P. Merritt and Chancellor Franklin Murphy, an agreement was reached early in 1963. JACL made a grant of $100,000 to UCLA which, as the host institution, took on co-sponsorship of what was to become known as the Japanese American Research Project. For its part, UCLA formed an advisory board chaired by Dr. Franklin P. Rolfe, dean of the College of Arts and Sciences, and an executive committee chaired by Dr. George Mowry, dean of Social Sciences. Dr. Miyakawa, on leave from Boston University, was named project director. Dr. Robert A. Wilson of the history department, a Japan scholar, was appointed to administer the fund. The JARP committee served as the contact between UCLA and the JACL membership. Thus, we were introduced to a trail-blazing enterprise—a partnership between a major university and an ethnic group seeking to learn more about itself and to share that knowledge with others.

Dr. Gladys Ishida Stone, a research associate in sociology, and her husband, Dr. Gregg Stone of the University of Minnesota, undertook construction of the all-important Issei survey. To gather as much information as possible before time took its inevitable toll on the surviving Issei, they designed a seventy-three–page questionnaire requiring an average of nine hours to administer. The massive and often baffling task of netting a national sample of more than a thousand comprehensive Issei interviews fell upon JACL chapters scattered throughout the nation with countless local volunteers compiling residence lists and conducting bilingual interviews. Without their help the survey would not have been possible.

Meanwhile, Dr. Miyakawa and UCLA were successful in obtaining a $140,000 grant from the Carnegie Corporation to ensure completion of the research project. Joe Grant Masaoka was hired to expedite the collection of documentary materials. He and Dr. Wilson traveled widely, taping interviews, gathering and assembling a mass of material. All of this collection—some 840 cases, the largest of its kind—has been classified and catalogued at the UCLA Research Library under the direction of chief librarian Robert Vosper. Joe Grant Masaoka carried out his duties with great enthusiasm and dedication and his untimely death in 1970 was a grievous loss.

When Dr. Miyakawa returned to Boston in 1966, Dr. Gene N. Levine, a survey specialist, was named to head the sociological study and Dr. Wilson became head of the historical branch of the project. JACL's history project was becoming far more comprehensive than its originators dreamed possible. But its value was attested to by a $400,000 grant from the National Institute of Mental Health to complete the Issei and Nisei sociological surveys and expand the latter to include the Sansei generation. With Dr. Levine as principal investigator, the study involved 1,047 Issei, their 2,339 Nisei offspring and 840 grandchildren eighteen years of age and older. His findings will be contained in his treatise, *The Japanese American Community: A Three-Generation Study,* co-authored by Dr. Robert Colbert Rhodes, scheduled for publication by Praeger Special Studies in New York. Its companion study also directed by Dr. Levine, *The Economic Basis of Ethnic Solidarity: A Study of the Japanese Americans,* by Dr. Edna Bonacich and Dr. John Modell, is forthcoming. Because of the depth of these studies and the unhurried pace of academia—which most of us were not accustomed to—there were long periods with no apparent progress. To fill this gap the JARP committee in 1967 commissioned two books, a "popular" history by

Bill Hosokawa, a journalist, and a "scholarly" book that would stand as an academic reference by Dr. Wilson.

Hosokawa resigned from the committee and took on the task of producing a book manuscript that, while historically accurate, would capture the broad, dramatic sweep of the Japanese American experience. His *NISEI: The Quiet Americans* was published in 1969 by William Morrow and Company, Inc. It enjoyed remarkable success, soon appeared in quality paperback, and was widely distributed. It became assigned reading in college ethnic-history classes, and countless term papers were composed with *Nisei* as the primary source of information. In that it circulated the story of Japanese Americans, the book admirably met JARP's primary goal. But additionally, it served two unanticipated purposes. As a commercial success it helped to replenish JARP's treasury so that other projects could be assisted, and it made publishers aware of Japanese American history while encouraging Japanese Americans themselves to write for publication. Hosokawa reviewed several dozen book manuscripts for aspiring writers, several of whom were published.

With JARP's encouragement, or under its auspices, several other books and monographs on Japanese Americans were prepared and published. JARP commissioned Frank Chuman's *The Bamboo People,* an exhaustive study of the legal history of Japanese Americans, which was published in 1976 by Publisher's Inc. Completed, but still unpublished, is Dr. Masakazu Iwata's *Planted in Good Soil: Issei Contributions to U.S. Agriculture,* a remarkably detailed review of the Issei experience in farming. Both of these valuable studies were given impetus by Dr. Wilson. Two other books need to be mentioned. Under JARP auspices was *East Across the Pacific: Historical and Sociological Studies of Japanese Immigration and Assimilation,* edited by Hilary Conroy and Dr. Miyakawa and published by CLIO Press in 1972. Also stemming from JARP was Dr. Modell's *The Economics and Politics of Racial Accommodation: The Japanese of Los Angeles, 1900–1942,* published by the University of Illinois Press in 1977.

Nearly two score scholarly papers and Ph.D. dissertations have been produced. Among them is one entitled *The Japanese American Community: A Study of Generational Changes in Ethnic Affiliation,* by Assistant Professor Darrel M. Montero, now of the University of Maryland. Ironically, news stories based on his study of a once-despised ethnic group referred to it as a "superminority." JARP also helped to fund Professor Yasuo Sakata's investigation of documents relating to Japanese Americans in Tokyo Foreign Ministry archives, and his translation of some of the more important papers.

The swelling mass of research materials both aided and hindered Dr. Wilson's efforts to produce the scholarly history. Keeping his manuscript reasonably concise became a necessity in view of escalating publishing costs. Wilson welcomed assistance from Hosokawa, a veteran editor, in shaping his manuscript to publisher's requirements. Thus, this volume, complete but concise, came to be published with Wilson and Hosokawa listed as joint authors. Their title, *East to America,* underlines the essence of the Japanese American story—a people who sailed eastward, not westward as the European immigrants had done, to a new life in the New World, with that difference carrying many profound implications which are treated in the book.

At the time the Japanese American community was asked to help fund the Issei History Project, donors of larger amounts were promised a copy of the scholarly volume as an expression of appreciation. This is that volume. It was a long time in coming, but members of my committee and I feel it was well worth the wait. With its publication the work of the committee has neared its end.

On behalf of the JARP committee and for myself, I wish to thank the donors for their generosity and patience. I also wish to take this means of thanking members of my committee for their loyalty and support, particularly Mike Masaoka and Yone Satoda for the key roles they have played from the very beginning, and my long-time JACL secretary, Sumi Shimizu, for her invaluable assistance.

SHIGEO WAKAMATSU

Chicago, Illinois
February 1, 1980

I ✿ The Earliest Sojourners

Their story lacks the epic elements that would inspire the pen of a Winston Churchill. No princes of church or state are found in it. Yet the history of the Japanese in the United States is an important and dramatic one told until recently only in fragments or from the posture of special pleading.

Their story is of a diligently tenacious people who wished only to be left alone to rear their families and work out their individual destinies. That the American majority for many decades denied them even this elementary dignity underscores the drama of their struggle and magnifies the dimensions of their ultimate triumph.

In both numbers and physical stature the Japanese were a small minority cast among the overwhelming mass of burly European immigrants. They compensated for their deficiencies with patience and endurance, accepting conditions which others found objectionable or unendurable. Two Japanese words describe the stubborn philosophy that enabled them to overcome: *gaman* and *gambare*. Both defy direct translation, for the depth of feeling in the original Japanese is lacking in the English equivalents. To accept *gaman* is to persevere, to endure the unendurable. The essence of *gambare* is contained in a contemporary expression—to hang tough. *Gaman* and *gambare*, plus much more, were the contributions of the Japanese to the cultural pluralism of America.

During the decades when immigration was predominantly from Northern Europe, there was a widespread notion that America was a melting pot which one day would produce a homogeneous culture and people. That has been changed by more recent realization that ours is a nation of minorities. While acculturation and integration do take place, the process is slow and often only partial. Many elements in the population retain aspects of ancestral culture which they find desirable or easily accommodated. Many observers regard this nation today as a complex made up of many only partly blended cultures.

The Japanese have contributed to this blending. Unbeknownst to many, the Japanese have exerted a subtle and—contrary to the real or imagined fears of generations of anti-Orientalists—usually propitious influence on the nature and quality of a broad spectrum of American life.

But for much of the century of the history of the Japanese in the United States, they were considered a sinister element, mistreated, discriminated against, and, as the ultimate irony, herded into wartime concentration camps on the grounds of their alleged unassimilability. Chinese immigrants, first on the scene, were the first to feel the sting of the West Coast's incipient anti-Oriental racism that kept political dynasties in office. The Japanese, who came to take over the jobs an earlier generation of Chinese had held, also inherited the prejudices.

This study will concentrate on modern immigrants from Japan and their descendants. However, there were a number of inadvertent immigrants in an earlier time thanks to the *Kuroshiwo,* the Black or Japan Current. This is a mysterious but powerful river rising in the tropical latitudes of the Western Pacific. It moves northward to about the parallel of Tokyo, then transcribes a great eastward arc which takes it off the Aleutians and then southward along the western coast of North America. It is perhaps the greatest of the ocean currents and it has exerted both a benign and baleful influence on Japan and its people. It moderates the climate of much of the islands and enriches the coastal fisheries. But it also lies in wait for unfortunate fishermen in disabled craft. Western whalers and clipper ships during the late eighteenth and early nineteenth centuries with surprising frequency encountered crippled Japanese junks helplessly adrift on the *Kuroshiwo.*[1]

No doubt most of the mariners aboard these frail craft would have perished had they not been rescued. But it would seem reasonable that some Japanese, through the centuries, made landfall on North America and struggled ashore, either to fall victim to the natives or settling among them. If indeed the distant ancestors of the American Indians made their way across a landbridge from Asia, the seafarers were in position to make a late contribution to the genetic pool.

This is conjecture. Entirely historical, however, is the story of a group of Japanese who reached Acapulco aboard a ship named the *San Buenaventura* in 1610.[2] The previous year Don Rodrigo de Vivero y Velasco, retiring governor-general of the Philippines, had left Manila aboard the galleon *San Francisco* en route to New Spain. A typhoon drove the ship onto the Japanese coast where it was destroyed. Don Rodrigo and many of his companions were rescued.

The Japanese offered the Spaniards use of a ship built by the Englishman, Will Adams. Renamed the *San Buenaventura,* the ship sailed for Acapulco in July, 1610, with a number of Japanese merchants as passengers. They returned to Japan a year later. This was almost a decade before the colonization of New England. These were the first Japanese, of whom we have written record, to set foot in the Western Hemsiphere.

The first Europeans to reach Japan probably were three Portuguese sailors. Accounts differ, but one version indicates they had engaged in an unsuccessful mutiny somewhere off Thailand, then known as Siam, escaped to a Chinese ship, and came ashore in Southern Kyushu in 1543. Six years later the famous Jesuit missionary, St. Francis Xavier, brought Christianity to Japan. During the next century Spain, Portugal, Holland, and Great Britain competed for trade and influence while the Japanese busily absorbed knowledge about the West. Tensions, however, grew between Japanese leaders and the various European visitors. By 1623, British traders left Japan, and a year later all Spaniards were expelled. In 1639 all Europeans except the Dutch were driven from the country. Japanese were forbidden to go abroad. Ocean-going ships owned by Japanese were destroyed, and the nation began more than two centuries of isolation. Trade with the Netherlands was permitted sporadically through Deshima, an island in the port of Nagasaki.

Government rules, however, could not block the flow of the *Kuro-shiwo.* How many junks drifted across the Pacific in its grip during the period of isolation is unknown. For most of those years there was no one on the Pacific Coast of North America to record their coming. We must leap forward two centuries in time to learn that a disabled Japanese junk had come aground near Cape Flattery on the Olympic Peninsula of Washington in March, 1833.[3] Only three of the crew had survived. They were quickly enslaved by Indians. Dr. John Mc-Laughlin, chief factor of the Hudson's Bay Company at Vancouver on the Columbia River, sent out a force to take custody of the castaways. Ultimately, the company returned the Japanese to the China coast.

Since foreign vessels were unwelcome in Japan, most of the Japanese rescued at sea by Western ships were put ashore in Hawaii or China. A few seem to have joined the crews of the rescue ships, eventually to be set free at their home ports. This may help to explain curious instances of Japanese reported in such an unlikely place as Columbia, South Carolina, in 1861.[4] Such a man may well have been a castaway who saw little possibility of returning to his homeland and settled down to make the best of his opportunities.

The stories of two such men are of particular interest. Their names are Nakahama Manjiro and Hamada Hikozo. Manjiro, or John Mung as he was known during his American odyssey, was the first Japanese in the United States of whom there is written record.[5] In 1841 he was rescued with four fellow fishermen from a Pacific islet where they had been marooned for six months. Ultimately, the master of the vessel, after dropping off Manjiro's companions at Honolulu, took him to Fairhaven, Massachusetts, where he was sent to school. Following a variety of adventures, Manjiro finally reached Kagoshima in Southern Kyushu after a ten-year absence from Japan. Fortunately for Japan, the authorities did not execute Manjiro, which was the penalty for going abroad. Before his death in 1898 he served his country in many important ways in a period during which Japan was making desperate efforts to catch up with the Western World. Manjiro, so far as we know, was the first Japanese to achieve a real command of English and his education and experience in the West enabled him to rise to eminence. Although he began life as a lowly fisherman, he was granted the right to use a family name. He chose Nakahama, the name of his native village.

Manjiro is not part of the immigrant story except in the sense that his decision to go on to New England with his rescuer marks him as an adventurer seeking his fortune rather than one intent upon hurrying back to his homeland. In this sense he was like the "birds of passage" among Japanese immigrants of later years—those who returned home to live after sojourns of varying length in the United States. But in another sense he was the forerunner of the students who, after the reopening of Japan by the Perry expedition, went or were sent abroad to learn the skills the nation needed to survive.

Hamada Hikozo (Joseph Heco) was also a bird of passage.[6] Rescued by Americans from a disabled junk in 1851, he and sixteen companions were brought to San Francisco. After a year they were sent to Hong Kong but they had no means of returning to Japan. Before long, Hikozo was back in San Francisco where B. C. Sanders, the collector of customs, took him under his protection. In 1853 he reached Baltimore with Sanders who enrolled him in a Cathloic school. There Hikozo was baptized Joseph Heco, the name by which he is best known. Heco seems to have spent a good deal of time traveling from one side of the continent to the other. By 1855, he was back in San Francisco. The financial panic that year left Sanders in difficulties, and Heco's formal education soon ended. Back in Baltimore, Heco was naturalized as an American citizen on July 7, 1858. Shortly afterward he joined the Brooks surveying expedition in the Pacific as a clerk. After a few months of service he went to China. By this time Japan had established relations with the United States. Heco found a position as unofficial interpreter for E. M. Dorr, the newly appointed American consul at Kanagawa, and returned once more to Japan.

At this point it is necessary to take note of Commodore Matthew Calbraith Perry's expedition that ended Japan's isolation. On July 8, 1853, Perry's fleet of four warships sailed into Edo (now Tokyo) Bay. Pointing his cannon at the Japanese, he suggested it was time to establish relations with the United States. President Millard Fillmore had commissioned Perry's mission in the interests of "friendship, commerce, a supply of coal and provisions, and protection for our shipwrecked people."

Despite the peaceful intent of the mission, Perry's ships were heavily armed. Two of them were the first coal-burning paddle-wheelers in U. S naval history. After a six-day stay, Perry left for South China waters, promising to return in the spring for an answer to the American overtures for a treaty.

This was, in effect, a manifestation of unabashed gunboat diplomacy but the Japanese were in no position to resist. The Tokugawa Shogunate, which had ruled the country for more than two centuries, was painfully aware of its weakness. It had little choice but to accede to American demands. Perry returned the following March as he had promised with a larger fleet. On March 31, 1854, Japan and the United States signed the Treaty of Kanagawa. Thus ended an era, and the modern Japan was born. Soon Japanese missions and groups of students would go abroad—the feudal government began issuing passports for foreign travel in 1866. But immigration as such would not begin in any numbers for more than three decades.

Although Manjiro was back in Japan at the time of Perry's visits, there is no record he played any direct part in the negotiations. Some sources indicate the Japanese authorities were still unsure of Manjiro's loyalty and kept him in the background. Joseph Heco, however, appears during the period in which details of Japan's new relationship with the United States were being worked out.

He was aboard the U.S.S. *Mississippi* when it dropped anchor at

Nagasaki on June 18, 1859. Among its passengers were Townsend Harris,* the first minister to Japan who shortly would go on to establish the U.S. legation in Edo; Consul Dorr, and his interpreter, the ubiquitous Heco. This was Heco's first visit to Japan since he left eight years earlier, but he returned as an American citizen and a Christian.

The paths of Heco and Manjiro crossed at least once. When in 1860 a Japanese mission was to be dispatched to Washington to ratify the commercial treaty negotiated by Harris, Manjiro was appointed a member of the staff. Leaders of the Japanese mission met with Consul Dorr aboard the *Kanrin Maru* in Edo Bay. Heco interpreted for the Americans and Manjiro for the Japanese.

By late 1861, Heco was back in the U.S. and early the following year he met President Lincoln in Washington. While in the capital he was able to get official appointment as interpreter for the Kanagawa consulate. He returned to his duties late in 1862 and worked about a year before resigning to go into business. In June of 1864 he founded *Kaigai Shimbun*, the first privately published Japanese-language newspaper. Japanese officials dealt with Heco as an American citizen and he seems to have derived both status and security from it.

Although both Heco and Manjiro were in the United States for considerable periods, neither is a statistic in U.S. immigration records. In fact, early U.S. statistics for the Japanese present many difficulties and cannot be used with confidence. It seems certain that many Japanese who traveled as steerage passengers were listed as Chinese. Between 1871 and 1882, the only Japanese recorded as arriving in the United States entered Atlantic ports. No Japanese were noted as arriving in San Francisco during those years and that is obviously incorrect.

A brief civil war preceded the restoration of Japanese imperial rule in 1868 and some who had fought on the wrong side fled to the United States to seek political sanctuary for a short time. Presumably, most of them returned when it became apparent no reprisals would be made. We know that a group of Japanese political refugees arrived in San Francisco in 1868 and settled for a time in Alameda County, but they do not appear in immigration statistics for that year.

From other records it has been determined that at least two Japanese arrived in the United States in 1861. They probably were the

---

* Harris had served as the U.S. consul general since August, 1856, in Shimoda. He was at the time returning from a furlough to China during which he was notified of his elevation to minister to Japan.

first to enter this country other than by accident and with the intention of remaining for a while. The first is nameless; he appears to have been a servant who arrived with his employer in San Francisco. There is much better, but still inconclusive, record of the other, Suzuki Kinzo.

In the archives of the Oregon Historical Society is an unpublished manuscript by George Himes relating Suzuki's story. It apparently was written about the time of the Russo-Japanese War. Himes remembered Suzuki and, probably because of renewed interest in Japan, interviewed an aged Portland merchant who had been responsible for Suzuki's arrival. According to the Himes manuscript, the merchant visited Hakodate in 1861 on a trading voyage. He met Suzuki and learned feudal authorities had put a price on his head. He managed to get the fugitive aboard his ship and brought him to Portland.

Nothing is reported about Suzuki's origins, but since he had a family name, a right enjoyed at the time only by the elite, he probably was a member of the samurai class. He well may have belonged to the group opposing government policy which was the target of the Ansei Purge of 1861. In Portland, Suzuki entered high school and excelled in mathematics and history. He joined his benefactor's firm and was visiting San Francisco when by chance he met members of a Japanese mission en route to Washington. Some of them were old acquaintances. As a result of the meeting, he joined the Japanese foreign service and served, among other places, in London where his knowledge of English made him particularly useful. It should be noted the Himes manuscript is based largely on the memory of an elderly man.

Stories of other Japanese arriving in the United States in that early period are similarly poorly documented. Much of this history does not rise above oral tradition and folklore. Furthermore, researchers are frequently at the mercy of newspaper accounts, a notoriously weak reed upon which to lean in writing history.

For example, the story of Takahashi Umekichi can never be more than an account lying between possibility and probability. Professor Robert Wilson located Takahashi's headstone in 1967 in an abandoned cemetery in Reno, Nevada. According to the inscription, Takahashi entered this country in 1867 and died in 1907. The only other information about him comes from a 1961 newspaper interview in which Matsuda Takechiyo recalls a conversation he had with Takahashi in 1906.[7] What this amounts to is the recollections of two elderly men, one of whom may have wished to exaggerate his social origins, and the other reporting on experiences more than a half-century earlier.

According to this account, Takahashi was a samurai on the losing Tokugawa side in the civil war that preceded the Imperial Restoration. Takahashi fled to Kobe and found his way aboard an American ship which took him to a U.S. port, probably San Francisco. So far as is known, he remained in this country until his death, which would make him the only one of the early arrivals to live continuously in the United States. If the account of his experiences is reasonably correct, Takahashi has the best claim to being the first of the real immigrants.

Historians are on only slightly firmer ground regarding the Japanese referred to earlier who settled in Alameda County in 1868.[8] Even here the only evidence about this group appears in a San Francisco newspaper in mid-1869. It reported that more than a year previously an undisclosed number of Japanese "gentlemen of refinement and influence in their own counrty" had settled on the east side of San Francisco Bay. They apparently were aided by a Mr. Van Reed whose son, Eugene, was consul for the Hawaiian government in Japan. These Japanese were also Tokugawa supporters who sought refuge abroad. They leased land in Alameda County and sought the tutelage of local farmers. It appears likely that when they learned the new imperial government would not punish the defeated Tokugawa minions, they returned home. In any event, census takers in 1870 found no Japanese in Alameda County, and only eight in the entire San Francisco Bay area.

The single most important event in the Japan of this period was the restoration of the imperial family to power. For more than two centuries the country had been governed by regents, called Shogun, of the Tokugawa clan. Their influence was at a low ebb when Commodore Perry arrived, and the Shogunate was forced to negotiate with Western powers from a position of weakness. Loyalists pushed strongly for an Imperial Restoration. After the Tokugawa forces were routed, a teen-ager, Mutsuhito, later to take the name of Meiji, was restored to power in 1868. Thus, 1868 became the first year (or *gannen*) of the Meiji era. It was also the year that a group of Japanese laborers sailed without sanction for the kingdom of Hawaii. They were to become known as *Gannen Mono*, or "first-year people." Their experiences will be noted later in this chapter.

One year later a company of Japanese led by a German merchant, John Henry Schnell, arrived in California to set up what was to become known as the Wakamatsu Tea and Silk Colony. Today a state historical marker at Gold Hill in El Dorado County commemorates this ill-fated project. The party arrived on June 9, 1869, at the Granger ranch at Gold Hill which Schnell was in the process of buying.[9] The deed to the property was recorded in his name two weeks later.

John Henry Schnell and his brother, Edward, were from Darmstadt in the South German state of Hesse. They had gone to Japan as traders and became involved with the pro-Tokugawa forces during the Restoration struggle. John Henry was in Wakamatsu, the capital of Aizu fief, in 1868 when it was captured by imperial forces. The details are murky, but apparently he decided to take some of his defeated friends to California to begin a new life as growers of tea and silk. How he got them out of Japan remains a mystery. The government was still upset by the unauthorized departure of the *Gannen Mono*. The question of proper passports for them is part of the controversy and there is no record of passports being issued to Schnell's party.

The enterprise was in difficulties virtually from the beginning although there was no lack of encouragement from Americans. Newspaper articles and editorials beginning on May 27, 1869, indicate many Californians held high hopes for Schnell's group. Sericulture had been undertaken by Louis Provost at San Jose and business leaders were hopeful of establishing a sizable silk industry. When it was discovered the Wakamatsu colony had begun development of land beyond the boundaries of the property Schnell had purchased, Congress on February 27, 1871, approved a bill to "enable J. H. Schnell, of California, to enter and pay for a section of public land in California for his Tea Colony." [10]

A combination of factors probably contributed to the project's ultimate failure. One may have been Schnell's ineptness. Another probably was a climate inhospitable to tea plants and mulberry trees. Again, Aizu fief was not a tea-producing district and Schnell was relying on inexpert help in launching a difficult venture in an alien environment.

A deputy federal marshal in July, 1870, recorded the names of twenty-two Japanese, including Schnell's wife, at Gold Hill.[11] Curiously, the name of Okei is not included. It was the discovery of her grave in the early 1930's that aroused new interest in the Wakamatsu colony. The original stone over her grave bears this epitaph: "In memory of Okei, died 1871, age 19 years, a Japanese girl." She is believed to have been nursemaid for the two Schnell children.

The Japanese who accompanied Schnell were from a feudal society and must have regarded him as a patron or feudal lord to whom they owed allegiance and service. If so, Schnell did not reciprocate. At an unknown date, probably sometime in 1872, he left the colony with his wife and children and never returned. It is not known whether Schnell was using his own funds to finance the venture, or was drawing upon resources of the business he and Edward owned. One can only wonder whether Schnell abandoned the project as a result of his brother's refusal to put more company funds into the colony.

There is no clear picture of what ensued at Gold Hill. Possibly the Japanese appealed to Charles Wolcott Brooks, honorary consul of Japan in San Francisco. Unfortunately, Foreign Ministry records that might have shed light on this episode were destroyed in the Tokyo earthquake and fires of 1923. Most members of the colony disappeared from view. There is record of only two in addition to Okei. One, Sakurai Matsunosuke, made his living in the area as a carpenter for about thirty years. He is buried at Coloma, not far from Gold Hill. The other was Masumizu Kuninosuke, who died in 1915. A moss-covered headstone marks his grave at Colusa, California. A family of mixed black, white, Japanese, and Indian blood living in Sacramento claims Masumizu as an ancestor, making them the only known descendants of a member of the Wakamatsu colony still residing in the United States.[12]

Let us return briefly to the *Gannen Mono* who, with the exception of diplomatic missions, students, and shipwrecked fishermen, were the first Japanese to go to the New World of whom we have certain record. As noted earlier, their destination was Hawaii. Following the discovery of the islands by Captain Cook in 1778, Hawaii underwent swift and vast changes.[13] The islands developed into a major whaling base. But with the decline of the whaling industry following the discovery of petroleum, sugar plantations developed.[14] The native Polynesian population, put to work in the fields, was soon decimated by diseases introduced by the whites. Since Western ships had been calling in South China ports since late in the eighteenth century, it was natural that Chinese coolies should be recruited for plantation labor.

But this proved to be no long-range solution, partly because of the disinclination of the Chinese to remain on plantations, and partly because of the criticism of Americans and Britons who had been warring on the slave trade. The conditions under which some of the

Chinese were transported abroad differed little from those of the traffic in African blacks.

In 1865 an American businessman, Eugene M. Van Reed, was appointed the kingdom of Hawaii's consul general in Japan.[15] One of his assignments was to negotiate a treaty of friendship and commerce. To his consternation, the Japanese, showing their Confucian prejudice against merchants, rejected him as a proper person to sign such an important treaty. He also ran into trouble when the Hawaiian Board of Immigration instructed him to recruit Japanese contract laborers. Van Reed had begun his negotiations with a regime about to be overthrown. On May 9, 1868, the day before his laborers were to sail, the new imperial regime assumed authority in Yokohama and refused to sanction their departure.

After a week of fruitless effort, Van Reed without authority sent 149 Japanese (including six women and one child) to Hawaii aboard a British vessel. They arrived at Honolulu June 19.

Japanese authorities were incensed at this "kidnapping" of their citizens.[16] Soon Van Reed came under criticism by both the Japanese laborers and their employers. The men his agents recruited were from the streets of Yokohama, unaccustomed to farm labor, and proved to be inadequate workmen. Many of the plantation overseers were former seafarers who brought a forecastle discipline to the plantations and proved to be harsh taskmasters.

The laborers' complaints brought a Japanese investigator to Hawaii in December, 1869. Forty of the laborers were released from their contracts and allowed to go home. The remainder served out their three-year agreements, with only seventeen electing to return to Japan when their contracts expired. It is likely that some of the *Gannen Mono* moved on to the United States to continue their work abroad, but as a group they disappeared. When the next shipload of Japanese reached Hawaii in 1885, there is nothing to suggest that their predecessors played any important role in smoothing the way for them. There is record of one member of the *Gannen Mono* dying on the island of Maui in 1936 at the age of 102.[17]

Despite the individual tragedies and triumphs experienced by these early sojourners, they made little impact either for better or worse on the American scene. That destiny was reserved for those who arrived later.

II ❦ Go East, Young Man

Some writers have contended that in the early years of its relations with the United States, Japan prohibited emigration of laborers because it did not want to damage its developing image as a modern nation. They assert that only after negotiation of a labor contract convention with the kingdom of Hawaii in 1885 did Japan acquiesce in the emigration of its citizens. However, it seems clear Japan at this time had no firm policy regarding the movement of its citizens abroad.

Those who came to the United States in the early years were a diverse group representing virtually the entire social spectrum of Japan—samurai loyal to the Tokugawa forces seeking what amounted to political asylum, students sent by the new imperial regime to prepare for government positions, students who financed their own studies, seamen who jumped ship, and sundry adventurers. In addition, in the years between 1868 and 1881, the records show 260 passports were issued to craftsmen and laborers. That some were issued suggests the absence of any real policy against emigration abroad. In fact, there is reason to believe the government was thinking less in terms of permanent departure of its citizens than in the tradition of *dekasegi*—people who left home temporarily for employment to supplement agricultural income—a common practice in old Japan.

The very diversity of Japanese coming to the United States presents difficulties in portraying them as an entity. A more meaningful analysis can be made by considering those who came prior to about 1891 as a group, and then dealing with those who came from that time to about 1924—when Oriental immigration was halted by restrictive laws—in a separate category.

Because of the unreliability of U.S. immigration statistics during that early period, reliance must be placed on the Imperial Statistical Annals of Japan (*Nihon Teikoku Tokei Nenkan*). But even here accurate figures are elusive. Passports were issued only for single trips abroad. Upon return to Japan the traveler had to surrender his passport and get a new one for a subsequent trip. Professor Yamato

Ichihashi reported one Japanese had made forty trips abroad, and each departure appears as a new statistic.[1]

Virtually all students sent to the United States at government expense fall in the period before 1891. They studied for the most part at eastern universities—Harvard, Yale, Rutgers, and other long-established schools. Since they were chosen from the elite, many went on to achieve distinction.[2]

Students who came at their own expense were usually earnest young men, some of whom founded the *Fukuin Kai* (Gospel Society) in San Francisco. In contrast to coarser elements of the Japanese population, they seldom gave Japanese consular officials concern about their reflection on Japan's image abroad.

Many of these students were motivated by the reports of earlier visitors to the United States. One who was particularly influential was Fukuzawa Yukichi, founder of Keio University and a newspaper publisher. We can imagine him saying to Japanese students (*shosei*), "Go East, young man."

Turbulence in Japan contributed to the number of young people leaving for study abroad. Many feared past political activities had made them vulnerable to punishment. Only seventeen passports were issued to self-supporting students in 1883, but the next year the figure leapt to 198 and remained near or above that level until 1902 when it increased to more than a thousand for reasons to be considered later.

Though not emigrants, businessmen received passports in numbers consistent with the pace of Japan's modernization. Only 157 were issued passports between 1868 and 1881, an average of about eleven a year.[3] Thereafter, the numbers rose steadily, reaching 275 in 1891.

Japanese statistics for passports issued and U.S. figures for entries are in wide disagreement in the 1880's. Curiously, the U.S. census for 1890 found 2,039 Japanese in the total population, a figure reasonably consistent with the cumulative total for Japanese immigration, but making no allowance for those who returned to Japan. Statistics for Japanese returning to their country were not kept by the United States until 1908. Also, it is probable that many Japanese were not counted at all by the census takers in 1890.

Despite the good intentions of most individually financed students, some found distractions. They had come on a shoestring and were unable to go beyond the Pacific Coast. For the most part they remained tied to the cities, sometimes going to work as domestics—called schoolboys—to learn American ways and earn room and board while attending night classes. They seldom became involved in the labor gangs under the control of labor contractors. Indeed, some who became competent in English became labor contractors themselves and employed other students as clerical help. Professor Ichihashi tells of one *shosei* who became a banker with the Mitsui interests. Another, Morinaga Taichiro, learned candy-making in Oakland and returned to Japan and built a very successful career as a confectioner.

There were also unique personalities such as Matsudaira Tadaatsu who came as a student in 1872, was graduated from Rutgers in engineering, and worked at his profession apart from other Japanese until his untimely death in 1888 in Denver, Colorado. Onuki Hachiro was another of this singular breed who achieved success while isolated from other Japanese. Onuki, or Hutchlon Ohnick, to use the name he adopted, was awarded a franchise in Phoenix, Arizona, to produce illuminating gas and electricity. These two companies provided the base from which the Arizona Public Service Company developed.

By 1891, there were large numbers of students about whom the Japanese government had genuine concern. When Mutsu Munemitsu was appointed Resident Minister to the United States in 1888 he was instructed by Foreign Minister Okuma Shigenobu to stop in San Francisco en route to Washington and report on the Japanese community. The Foreign Minister in his instructions to Mutsu stated:[4]

> In recent years, an increasing number of Japanese have gone to the United States of America and landed at San Francisco on the pretense of studying or engaging in trade. It is apparent, however, that most of them had no definite objectives to attain in America from the first. Consequently, a large number of those Japanese who now reside in San Francisco, I am informed, have idled away their time and quickly exhausted the small amount of funds in hand which they brought from Japan without accomplishing any purposeful tasks. The resultant destitution has, therefore, compelled them to work as servants, waiters, or other menial labor. Furthermore, from the consular reports and articles appearing in local American newspapers which H.I.M.'s Consul in that city has sent to me, I have also learned that among these Japanese residents are many undesirable individuals upon whose unruly conduct and misbehavior Americans often look with scorn. I believe that shameless activities of such undesirable Japanese will no doubt impair Japan's national honor and dignity.

I therefore beg your excellency to stop over in San Francisco for about a week on your way to assume your appointed post in Washington, D.C., in order to make inquiries into this matter, and to make a full report of your finding with respect to the conduct and behavior of the Japanese residents in that city, their occupations, their living standard and conditions, and the probable outcome of their stay in America.

Mutsu communicated his findings to the Foreign Minister in private correspondence. In his report he stated *inter alia*: [5]

Soon after my arrival in San Francisco, I began my inquiries into this matter. I first had discussions with H.I.M.'s Consul Fujii on several occasions. I then had interviews with some of the Japanese merchants and the so-called *shosei* [students] residing in this city. In these talks, there appears to be a consensus of opinion with respect to the undesirable and deplorable situation which has been created by the clustering of such large number of knavish *shosei* here in this city . . . These self-styled *shosei* are all very young and have no steady jobs. As is usual with the *shosei* in Japan, these young students here are all men of little means and, consequently, work as menial laborers to gain a bare livelihood. Although some of them seem to have hoped, when they left Japan, to pursue a course of study in America, it is obvious that a penniless person cannot undertake such an ambitious task as the pursuit of knowledge without specific objectives and no funds . . . Their life and experiences as servants have, it seems, fostered the so-called mercenary spirit in them; hence, they are extremely rude in their manners and disgustingly vulgar in their tastes. Today, they all have lost interest in their original aims which they hoped to accomplish upon their departure from Japan . . .

In this city, these 2,000 Japanese residents have established numerous associations or organizations. Each of these associations or organizations has usually rented a room or two so that, by also serving simple Japanese food, [these indigent laborers] can live on twenty to thirty cents a day. . . .

As for the aforementioned associations or organizations which are numerous in this city, they can be classified, I believe, into two major categories: religious and political. Such associations as Fukuin Kai and Nihon Seinen Kai are religious. Among the members of these religious associations are many who are not dissolute. In fact, a few American ministers are, in one capacity or another, connected with some of the religious associations. On the other hand, almost all the members who belong to political organizations such as Yushikai, Seinen Kai, and Kakumeito, are radical in politics and rude and wild in manners. It is indeed the members of these political organizations who regard the staff of the consulate as their enemies and often try to circulate groundless rumors to slander these officials . . .

Contrary to our expectations, therefore, these *shosei* will not, upon returning to Japan, contribute anything valuable to our efforts to transform our country.

. . . In view of the existing situation I have just described, I have instructed H.I.M.'s Consul Fujii . . . to regard those *shosei* who are employed as menial laborers as *dekasegi mono*.

The concluding comment by Mutsu suggests that genuine *shosei* were treated by the Japanese Consulate in a manner different from that accorded workers coming to America for employment. This would suggest that students were regarded as potential members of the Japanese elite and a higher value was placed on them than on common laborers.

Before the turn of the century, Japanese were found in considerable numbers in the San Francisco demimonde. Japanese Consul Chinda Sutemi reported on the subject to the Foreign Ministry in Tokyo on March 10, 1891, in the following terms:[6]

With regard to the unlawful profession that some Japanese women of ill fame pursue in San Francisco, my predecessors at this consulate, I believe, have already reported to your excellency on a number of occasions. It has come to my attention that, as the number of Japanese prostitutes and operators of houses of pleasure in this city have, in recent years, steadily increased, their ignominious conduct has begun attracting public attention and often resulted in scandalous publicity in local newspapers. It is indeed a deplorable situation that their being the cause of public scandals must cause unnecessary hardship in our endeavor to maintain the reputation of the Japanese as a whole.

By this time, a number of Japanese saloons had begun operations in San Francisco relying almost entirely on a Japanese clientele. And in 1892 the Japanese brothel operators had banded together in a new organization. The San Francisco *Report* on May 4, 1892, commented on this development in a lengthy article which said in part:

While the respectable members of the Japanese colony, which, by the way, is increasing rapidly, are lamenting the present condition of affairs and are doing their best to suppress the disgraceful traffic with their country women, they are heavily handicapped by a society of Japanese recently formed for the sole purpose of blackmail, and of trading in the women off whose earnings they live. The new Japanese organization is composed entirely of the most disreputable elements. It has been appropriately named the Gorotsuki Club—the nearest interpretation of which is a "hard crowd."

In July, 1891, Consul Chinda sent his secretary, Fujita Yoshiro, on an inspection trip throughout the Pacific Northwest to determine the circumstances of the Japanese living in that region. On his return he reported his findings in part as follows: [7]

In Seattle, there is one grocery store and ten restaurants owned or operated by Japanese, and approximately 250 Japanese live there at present. Of these 250, only forty who are either the proprietors or employees of the grocery store or the restaurants have steady jobs. The remaining two hundred Japanese residents are, if not prostitutes or proprietors of houses of pleasure, either gamblers or pimps. Furthermore, some of these restaurants are operated as part of the houses of pleasure, or run separately by the proprietors of such houses. In other words, five or six restaurants are actually connected, in one way or another, with prostitution in this city. Thus, in Seattle, I can name only ten individuals who have absolutely nothing to do with prostitution or gambling and are indeed engaged in legitimate business or occupations in a strict sense.

From Seattle, Fujita went on to Port Blakely on Bainbridge Island where about eighty Japanese were employed in a sawmill. He found them to be a mixed group of sober, industrious workers and habitual gamblers. On the morning of his arrival he found some thirty of the total of eighty Japanese employees were not at work, but gambling in the shack provided for their housing.

In Tacoma he found a Japanese community of about ninety which was a happy contrast to the Seattle group. He commented that "all the Japanese residents are indeed enterprising young men, and many of them have already gained the confidence of Americans living in this community."

In Spokane, Washington, he found an approximation of the conditions he encountered in Seattle. Of the approximately sixty Japanese in that city, forty-seven were prostitutes, pimps, or gamblers.

In Portland, Oregon, he found that about half the Japanese population of about 130 were connected with the demimonde. He commented in his report to Consul Chinda: [8]

> Like in other cities in the Pacific Northwest, Japanese prostitutes also live in Portland. There are, at present, nineteen to twenty of them. As I did in Spokane, I asked a Japanese who was regarded as boss by his fellow Japanese gamblers here in this city to accompany me when I visited each one of the houses of pleasure which were operated by Japanese. Most Japanese men I met with there tried to avoid seeing me or having a conversation with me. Significantly, most of these Japanese prostitutes, as was the case in Spokane, came out to talk to me . . . Then, I learned that most of these women came from Seattle, having been brought by Japanese sailors who had jumped ship. These sailors, either as a prostitute's husband or as her employer, have forced these Japanese women to practice prostitution. At present, there are about forty of these pimps in this city, . . .But, to my surprise I found two or three former students among these pimps. These students, I was told, gave up the studies they had undertaken in San Francisco and drifted to this city . . .
>
> On my way back to San Francisco, I have made inquiries concerning the presence of Japanese at every train stop. As a result of these inquiries, I have learned that there is a group of Japanese in almost all of these places. These Japanese were, however, either prostitutes or their employers; none of them were engaged in legitimate business or occupations.

It is small wonder that Japanese diplomatic and consular officials were constantly reporting to the authorities in Japan these conditions among Japanese in America. In 1891, Japan was still engaged in her program to win full sovereignty as a nation-state. The end of the unequal treaty system in Japan remained as a major diplomatic preoccupation and Japan's image was of great concern to her representatives abroad. But the anti-Japanese movement when it came was not based on objections to the moral behavior of the Japanese. The white community was in a poor position to point the finger of scorn at the Japanese. Most of the prostitutes and the vast majority of their patrons were from the Caucasian community.

As the decade of the 1880's wore to its end, Japanese who were classified as common laborers in imperial statistics were approaching the number of students coming to America annually. According to U. S. immigration figures, 14,881 in the ensuing decade came in all categories. The Imperial Statistical Annals present the following picture for passports issued for the mainland United States in certain categories. We will eliminate from the totals the passports issued to officials, tourists, and government-supported students.[9]

PASSPORTS ISSUED—DESTINATION U.S.A.

Year	Students	Commercial Business	Fishery Agriculture	Craftsmen	Laborers	Others	Total
1880	11	12	—	—	11	1	35
1881	1	16	—	12	21	3	53
1882	9	15	—	5	12	8	49
1883	18	16	—	1	6	5	46
1884	202	19	—	3	43	6	273
1885	175	22	—	0	100	10	307
1886	237	38	—	3	44	3	325
1887	264	97	—	0	88	5	454
1888	224	150	—	5	350	14	743
1889	195	171	—	13	184	25	588
1890	198	172	—	15	184	33	602
1891	232	275	1	33	246	661	1,448
1892	239	373	860	427	291	139	2,329
1893	220	492	404	147	340	320	1,923
1894	182	236	593	94	257	134	1,496
1895	193	297	30	5	424	89	1,038
1896	211	360	8	23	1,066	77	1,745
1897	244	390	527	84	608	70	1,919
1898	325	805	135	11	1,287	248	2,811
1899	481	1,882	87	170	3,742	444	6,606
1900	437	2,159	1,463	1,540	4,366	536	10,501
1901	508	627	39	12	83	681	1,950
1902	1,283	1,531	96	51	249	1,859	5,069
1903	1,340	1,745	87	50	223	1,724	5,169
1904	1,251	1,009	00	43	161	935	3,399
1905	868	443	167	17	263	1,319	3,067
1906	2,825	1,215	1,046	22	462	2,851	8,421
1907	2,972	1,246	1,561	20	664	3,092	9,555
1908	383	592	837	28	534	808	3,182
1909	134	432	288	4	410	693	1,961

Although the Japanese statistics show a sudden advance in 1884, it was not until 1886 that the U.S. Bureau of Statistics reported the arrival of more than one hundred Japanese in a single year. At no time in the period to 1908 and the enforcement of the Gentleman's Agreement are the Japanese and American statistics in agreement.

III ❦ The Invisible Baggage

The coming of Japanese immigrants to this country is closely linked to the Chinese although the latter began arriving many years earlier. The fact that American ships had been calling in Canton since late in the eighteenth century, more than a half-century before Japan opened her ports to the West, made it natural that Chinese labor should be recruited to do the menial work for Americans who had settled in California. By the time gold was discovered at Sutter's Mill in 1848, several thousand Chinese were already in the territory. By 1860, census takers were able to list 34,933 Chinese. In the absence of specific legislation, both European and Asian immigrants were admitted quite freely in this period. In fact, Chinese immigration was encouraged in order to meet the need for cheap labor on farms and in cities, and in the construction of the Central Pacific Railroad. But the welcome quickly turned to hostility when hard times descended on the West and Californians found the Chinese competing directly for their jobs.

The formation in 1877 of the Workingmen's Party in California, headed by Dennis Kearney, led to the crystallizing of an anti-Chinese movement. Under political pressure from the West the United States in 1880 negotiated a treaty "to regulate, limit or suspend" the immigration of Chinese laborers. This agreement was superseded in 1882 by the so-called Chinese Exclusion Act: Congressional legislation banned Chinese immigration for ten years and prohibited naturalization of those already here.

The legislation singled out the Chinese for discriminatory treatment. It did not prohibit immigration by other nationalities, but there was no immediate influx of Japanese. The census of 1890 showed only 2,039 Japanese residents—there probably were a few more—compared with 107,488 Chinese.

Although of similar racial stock, there were easily distinguishable differences between the two nationalities. For one thing, the Japanese had quickly adopted Western clothing and Western hair styles; the Chinese adhered largely to their traditional clothing and wore their hair in plaited queues, the style imposed upon them by their Manchu conquerors in the seventeenth century. The Chinese were primarily of the coolie class, capable of enduring conditions whites would not tolerate, while working diligently at backbreaking tasks. By contrast, as we have seen in the previous chapter, there was a large percentage of students and merchants along with the gamblers, pimps, and seamen among the Japanese.

Even so, the Japanese represented a cultural tradition far different from the Judeo-Christian ethic and Graeco-Roman institutions that were the basis of the American nation. The nature of Japanese culture is important to this study of one special group among the many in American immigration history.

The island nation from which the Japanese came was an ancient land with a well-developed culture.[1] The oldest written records go back to A.D. 712, but they purport to present a history of developments nearly fourteen centuries before that time. During the first centuries of the Christian Era, Japan profited from sporadic continental influences. However, it was still a rather primitive nation, if that, when she came under the direct cultural influence of China in the sixth century, a time when the West was entering its dark decline from "the grandeur that was Rome."

Developing Chinese Buddhism and Buddhist missionary zeal were responsible for the development of regular and, in time, official contacts between China and Japan. The continuing Japanese interest in Buddhism provided the track along which many cultural influences— the written language, arts and crafts—flowed into Japan from China.

As the generations passed, Buddhism provided a heavy metaphysical overlay of the indigenous Japanese cult of Shinto. Indeed, Shinto may have survived the more than a millennium of Buddhist domination only because its mythology provided the basis for the Imperial Institution.

In the period when Japan borrowed so heavily from China, the Japanese were aware they were becoming a cultural daughter of China. But Japan's long history has been characterized by a swing of the pendulum between action and reaction, and by the ninth century she began to withdraw into herself to digest what she had borrowed and to synthesize a culture which was distinctly Japanese, not just a pale echo of the Chinese. She was, and she remained, independent. But she became provincial in attitude, a quality of mind and spirit that Japanese immigrants in America referred to as *shima-guni konjo*, literally "island country mentality."

With the establishment of the Kamakura Shogunate in 1192, imperial authority was submerged and a system of military chieftains ruled with varying effectiveness until the Restoration in 1868. Military values became a part of the ethics and attitude of the elite, and a term, *Bushido* (the way of the warrior), was coined for the samurai value system.

After the arrival of Europeans in the sixteenth century, the political implications of missionary activity—the fear that widespread conversions to Christianity were a prelude to political domination—led to the expulsion of all but the Dutch. Christianity was proscribed although small pockets of the estimated 300,000 converts maintained the faith.[2] As late as 1868, fourteen years after the Perry expedition, anti-Christian edicts were being issued. But in 1873 religious freedom was restored. Christian missions, largely from the United States, enjoyed considerable success, particularly among the upper class. By 1890, some 90,000 Japanese had been converted. Japanese immigrants who became Christians could do so in the full knowledge that this was acceptable back home.

In 1600, when the Tokugawa Age began, the Christian threat to Buddhism was replaced in part by growing interest in the social philosophy of Confucianism. By the nineteenth century, Confucian ethics and philosophy showed more vitality than Buddhism.

The Tokugawa Age was dominated by a powerful military regime which stopped short of complete centralization of power and permitted a great degree of autonomy in the feudal domains. Nevertheless, it provided Japan with its first real central government, encouraged entrepreneurial activity, and produced an economy far more sophisticated than might be expected in a politically feudal land. At the same time, the people were confronted with myriad rules and regulations which governed virtually every activity. In time the people became comfortable with these required patterns of behavior.

In this new age, Japanese culture, which had been dominated by a Buddhist and a military elite and by the old court aristocracy, was gradually transformed into one in which the townsmen commoners exerted a decisive influence in many aspects of the arts. The older art forms persisted but with declining vigor. And the economy was increasingly dominated by commoners who were, nevertheless, among the most affluent members of society.

As the nineteenth century dawned and Westerners began knocking at Japan's closed doors, the old order—political, social, and economic—showed signs of decay. Power relationships and all that went with them were eroding. Basic premises, hitherto unquestioned, were now being challenged. With this growing restlessness, that large segment of society which felt a decreasing vested interest in the status quo began to raise questions which went to the heart of existing political and social theory. Within the elite class many samurai sought relief from their growing poverty by employment and even minor entrepreneurial activity, roles which they would have proudly disdained in better times.

Soon after the opening of Japan by Commodore Perry, even the Tokugawa family and its traditional supporters were no longer of one mind on national policy. A large number of the great feudal states, the *han*, from the beginning of the age in 1600 had remained hostile to the Tokugawa family and its monopoly of power at the national level. Men from these *han* discovered in the idea of Imperial Restoration the means for bringing down the Tokugawa Regime. Well before the coming of Perry the theory had been advanced, very cautiously it is true, that the Tokugawa were usurpers of power that properly belonged to an Imperial Institution which had not exercised real national control for nearly a thousand years, if indeed it can be said that the Throne had ever done so.

The Japan to which Perry came was a country facing growing and serious internal problems, but still characterized by political stability. And it was a nation which had been in seclusion since 1638. Prejudice against the stranger was deeply imbedded in the attitude of the people. In fact, a Japanese felt completely secure only in the immediate circle of his own family. The old proverb ran, *"hito wo mitara, dorobo to omoe"* (when you see a stranger, regard him as a thief). Japanese in the villages were suspicious of men from other villages. Men of one *han* placed little trust in men from other *han*. The most complete stranger, of course, was the foreigner, a proper object of total distrust.

The Japan that Commodore Perry found was a divided and fragmented society.[3] There was little national consciousness among the masses of the people. They regarded themselves primarily as men of Satsuma, Choshu, or some other of the more than 250 fiefs which made up the country—that is, they so regarded themselves when they thought in more than immediate-family terms, which was seldom or never for the peasant masses.

Clearly the old order was faltering. Out of this crisis came the end of the Tokugawa Regime in 1868, nominal Imperial Restoration, and in 1871, the end of the old feudal barons as the center of regional power and loyalty. In less than a generation then, following the opening of Japan to foreign influence, the old order was brought to an end, but out of the welter of crises and conflicts that attended this development came no clear view of alternatives to what was being destroyed.

The moral and ethical values of Buddhism and Confucianism remained as generalized guides in daily living, but all else was uncertain. Imperial Restoration in 1868 had meant to some only that the Emperor instead of the Tokugawa Shogun presided over the feudal order. To others it meant only a beginning of a vital transformation. Some leaders were consumed by one grim thought, that Japan must find the means to survive in the predatory and threatening world of nineteenth-century imperialism.

The means to national power was sought through an examination of the sources of power which had made Western nations so strong. After a period of analysis and assessment, the members of a developing oligarchy began to borrow from the West those aspects of Western civilization which, they concluded, were the significant sources of strength. For many years after the Restoration there was an excessive admiration of things Western, and something of a denigration of things Japanese.

As Professor John W. Hall describes this:

> Rabid converts to Western ways turned their iconoclastic attacks on all of Japan's past, its government, art, literature, philosophies, as products of a benighted, barbarous culture. Western ways for many became a compulsive fad, as Japanese avidly put on Western-style suits and hats, grew out their hair, sported watches and umbrellas, and learned to eat meat. The country as a whole rapidly adopted Western material culture, sometimes with thoughtless avidity.

In 1871 the Meiji leaders, in an effort to weaken the old regional loyalties, abolished the *han* and created new administrative entities called *ken* (prefectures) to replace them. At the same time, the former feudal lords were ordered to take up residence in Tokyo. By thus removing the feudal families, the leaders around the Throne sought to destroy the traditional local relationships. But, in this effort they

were not entirely successful. Local attachments remained strong, to
be expressed even in the developing oligarchy by the *hambotsu*, or
cliques of leaders from certain of the old *han*.

The leaders of the new Japan were obsessed with the need for
speed in achieving what they called *fukoku-kyohei*, by which they
meant a strong and prosperous state. In seeking the means for this,
they quickly decided to institute a system of universal education and
universal military conscription, even before they had reached any firm
conclusions concerning other requisites for national strength. The
decade of the 1870's in Japan witnessed a lengthy study of the West
and a continuous dialogue among the leaders concerning the nature
and extent of change to be undertaken. What features of Western
societies lay at the heart of the national strength of Western states?
How much of traditional Japanese culture stood as an impediment to
national strength?

By the beginning of the next decade certain decisions seem to have
been reached. Western religion, philosophy, and related aspects of
Western culture were not, it was concluded, important sources of
national strength. Japan could safely continue on her traditional ways
in these aspects of culture. While change had occurred in Japan
during this decade of decision, it had not altered in any important
way the philosophical and ethical heritage of the feudal past. The
new decade of the 1880's was to see an acceleration of the transformation begun in the 1870's in science, technology, and even in
the structure of government. One scholar has referred to the resulting
blending of things Western and things Japanese as involving "Western
theory and Eastern practice."

This was the historical tradition to which the immigrants were
heir. The values, ideals, behavioral predispositions, psychology, and
philosophy they brought with them might be likened to invisible baggage that profoundly influenced their adjustment to life as an alien
minority within the diverse American population. Some of these
values were unique. Others involved only an unusual degree of application by the Japanese of values long a part of the Judeo-Christian
ethic.

It is the opinion of two noted students of Japanese American life
that these values have persisted among the citizen-children of the
Issei, the *Nisei*, and their grandchildren, the *Sansei*, and that Japanese
Americans today stand somewhat apart from other Americans as a
subculture (Harry H. L. Kitano)[4] or as a subnation (William Petersen). In view of the fact that American life has proved a solvent for

much that was worthwhile in the values which the European immigrants brought with them, the unusual persistence of Japanese values in Japanese American life compels us to take notice of them.

In two important ways the incoming Japanese differed sharply from the population they joined. From the long feudal age in Japan they inherited a presumption of inequality in contrast to the, at least theoretical, assumption of equality among Americans. The hierarchy of status which characterized Japanese values meant necessarily that emphasis was placed upon "knowing one's place" in this scheme of things. Even the Japanese language provided ample ways in which one acknowledged his relationship to others as superiors, inferiors, or equals.

Since one assumed one's "proper station" in society and discharged the appropriate duties and obligations, there was little room for "individualism" as understood in the West.

These basic attitudes were brought to America and once they were firmly established and enforced by social pressures, not many "mavericks" appeared among the Japanese immigrants.

The development of a coherent system of values from Japanese norms awaited the growth of urban centers in America, the establishment of families, and the arrival of the Nisei generation. Within this system was a family structure characterized by strong paternal authority. Its other attributes were ability to endure prejudice, concern for the reputation and well-being of the ethnic community, and modesty carried to unusual extremes. These were values which enabled the Japanese to achieve a functional compatibility with American middle-class norms.

But before we inspect the culture baggage in greater detail, we must know more about the Issei, the first generation of Japanese to become permanent or semi-permanent residents of the United States.

IV ❀ The Push and the Pull

The year 1891 is significant in this study since it was then that the number of Japanese entering the United States reached 1,000 for the first time. Total immigration that year from all countries was 560,319.

That date is also a convenient milestone for noting a change in the "kinds" of Japanese who entered the United States. Until this time a large percentage of those coming to this country were students drawn from the elite, businessmen, and drifters.

The new immigrants were largely young, single men intent on personal gain. Many were uncomplicated farm boys, younger sons with no prospect of inheriting land. Few had any intention of remaining beyond the time necessary to accumulate the thousand dollars of which they often spoke. That sum was regarded as sufficient to buy land which would provide them with a secure life in Japan.

Since they had no intention of remaining in America permanently, they felt little need on arrival to come to grips with American life and institutions. But as time passed and the Japanese economy developed, these workers were compelled to enlarge the size of the necessary nest egg. Inflation in Japan simply meant more dollars were needed to realize their hopes. At the same time, many found that economic and social harassment made putting away any amount of money a difficult matter.

One of the great ironies of Japanese American history is that few of the immigrants would have remained permanently in the United States if they had been permitted to achieve their limited economic goals. But they were molested at every turn, their objectives frustrated by discrimination and denial of opportunity. Unable to save the necessary sums, some were forced to become permanent residents in America. Thus the anti-Japanese forces, in some measure, were responsible for the present size of the Japanese American community. Small though it is today, it probably would have been much smaller had no anti-Japanese movement developed.

Faced with the need to adjust their goals, numbers of the immigrants began to think of long-term stays. This necessitated seeking permanent livelihoods, establishing families, and facing the problems of acculturation, adaptation, and integration. Others drifted along, unable or unwilling to go home, but still not fully reconciled to permanent residence in America. Those who stayed were the Issei.

Professor Frank Miyamoto of the University of Washington suggests a new period in the history of Japanese Americans began about 1907 when further immigration of common laborers from Japan was halted by the so-called Gentlemen's Agreement. He calls this the "settling period" in contrast to the earlier "frontier period" of Japanese immigration. This means the Japanese were moving toward genuine immigrant status rather than simply transient workers from Japan. This phenomenon will be studied in greater detail in other chapters. At this point we return to the forces that impelled the Japanese to come to the United States. Both a "push" and a "pull" were involved.

There is an inertia in human behavior which is not easily overcome. Either crisis conditions at home (the push), or a powerful attraction from abroad (the pull), is required before people act. In its simplest terms, the theory holds that migrants may be impelled to leave their homelands by circumstances that push them into fleeing intolerable conditions. Conversely, the lure of real or imagined opportunities in another land moves people to seek the better life.

The push may be a sudden event, such as the potato famine in Ireland which led thousands to flee to America. Or the push may come from more slowly moving forces, such as overcrowding. In the last half of the eighteenth century and the first half of the nineteenth, Europe's population grew by about 75 percent. There was not enough land to provide livelihoods for younger sons, and the developing industrial revolution could not absorb enough of them. From peasant villages throughout Europe tens of thousands sought refuge in America. Those who were not skilled craftsmen became additions to this country's pool of unskilled labor.

The Japanese, on the other hand, were not pushed out of their homelands as many Europeans had been, and most left with no real feeling of alienation or permanent separation. In this sense, the Japanese sojourners were "birds of passage," and do not conform to the usual definition of immigrant, although many did in time give up expectations of returning permanently to their homeland.

How infinitely few Japanese qualified as immigrants is to be seen in these figures. Between 1860 and 1920, some 28,592,382 persons arrived in the United States as immigrants. Of this number 246,400 were Japanese, which figures out at about .0086 percent of the total. The census of 1920 found only 111,010 Japanese, which included their American-born children. Even taking into consideration the number of Japanese who died in the United States, it would appear that more than half of those who entered the United States, perhaps as many as 150,000, returned to the Old Country after sojourns of varying lengths.

However, economic pressures provided a major push for the peasants who made up the bulk of the post-1891 migration. In order to achieve fiscal stability, the new leaders of the Meiji Regime transformed the traditional feudal tenure in land into private-property rights. The new legal owners were usually the previous cultivators; those who had tilled the land were given right to it. But this was followed by setting land values as a tax base. And in the absence of other sources of revenue, the land tax became a heavy burden. It is no exaggeration to say that the modern Japanese state was created by wringing from peasant cultivators just about that portion of their yields that was normal in feudal times. And, of the feudal scene, it was said that taxes were imposed upon farmers "to such an extent that they could neither live nor die."

While the cultivator was freed from the oppressive bondage of feudalism, he was also deprived of that compassionate paternal consideration which the lord could and sometimes did exercise in times of distress, but which the state in its search for a stable source of revenue would not. Fluctuations in the market added to the burdens of the farmer, and for many it meant ultimate loss of status as independent producers as they mortgaged or sold their lands to pay their taxes and finally sank into tenantry. And, of course, poor harvests such as occurred in 1889 meant famine in the countryside and the growth in numbers of landless agricultural laborers. The ultimate consequence of these circumstances when added to the growth of population in the countryside has been well described by one scholar in the following terms: [1]

> This vast body of small peasant proprietors, tenants and half-tenants, cultivating in ever larger numbers minutely parceled plots of land, historically forms the reservoir of Japan's stagnant and potential surplus population. The atomized, minute-scale cultivation is quite inadequate to give them a net income suf-

ficient to eke out even a bare subsistence, so their women must engage in some form of domestic industry while the men seek part-time employment as coolies working on roads, railway construction and the like. That section of stagnant surplus population which was not afforded the protection of the family system was forced to seek its livelihood in the cities. Those who could not enter the factories became rickshaw-men, longshoremen, coolies, in a word the lowest stratum of unskilled labor.

The socio-economic dislocations implicit in this situation were sufficient to provide the motivation for many to go abroad to secure the money by which a deteriorating family situation might be redressed. The significant amounts of money remitted by Issei back to families in Japan undoubtedly moderated the distress in the countryside and very probably saved some families from immediate disaster.

The elitists in the Japanese foreign service were not unaware of the low social status of the immigrants. Although the following quotation covers a period somewhat earlier than the decades of heaviest immigration, the official attitude is revealing. The Japanese consul in New York, Takahashi Shinkichi, in an official message to the Foreign Ministry on February 13, 1884, commented about growing problems with Japanese immigrants: [2]

> In seeking for an answer to the question of why these undesirable Japanese began to arrive suddenly in increasing numbers two years ago, I have come to the conclusion that these Japanese laborers must have been recruited in Japan and brought to this country to replace the Chinese laborers whose passage to this country was stopped in 1882. It is indeed the ignominious conduct and behavior of indigent Chinese of inferior character, however, that brought upon the Chinese as a whole the contempt of the Westerners and resulted in the enactment of the legislation to exclude them from the country. Hence, if the Japanese government fails to take any effective steps at this time in regard to the control of the passage of these indigent Japanese laborers to the United States, it is apparent that the Japanese will soon follow in the wake of the Chinese.

In passing, it should be mentioned that some of the snobbish scorn for Issei as a group persisted for decades among consular officials and representatives of Japanese trading companies stationed in West Coast cities who moved in social circles quite apart from the Japanese American communities.

Some Issei, in explaining the push that motivated them, contend they "fled" Japan to escape universal military conscription which was instituted in 1873. All male Japanese were theoretically responsible for military service between the ages of twenty and thirty-two, the terminal age later being advanced to thirty-seven. It may be doubted that very many were initially impelled to leave Japan for this reason, but some undoubtedly stayed on in America longer than originally planned to escape service.[3] Residence abroad entitled a Japanese to continuing exemption until his return. And if he had then passed the upper age limit he was no longer vulnerable.

Many Issei, no doubt, took note of Japan's militarism and the international disapproval which it provoked and were able to persuade themselves later in life that desire to avoid personal involvement had played at least a part in their decision to emigrate. However, so very few had any real intention of leaving Japan permanently at the outset of their personal odysseys that we may regard such Issei allegations, for the most part, as products of understandable self-delusion.

Of greater importance in the push of Japanese conditions were the socio-economic dislocations at the end of Japan's major wars. During the Sino-Japanese War (1894–1895) emigration to the United States fell sharply, but three years after the war ended, the emigration figures again reached those attained in the year that the war began. The same pattern prevailed during and after the Russo-Japanese War (1904–05).

Demobilization presented severe problems as servicemen were returned to the civilian economy. Many Japanese soldiers encountered difficulties in resuming normal lives in a society which had managed without their productive services. Particularly after the Russo-Japanese War, veterans came to the United States in considerable numbers.

Most of the migrants came from prefectures in Western Japan, areas where agrarian distress was greatest.[4] But a push of the spirit must also be taken into consideration. These districts historically had produced the most venturesome of the Japanese. The pirates of medieval Japan were from this area, as well as seafarers of more conventional kinds.

In discussing the causes of emigration from Japan, Yoshida Yosaburo wrote in 1909: [5]

. . . A large proportion of the Japanese emigration comes from the peasant class in the districts of the south; and growing population, economic pressure and inducement or attraction combine to cause their emigration. No doubt there are countless minor causes operating on individuals, such as ill-luck in business, a bad crop of rice, sudden death of the devoted wife, frequent visits of the bill collectors, or simply desire to see America. But the fundamental and principal causes are those already mentioned.

A number of scholars have studied Japanese passport data and have identified the prefectures from which the Japanese came from 1899 to 1903. The regions were not the most populous of Japan, but they were the districts in which the struggle for existence was most severe. The tabulations were as follows: [6]

District	No. of Passports Issued
Hiroshima	21,871
Kumamoto	12,149
Yamaguchi	11,219
Fukuoka	7,698
Niigata	6,698
Wakayama	3,750
Nagasaki	3,548
Hyogo	3,532
Okayama	2,176
Miyagi	1,613
Fukushima	1,613
Ehime	948
Aichi	767
Fukui	683
Shiga	646
Saga	624
Twenty-seven other districts	5,041

These statistics support the contention that the Japanese came largely from the Inland Sea districts and from Kyushu. The lure of America is aptly described by one Japanese writer in the following terms: [7]

No advertisement has ever appeared in the Japanese newspapers inducing emigrants to go to the United States. But the most effective advertisement is the stories of success of Japanese in America, which occasionally appear in the papers and magazines. Whenever certain Japanese return to Japan they talk with the newspaper reporter, telling how they struggled in a penniless condition, how they saved money, what industry they started, or how many acres of land they own in America. Such articles in a local newspaper, accompanied by illustration, usually make a strong impression upon the young peasant or rough country lad. Thus, the account of success of Mr. Kinya Ushizima (sic), the "potato king" in California, appeared many times before the public and, it seems, induced many emigrants to leave home, especially from the district of Fukuoka, from which Mr. Ushizima himself migrated many years ago. The success of Mr. Domoto, as the greatest flower raiser west of the Rockies, attracted many young farmers from his native district of Wakayama.

There have been many pamphlets published, some printed in more than thirty editions, under such titles as "How to Succeed in America," "Guide Book to Different Occupations in America," "Guide Books to America," "The New Hawaii," etc. All these books are written by those who returned from America or are still residents in this country. Generally speaking, they have exaggerated the abundance of opportunities in the United States and have stimulated emigration in over-attractive descriptions. Correspondence with Japanese laborers who are already in this country has also some influence. But the sphere of this kind of inducement is very narrow, limited to the correspondent's relatives or friends at home. The inducements and attractions above mentioned are the result of the simple fact that labor earns more in America than in Japan.

Whatever the conditions in Japan which constituted the push, and however influential the conditions in America which constituted the pull, it still required courage and the optimism of youth before a lad would leave the known and venture into the unknown. Each individual was, of course, influenced by his family circumstances and by family counsel.

The decision to go to the United States sometimes was based on unique circumstances, as illustrated in the family history of U. S. Senator Daniel K. Inouye. A fire broke out in his great-grandfather's home and led to destruction of other dwellings. Village elders assessed damages against the Inouye family which never could be paid under normal circumstances. The family decided the eldest son should go to Hawaii to earn the money to discharge this family debt. The years of labor necessary to meet this obligation led to the planting of roots in Hawaii and the senator's grandfather did not return to Japan even after the debt had been paid.

Beyond question many Japanese experienced both push and pull. The push may have come from the knowledge that there were minimal opportunities in Japan; the pull from visions of opportunities to learn new skills as well as earn money to enable them to achieve success after returning home.

In addition to these elements, the matter of "enticement" must be considered. Profit-making emigration companies developed in Japan to help young men go abroad, offering to find jobs and painting glowing pictures of opportunities to be found in America. In this the emigration companies were abetted by foreign shipping firms which were interested only in the fares they could sell. One notorious case occurred in 1891 when fifty-three Japanese arrived in Portland on two vessels of the Apton Steamship Company.[8] The firm through a Japanese agent recruited men in Okayama and Wakayama prefectures for promised employment in railroad construction. But there were no jobs and the Japanese encountered severe difficulties before they found employment on their own. There is no reason to believe this was an exceptional case.

By 1900, there were eleven emigration companies operating in Japan, many with agents in the United States to collect from Japanese laborers sums advanced to them for passage, clothing, etc., all provided with suitable markup for commissions. It must be remembered that few members of the peasant class could accumulate sufficient funds to go abroad without assistance.

Because the Japanese government was concerned about its image abroad, it passed legislation in 1894 requiring emigration companies to be responsible for returning workers who became ill, indigent, or public charges. If the worker went abroad under his own auspices he had to provide two sureties who would assume the same responsibility.

Despite these restrictions substantial increases in emigration are revealed in the Imperial Statistical Annals. In 1896 when the above law became effective, 1,764 passports to the United States were issued. In 1899 the figure rose to 6,942 and the following year it leapt to 10,562, of which 4,175 were to persons classified as laborers.

Hostile reaction on the West Coast to such sharp increases resulted in an order by the Foreign Ministry instructing prefectural governors to stop issuing passports to *imin* (laborers) immediately. The result was dramatic. In 1901 only eighty-three passports were issued to laborers and the total fell to 1,986. Clearly the immigration companies were caught off balance, but they quickly recovered. In 1901, 508 passports were issued to students, and 625 to commercial businessmen. In 1902 student passports soared to 1,283, and business passports to 1,531.

This sharp rise in these two categories caused the Foreign Ministry in 1903 to instruct prefectural governors to investigate applicants' background and qualifications more thoroughly. The governors were ordered to require applicants to meet the following qualifications: [9]

A. Merchants

    (1) An applicant must have experience in the line of business in which he is going to be engaged in the United States.

    (2) An applicant must be able to prove that he has in his possession ¥3,000 in cash ($1,500 at the then rate of exchange), in goods, or in both. The above amount does not include funds to cover travel expenses.

    (3) An applicant must have adequate facility in the English language, or prove he will be able to hire an interpreter.

B. Students

    (1) An applicant must be a graduate of middle school.

    (2) An applicant must have ¥700 ($350) at the time of departure. Or an applicant's parent or guardian must be able to prove he can defray all necessary expenses while the applicant is in the United States.

    (2) An applicant must be under thirty years of age.

The effectiveness of this directive is difficult to evaluate. It came on the eve of the Russo-Japanese War (1904–05) and there was little decline in the number of student passports issued in 1904. There was, however, a substantial decrease in commercial passports. In 1905 both categories showed sharp decreases, but the upswing was renewed immediately after the war.

Throughout the years charges have been made that Japan attempted to solve its "population problem" by flooding America with its "undesirables." Such allegations appeared in many Western newspapers, particularly the Hearst Press which waged what it proudly called "a thirty-five-year war with Japan." However, the record shows an extraordinary degree of accommodation by Japan to the racial concerns of other nations, and deserves detailed attention.

It will be recalled that in 1868 the *Gannen Mono* left for Hawaii without Japanese government approval. Because of dissatisfaction with the experiences of these laborers, no other Japanese plantation workers had appeared in Hawaii until 1885. The next year a labor convention was signed between Japan and the kingdom of Hawaii. Under its terms the Japanese government undertook to look after the interest of Japanese laborers in Hawaii but took no responsibility for their recruitment or transportation. This action was followed by controls over the emigration companies and restrictions on passports discussed in preceding paragraphs. These were hardly the actions of a nation seeking to get rid of its people.

Ultimately, however, it was a convulsion of nature that set in motion a train of events that were to have a profound effect on the tide of Japanese immigration. On April 18, 1906, an earthquake rocked San Francisco. The city was ravaged by the fire that followed. (Japan, no stranger to such disasters, contributed $246,000 in relief funds, a sum larger than the total from the rest of the world.)

The earthquake damaged a number of school buildings. Using this as a subterfuge, the school board on October 11, 1906, ordered that all Japanese children no matter where they lived must attend the segregated school in Chinatown. There were ninety-three Japanese pupils, twenty-five of whom were American-born and therefore citizens. It was explained that many of the Japanese were older than their classmates and posed a potential danger. The statistics hardly supported this contention. Among the sixty-eight Japan-born, fifteen were girls. Of the remaining fifty-three, twenty-one were fifteen years of age or younger. Only thirty-two Japan-born students were of an age which might justify parental concern. The Japanese community was willing to accept the separation of these older students, but the blanket segregation order was a violation of Japan's treaty rights as well as the rights of Japanese American citizens.

The Japanese government protested in Washington. Tokyo knew, however, that because of the peculiarities of the American governmental structure national leaders could not be held responsible for actions within a state. The protest led to a bargain between President Roosevelt and the San Francisco officials who represented the viewpoint of the Asiatic Exclusion League. On March 13, 1907, the San Francisco school board rescinded its segregation order.

In return, U. S. authorities had approached the Japanese government with proposals that it tighten its policy of withholding passports from laborers. Although Tokyo had been offended by the school incident, it responded in the same accommodating spirit with which it had approached the "American problem" in the past. Japan agreed "to issue passports for America only to nonlaborers, laborers returning from a visit to Japan, the parents, wives, and children of domiciled laborers, as well as laborers who had an already possessed interest in a farming enterprise in the country." [10]

To placate the Asiatic Exclusion League, which had become a potent political force in California, the immigration bill then in Congress was amended to give the President power to prevent "secondary immigration" into the United States. The bill was passed February 18, and a month later—one day after the school board's action—President Roosevelt issued an executive order prohibiting Japanese laborers in Hawaii, Canada, and Mexico from entering the United States. Japan, of its own volition, applied the same prohibition to labor emigration from Japan to Hawaii. This restriction, which became effective the summer of 1908, was the final provision of the Gentlemen's Agreement [11] under which the two nations agreed on measures to choke off Japanese immigration.

But not even these drastic measures solved Japan's "American problem." What had been overlooked in the legalisms of high level negotiation was a matter as basic as biology and love of family. The young Japanese males who had migrated to the United States were denied by law, custom, and social pressures from taking Caucasian wives, even though in 1900 there were nearly twenty-four men for every Japanese woman. Men with the means could return to Japan to marry women chosen for them by the time-honored system of go-betweens. Others legally married picture-brides in matches made after an exchange of photographs.

U.S. immigration statistics show women began to arrive on the mainland in important numbers only after the admission of Hawaii as an American Territory in 1900. For a few years these women were, for the most part, wives of former plantation workers who were moving to the mainland. In 1902, for example, Japan issued passports for the United States to only 420 women, but immigration figures show the arrival of 3,856. Only after the end of the Russo-Japanese War in 1905 was there a sharp rise in the number of women leaving for the United States. In 1909, after the Gentlemen's Agreement had reduced the number of male immigrants, Japanese women entering the United States outnumbered men for the first time and they were never in the minority from then until all immigration was halted.

The picture-bride tradition was explained by the Japanese ambassador, Sato Yoshimaro, to the State Department in 1917 as follows: [12]

> . . . the places of actual residence of the parties concerned form no essential requirement for a marriage to be legalized. Such being the essence of formal marriage in Japan, a Japanese man residing in this country can marry a Japanese woman residing in Japan by personally affixing his seal to the document to be presented before the registrar in Japan, and the validity of such marriage is amply attested by the issuance of certified copy of the family registry bearing the official seal of the registrar, which document the so-called picture bride proceeding to this country is always provided with.

Though Japanese women often had little say in this matter and were expected to obey family dictates, we must, nevertheless, recognize the stoic fortitude with which Japanese wives faced an uncertain future in a strange country with a strange man. Japanese women faced a different challenge in America than did men, but they met it with a response equally courageous. In fact, the women never have received the credit they deserved for bringing stability and a sense of uplift to Issei life. Many of the women, having spent more time in the homeland, were better educated than their husbands and more familiar with Japanese cultural arts. Nonetheless, in view of the precarious economic circumstances their families faced, they became working wives who took on outside responsibilities in addition to childrearing and maintaining the home.

The more bitter exclusionists saw the picture-brides as little more than mindless beasts of burden and brood sows, increasing the Japanese labor supply and breeding U. S.-born citizens. The racists saw the arrival of women as part of a plot to circumvent immigration laws and, with the new families "breeding like rabbits," overrun the West Coast with a new generation of Orientals armed with citizenship.

Why did these women agree to come to America? They may not have been immune to the propaganda of those in Japan who stood to profit from emigration, but for most this was irrelevant. Marriage in Japan was a family rather than a personal matter. Marrying men who were virtual strangers was an accepted custom, and it mattered little whether the prospective groom lived in Japan or America. Whatever else she might be called on to endure in America, she would at least be mistress of her own household and thus escape the tyranny of the classic Japanese mother-in-law. For most, the question of push or pull had little bearing. Many came simply at the bidding of parents with a few, no doubt, looking for adventure and independence.

No reliable figures are available on the number of picture-brides, but at most they were only a handful, nowhere close to the hordes portrayed by the anti-Orientalists. One source estimates one in four Issei women was a picture bride. Since approximately 20,000 Japanese women emigrated to the United States between the turn of the century and the end of the picture-bride era two decades later, the total was roughly 5,000. By 1920, the sexual imbalance had been corrected somewhat although there were still 189 males for every 100 females in the Japanese population in America.

The Japanese press had reacted strongly to repeated American manifestations of prejudice over the years, but the government had been restrained. Yielding to American hostility, Tokyo announced it would cease issuing passports to picture-brides on February 28, 1921.[13] This declaration has been referred to as the "Ladies' Agreement." It was met with consternation by many Japanese bachelors who feared they were destined to remain unmarried.

But worse was yet to come. Japanese immigration was excluded altogether in the Immigration Act of 1924. Its implications will be treated in detail in another chapter.

As we have seen, Japan through the years attempted to adapt itself to the demands of American regional sentiment and national policy. It was unsuccessful because the conviction among many that America was being "mongrelized" resulted in anti-Japanese prejudice that was close to paranoia.

Japanese immigration was minuscule compared to that from Europe. Down to the exclusion act in 1924, no more than 400,000 had entered the U.S. mainland and the Hawaiian Islands, and the majority had returned to Japan. More specifically, the cumulative total of Japanese immigrants to mainland America through 1919 was 237,121; those who either returned to Japan or died numbered 155,783, showing a net gain of only 81,338. However, the 1920 census shows 110,010 "Japanese" in the U.S. mainland. The difference is accounted for by 29,672 Nisei who were American citizens by birth. But the majority of the 110,010 were concentrated in California, and this meant high visibility which magnified their problems and focused the discrimination against them.

V ✿ The Search for Land and Jobs

While numbers of immigrants were recruited in Japan by emigration companies and labor contractors, many others arrived in the United States virtually unaware as to what lay ahead. They depended on operators of boardinghouses and small hotels—some of whom doubled as employment agents or contractors—for help in finding jobs. This was particularly true after the United States began to enforce legislation forbidding contractual arrangements made before an immigrant entered the country; once a laborer was admitted, he could make whatever arrangements he wished. This accounts for the prominent role of Japanese labor contractors in the West.

San Francisco for decades was the principal port of entry, but other Japanese landed in Tacoma (which eventually gave way to Seattle as Washington's chief port), and Portland, Oregon. Usually it was sheer chance that determined where an immigrant went after arrival unless he had friends or relatives who preceded him. It was natural that most of them stayed fairly close to the port, and because of the need for unskilled farm labor, many found their first job in agriculture.

As the West Coast's leading port, San Francisco's connections with Japan go back to the earliest days. The *Kanrin Maru,* a sailing ship with a small steam engine, was the first Japanese vessel to call. It arrived March 17, 1860, with an official party of about 100, including several lords and Shimmi Buzen-no-Kami, first ambassador to the United States. Ten years earlier Manjiro had passed through the city on his way home. Decades later, the first sight of America for Japanese students and immigrants was through the Golden Gate.

By 1904, some 10,000 Japanese—one fourth of the total in the United States—were in San Francisco. This is not an entirely accurate picture since many probably were between jobs and in the city only temporarily. The Japanese American Yearbook of 1905 presents the following picture of the San Francisco Japanese community by

58

occupation and numbers just before the earthquake and fire of 1906 did great damage to the area:

Occupation	Adults	Children	Total Population
Government officials	10	4	14
Company and bank employees	29	3	32
Publishers of newspapers, magazines, and employees	96	5	101
Association officials	15	1	16
Schoolteachers	15	3	18
Physicians and employees	23	13	36
Dentists and employees	8	0	8
Curio dealers and employees	287	18	305
Grocery store owners and employees	67	12	79
Restaurant owners and workers			
Japanese food	157	14	171
Western food	135	13	148
Barbers	34	9	43
Shoemakers and repairers	119	12	131
Photographers and helpers	17	2	19
Transportation business operators and employees	22	3	25
Operators of employment agencies and employees	12	0	12
Operators of variety stores and employees	21	1	22
Operators of flower shops	4	0	4
Operators of laundries and employees	107	3	110
Bookstore operators and employees	11	4	15
Operators of watch repair shops and employees	7	1	8
Interpreters	9	3	12
Produce dealers and employees	12	2	14
Operators of confectionery shops and employees	15	0	15
Operators of shooting galleries	11	2	13
Operators of pool halls	11	1	12
Operators of bath houses and employees	19	7	26
Operators of tailor shops and employees	36	1	37
White-owned store employees	960	7	967
Factory laborers and sailors	450	0	450

Occupation	Adults	Children	Total Population
Cleaners	568	10	578
Schoolboys	655	0	655
Domestic workers	2,920	58	2,978
Boarders at various Japanese organizations	290	5	295
Keepers of hotels and boarding houses and boarders	1,478	64	1,542
Others	1,123	98	1,221
TOTALS	9,753	379	10,132

Of the children, 191 were born in the United States and therefore were Nisei.

The immigrants apparently felt a need to organize for various reasons, primarily social. The Yearbook shows there were organizations for immigrants from the following prefectures: Aichi, Ehime, Hiroshima, Ishikawa, Kagoshima, Mie, Nagano, Niigata, Okinawa, Sendai, Tochigi and Gumma, Tokushima, Yamanashi.

There were also a number of religious groups: *Fukuin Kai* (Gospel Society), *Kirisuto-kyo Seinenkai* (Christian Youth Organization), *Bukkyo Seinenkai* (Buddhist Youth Organization), *Mii Kyokai* (Methodist Church), *Seiko Kai* (Anglican), *Minami Mii Kyokai* (Southern Methodist), *Kumiai Kyokai* (Congregational).

Eight schools, most of them connected with church groups, taught English. There was also one Japanese-language school for children who, it was assumed, would return to Japan one day and had to become proficient in the mother tongue.

In addition there were associations for tailors, shoe repairmen, restaurateurs, barbers, janitors or houseworkers, a students' club, and a residence for women.

Because San Francisco was the center of Japanese immigration, it is not surprising that the first Japanese to enter the American agricultural labor force went to work in the Vaca Valley of Solano County a short distance inland. The Federal Immigration Commission in its 1911 report found they arrived in that area in the winter of 1887–88.[1] They replaced Chinese workers whose numbers were declining as a result of the Exclusion Act of 1882. By 1889, sixty Japanese were under contract to pick fruit. In the nearby Suisun Valley of Solano County, Japanese laborers began to arrive in the early 1890's. Census takers in 1900 found there were more Japanese in Solano

County than any other California county except San Francisco, Alameda, and Sacramento.

As the Japanese became more numerous they developed a business district in Vacaville. In 1908 it included "four provision and supply stores employing twenty clerks; three billiard parlors, one steam laundry, two restaurants (one serving American and the other Japanese meals), a barbershop, four lodging houses (two with 15-cent bunks and two with good private rooms), four confectionery stores and ice cream parlors, three transfer companies, and a bank." [2] In the adjacent Chinatown, along with more prosaic establishments, were fourteen gambling houses and a number of houses of prostitution, both of which were well patronized by the young, unattached Japanese.

In the Vaca Valley and elsewhere the Japanese were welcome at first as laborers. But the more enterprising among them were not content to continue working for others. By 1900, some Japanese were farming on a "share plan"—leasing land and paying the rent with a percentage of the harvest. Within a short time they moved to cash rental payments which enabled them to make planting and marketing decisions on their own and keep a larger part of the profits when income was good. By 1908, the Japanese owned 290 acres, not a substantial amount but enough to alarm some citizens. Farmers, who had been indifferent to the complaints of urban labor groups about Japanese competition, suddenly became aware of the issue when the Japanese began to work for themselves. The Japanese were diligent farmers. In addition, the Japanese entrepreneur was in a position to screen his people for the very best workers.

While Japanese laborers may have made their influence felt first in the Vacaville area, they reached other parts of the rural West shortly afterward. Here are the stories of some of them:

Florin District

Japanese seasonal laborers came to the Florin area, a few miles from Sacramento, in 1894 to replace aging Chinese workmen on grain and hay ranches. Soon the Japanese began to lease land and in 1898 some of them turned to strawberry culture. Overproduction, falling prices, and increased labor costs caused the Japanese to try viticulture. Their control over seasonal labor gave them an advantage about which the Immigration Commission in its 1911 report commented: [3]

Because of the strong desire of the Japanese to lease and the competition among them for farms, the rents paid have risen. Not only have they as a rule paid higher cash rents, in several instances (though few as compared to the total number of leases) they have practiced coercion by withholding necessary labor in order to gain control of desirable farms.

The Florin district was about twenty square miles or 13,000 acres. The Immigration Commission in 1909 estimated the Japanese through purchase or lease controlled about 2,300 acres. Even assuming that in the next four years they doubled their holdings to 4,600 acres, the picture of Japanese domination presented in 1913 to push for a law prohibiting Japanese control of lands is hardly justified.[4] As a matter of fact, many white landowners found they could realize more by leasing to Japanese than by farming the land themselves. Beyond question the Japanese contributed greatly to the productivity of the Florin district. From an area of low yield in hay and grain, it was converted to a high productivity. As H. A. Millis writing in 1915 put it: [5]

> . . . the leasing of their farms has appealed strongly to the landowners of the community. Much labor is involved in growing intensive crops, and leasing interests the laborer in the crop and gives a nucleus for the needed labor supply. In some instances farmers have said that they leased their land when it was sought lest they should be unable to secure the Japanese labor which had become almost necessary. Moreover, leasing for the growing of strawberries has been attractive to farmers who wish to develop "hay land" into vineyards. The tenant has leveled the ground, irrigated it, and set and cared for the vines while growing berries. And while this was being done, the land brought a rental considerably higher than it would yield if used for the production of hay or wheat. And finally, the Japanese have been willing to pay relatively high rents. As the purchasers of land also they have been willing to pay relatively high prices. By frugal living, long hours, and great industry they then have sought to make their profit.

Sacramento and San Joaquin Delta

Chinese laborers were responsible for much of the first reclamation work done on the Sacramento River delta. The Japanese who came after them helped reclaim the San Joaquin Delta and put it to the plow. The best known of these people was George Shima (properly

Ushijima) who with the backing of the Fleischacker financial interests in San Francisco erected dikes around islands in the San Joaquin Channel, drained the excess water, and converted them into fields. Little of this land was owned by Shima. He grew potatoes in vast quantities on leased land and became known as the Potato King. At his death in 1926 he left an estate estimated at $15 million.

Fresno

A number of Japanese sought employment in Fresno County, in the torrid Central Valley, in 1890 but were turned away. The following year thirty found jobs in the vineyards and from that small beginning Japanese labor became an important part of the local economy. The first leasehold is believe to have been entered into in 1900, and the first land purchase was made near Fowler the following year. By 1908, Japanese owned 5,745 acres.[6] In the federal census two years later, Fresno County listed 2,233 Japanese.

In Tulare County to the south, crews of Japanese were brought in for work in the citrus groves, sugar beet and hop fields.

Pajaro Valley

Beginning in 1892, Japanese found work in the hop yards and sugar beet fields in this area near the coast south of San Francisco and soon displaced the Chinese as the basic labor supply. As elsewhere, the Japanese were not content to remain as laborers and began to rent land. By 1909, there were approximately a thousand Japanese in the valley and thirty-seven Japanese-owned businesses were operating in Watsonville.[7]

During the early decades of this century Japanese fanned out from the port cities, first as laborers and then as entrepreneurs, into other areas such as the upper Sacramento Valley, the Salinas Valley, the Guadalupe and Santa Maria districts in Santa Barbara County, and the foothill orchard districts on the western slope of the Sierra range.

The Immigration Commission in 1909, relying in part on data in the Japanese American Yearbook, reported 16,449 acres were owned by Japanese in California and 137,233 held in various forms of leasehold. The following year Japanese-owned acreage had climbed to 17,035, and lease acreage to 177,762. California had about 11 million acres of improved farmland in 1910; the Japanese holdings amounted to less than 2 percent, a figure which scarcely justified the drive for anti-alien land legislation which was getting under way.

After several false starts (twenty-seven anti-Japanese proposals were introduced in the California state legislature in 1910), an alien land measure was passed in 1913. The assembly endorsed it 72–3, the state senate 35–2. Although the Japanese were not named, the law was aimed at "all aliens other than those eligible for citizenship." It prohibited further purchase of agricultural land by Japanese aliens. It permitted them to lease land for not more than three years, thus discouraging them from investing in long-term improvements. The obvious intent was to force Japanese, if they wanted to farm, to work as laborers or sharecroppers on white-owned land.

Attorneys for the Japanese soon found a loophole. Land could be purchased by the Issei in the names of their minor children-citizens. In 1920 the State Board of Control reported that in the previous year lands owned by Japanese amounted to 74,769 acres and leased lands had risen to 383,287 acres. However, total agricultural lands had risen to nearly 28 million acres.

Anti-Japanese forces pushed through even stiffer alien land legislation in 1920 with additional amendments in 1923. If they had been enforced, the lot of the Japanese farmers would have become difficult, indeed. However, following the 1924 Immigration Act prohibiting further immigration of Japanese, the anti-Japanese forces seemed to relax and the alien land laws were not effectively enforced.

Despite this kind of harassment, the Japanese became an important part of California agriculture. The value of their crops rose from $6,235,858 in 1909 to $67,145,730 just ten years later.

No small part of their success can be credited to special techniques used by the Japanese. Since supply and demand determined market prices, they learned to speed up the maturation of crops ahead of their competitors and also to bring along crops more slowly so they would have produce when others had completed their harvest. They also lost little time in entering the marketing end of produce—from jobbing, wholesaleing and shipping carload lots to distant markets, to operating retail stands. By developing the whole industry from producer to consumer they were able to keep the profits within the Japanese community, whether or not this was their original intention.

It is difficult to overemphasize the importance of agriculture in the history of the Japanese in the United States. In the summer of 1909, the Immigration Commission estimated, half of all Japanese in this nation—39,500 of approximately 79,000—were engaged in some phase of farming. And three of every four agricultural workers—

30,000—were in California. Perhaps 6,000 were independent operators, the others, hired hands.

As the Japanese on the farms grew in numbers and productivity,
the urban community also expanded, in large part to provide services. Gradually, the farm-urban ratio changed. By 1930, slightly
more than 43 percent of the total Japanese population of California
lived in cities of more than 25,000. And though the urban Japanese
depended primarily on their own people from the countryside, they
required and found clientele for their services among others.

Obviously, some Japanese who tried farming were unsuited for it.
This and language difficulties may help explain charges that the Japanese in early years failed to honor contractual agreements. H. A.
Millis, who conducted an extensive study of the Japanese for the Immigration Commission in 1911, wrote later on this point: [8]

> Much of it [the reputation for not living up to contracts] appears
> to have been due to their inability to understand all the details
> of a contract they could not read. In recent years more care has
> been taken to understand all of the conditions of the contract
> entered into and the charges of breach of contract have become
> much fewer. Another source of misunderstanding has been that
> some of the Japanese who think more in personal terms and less
> in terms of contract than Americans, have sought to secure a
> change in their leases when they proved to be bad bargains and
> have occasionally left their holdings in order to avoid loss. A
> third fact is that formerly some undesirable Japanese secured
> leases. These, however, have gradually fallen out of the class of
> tenants so that most of those who remain are efficient and desir-
> able farmers. The changes noted explain the statement of a
> prominent fruit shipper to the effect that ten years ago forty of
> each fifty tenants were dishonest, but that now the forty are
> honest and entirely trustworthy.

For the most part the Japanese sought individual opportunities to
lease or own land, but there is one conspicuous exception. In 1907
Kyutaro Abiko, a leader of the San Francisco Japanese community,
newspaper publisher, and head of the Japanese American Business
Promotion Company (*Nichibei Kangyosha*) purchase 2,000 acres of
what was considered wasteland near Livingston.[9] He persuaded a
number of Japanese to settle on this land on liberal terms, creating
what came to be known as the Yamato Colony. These Japanese

pioneered in a very real sense land which never had been cultivated. Ultimately, they were able to tie down the shifting sandy soil and produced fields that were much admired by their white neighbors. Members of the Yamato Colony became landowners before the first alien land laws were passed. They prospered, although Abiko did not. In the depression of 1913 his company, which was overextended by land purchases, failed.

Two other areas of notable Japanese success deserve mention. The first is rice-growing.[10] On the rich land of the lower Sacramento Valley the rice grew rank and did not mature before the rainy season. The idea that changed matters is attributed to a man named K. Ikuta who imported seed from early maturing varieties in Japan. His success attracted white farmers to rice culture. By the time of World War I, California was a major rice producer although the Japanese were responsible for only a small fraction of the crop. Even so, the Japanese Association of America in a memorial to President Woodrow Wilson asserted that Japanese farmers in 1918 produced one million sacks of rice.[11]

The other is chick-sexing. Using techniques developed in Japan skilled workmen identified male chicks soon after hatching. These can be discarded by poultrymen interested only in producing laying hens. Chick-sexing in the late 1930's became a professional monopoly of Japanese and Japanese Americans whose expertise was in high demand in all egg-producing areas.

Southern California

Perhaps because early Los Angeles was not an important port, Southern California did not attract Japanese in significant numbers until after the turn of the century. In 1880, Los Angeles was a sleepy little community of about 11,000. The census of 1890 found only thirty-six Japanese in Los Angeles County; in 1900 there were only 204. This was largely an urban group working at small business enterprises such as restaurants and bamboo-furniture shops plus a few railroad workers. But the first decade of this century saw a surge of Japanese into the Los Angeles area. The 1910 census listed 8,641 in the county, half of them in the city of Los Angeles. Many of those in the still-undeveloped county were railroad and farm laborers, but others farmed land which long since has been turned into heavily populated suburbs. The Los Angeles population was also augmented by Japanese who left San Francisco after the 1906 earthquake. Before long, Japan town in Los Angeles, not far from City Hall, became the center of the largest concentration of Japanese in the United States.

Imperial County

Census takers in 1900 found no Japanese in Imperial County. But by 1910 they began to lease land and became an important factor in the region's economy. The story in Orange County was approximately the same.

Commercial Fishing

While numbers of Japanese were making their way in farms and towns, a lesser number turned to commercial fishing. One report states they fished for salmon on the Sacramento and San Joaquin rivers before the turn of the century; another says they first fished commercially in the Monterey Bay area. The Japanese were involved in the salmon industry in Oregon and Washington as well, but only in the canneries since they were not permitted to fish commercially. In Southern California they harvested abalone commercially in 1899 but found little market among the white population. Masaharu Kondo, who studied fisheries and oceanography at Tokyo Imperial University, arrived in the United States in 1908 on a trip around the world. While in the San Pedro area he became interested in the possibility of developing a fishing industry off the west coast of Mexico. In 1912 he returned to San Diego, organized the M. K. Fisheries Company and obtained concessions to fish for lobsters, abalone, and tuna off Baja California.

Don Estes, writing in the *Journal of San Diego History*,[12] says:

> In the process of fishing for tuna these Japanese inadvertently introduced a technique that was to have a major technological impact on the American tuna industry. All of these men, familiar as they were with Japanese methods, fished for tuna by utilizing long, flexible, and exceedingly strong bamboo poles rather than with nets. The net method, known as seining, caught more fish, but in the process many of the fish were damaged or bruised. The result was that blood spots would show up in the cans of otherwise white tuna meat. By utilizing poles the Japanese fishermen were able to bring the fish aboard the boats without any damage to the meat. Once the San Diego canneries discovered this method, they promoted it among the entire west coast tuna fleet.

The tuna canneries were established in 1913 and the area near San Pedro called Terminal Island became almost a company town of Japanese fishermen and their wives who worked in the canneries. California Fish and Game Commission records show there were 491 Japanese fishermen, about 13 percent of the total, in the 1915–16 year. Four years later there were 1,316 Japanese fishermen or 28 percent of the total. By 1923, according to the United States Department of Commerce, Japanese made up 50 percent of fishing-boat crews in San Diego. Another report shows some 900 Japanese fishermen manned 250 boats out of San Pedro in 1929, with 180 fishermen operating thirty boats out of San Diego.

Pacific Northwest

California always has had the largest Japanese population and was the bellwether state both in development of community organization among the Japanese and movements hostile to them. However, Japanese came in considerable numbers to the states to the north. Oregon achieved statehood in 1859, thirty years earlier than Washington, and Japanese entered the port of Portland long before direct shipping lines from Japan came to Puget Sound. But Washington provided the immigrants greater opportunities and as early as 1900 the census takers found twice as many Japanese in Washington as in Oregon.[13] Seattle and Tacoma were the ports of entry from which they went out as gang laborers and where they returned when employment ended. Labor contractors organized crews of immigrants fresh off the ships and sent them as far east as Idaho, Montana, and the Dakotas to maintain railroad lines. It was not unusual for Japanese farm boys to get their first real view of the United States from a section-gang camp in the lonely reaches of the Rockies.

Other Japanese found employment in the sawmills that were busily turning logs into lumber. Japanese consular records show that in 1891 as many as eighty Japanese were among the 500 men working at a sawmill in Port Blakely on Bainbridge Island across Puget Sound from Seattle. A few began to start families about the turn of the century and some of the first Nisei were born there.

Salmon canneries on Puget Sound and along the Columbia River also provided seasonal jobs for early Japanese immigrants.[14] Here as in the California farmlands, the Japanese replaced aging Chinese laborers. When the salmon runs dwindled and canneries moved to Alaska, Japanese contractors again provided labor crews of bachelors, many of whom drifted to California farm jobs after the summer salmon season. These migrant laborers were referred to as "Alaska boys" and rather scorned by the settled Japanese community. In time the Issei laborers were joined, then replaced, by Nisei, many of them students who used their summer earnings to pay for college educations. And the Nisei in turn lost their jobs to Filipinos and Mexicans whose vigorous union activities had forced out most of the Japanese contractors by World War II.

Railroad jobs, which took the immigrants out of the port cities, also introduced them to other employment opportunities. Labor in the sugar beet fields of Spokane County established the Japanese in that area about 1900. In Washington as in California the Japanese were not content to work for others. The first Japanese-operated farms were started in 1903—east of the Cascade Mountains in Wapato in the Yakima Valley, and west of the Cascades in the White River Valley between Seattle and Tacoma.[15] The White River Valley, together with the adjoining Puyallup Valley, were to become centers of Japanese truck farming. Oddly enough, dairying also became important among the Japanese in this area. Since animal husbandry was of little importance in Japan, the immigrants had little experience in this industry but they made an important contribution to the milk supply of Seattle consumers and condensing plants.[16]

All these farmers operated on a precarious basis. The Washington state constitution prohibited land ownership by aliens unless they had declared their intention of becoming citizens. The Japanese, as aliens ineligible to citizenship, were caught in limbo. They became lease holders or renters and, in large part, undertook to convert swampy and logged-off land into farms, a feat that required an enormous amount of back-breaking labor. East of the Cascades much of the land cultivated by the Japanese was reclaimed from sagebrush on the Yakima Indian Reservation.

In Washington as elsewhere the charge that Japanese had driven white farmers from the best agricultural lands was absurd. However, as time went on, there was an element of truth in these complaints in that often the Japanese were willing to pay higher rentals than their white competitors for desirable property. But in a free, competitive society it only meant they could outcompete their white neighbors. The accompanying charge that the Japanese, like the Chinese before them, lived more cheaply than the white man meant only that they accepted the substandard accommodations provided by the white landowner, and that their aspirations for a better life for their children necessarily meant careful husbanding of resources for the future.

So long as they viewed themselves as sojourners, the Japanese felt little concern about their inability to buy land. But as the prospect of return to Japan receded, they found land ownership increasingly attractive. In time they, like the Japanese in California, found they could buy land in the names of their citizen-children or by corporate ventures. Washington closed these loopholes by amendments to the law in 1921 and 1923, but by then the Japanese were playing a substantial role in the farm economy as growers and shippers of vegetables. One of their more noticeable contributions was their neat and colorful retail vegetable stands at the Pike Place Public Market where handsome fresh produce was available at bargain prices.

One other notable Japanese contribution to Washington's economy was the introduction of the large Japanese oyster into Puget Sound about 1919. Two Issei, Joe Miyagi and Emy Tsukimoto, are usually associated with the first successful efforts to transplant this oyster at Samish Bay near Bellingham. They soon spread to other sheltered bays and make up a large part of the Northwest's seafood industry.

Although Oregon's climate and economy resembled Washington's, its Japanese population was much the smallest of the three coastal states. As in Washington the immigrants found employment on railroads, in lumber mills, salmon canneries, and on farms. Agriculture was largely in the Columbia and Willamette River valleys around Portland. In Oregon the Japanese inherited less anti-Oriental prejudice than in the other two states. Oregon was a conservative state. The Chinese had played an important role in its early development and the political and business leadership prevented the kinds of anti-Chinese movements that disfigured the history of California and Washington.

The report of the Immigration Commission in 1911 [17] describes Japanese truck and berry farms in Mt. Tabor, Russellville, Montavilla, Gresham, and other areas that were absorbed long ago by Portland's expansion. The Hood River Valley, up to the Columbia from Portland, attracted a number of Japanese. Hired initially to clear logged-off lands, some were given uncleared tracts as payment and were able to begin berry, apple, and pear production on their own. In adjacent Wasco County the Japanese made an abortive attempt to grow wheat, after which they concentrated on truck crops and tomatoes. Just north of Salem, another group of Japanese tilled the rich beaver-dam land at Lake Labish, for the most part on lease-hold. Until 1923 Japanese could purchase land in Oregon, but land ownership grew slowly. As elsewhere, the immigrants saw themselves as sojourners who wanted their assets liquid. By 1920, there were only 4,151 Japanese in the entire state and although many were urbanites, they owned only 2,185 acres. By comparison there were 17,387 Japanese in Washington and 71,952 in California. Even so, the xenophobia set in motion by World War I led to the passage in Oregon of anti-alien land legislation in 1923. Thus, land-ownership, essential to long-term planning, was denied to the Japanese in all three coastal states.

In 1920, 93,490 of the 110,010 Japanese on the American main-land were concentrated on the West Coast. Of the national total, nearly one fourth were American citizens by birth. Clearly, the Japa-nese were entering a new phase of their history in America. A rela-tively stable population was now in being. A measure of commit-ment had been made to life in America, although thousands of Issei returned to their homeland in the following two decades. Those who remained were largely family men whose commitment to Amer-ica was made on behalf of their children who knew no other home. Some scholars have referred to the next phase as the "settling period."

VI ❀ In Interior America

In the preceding chapter we examined the development of Japanese communities in the three West Coast states, particularly in the agricultural areas surrounding ports of entry. There were many Japanese, however, who settled in interior states. In fact, many thousands of young immigrants were in the mountain states at different times in their sojourn as they lived a roaming, almost nomadic life without commitment to any of the regions where they found employment.

Jobs on railroad section gangs introduced the Japanese to interior areas. In 1906, just before the Gentlemen's Agreement barred unskilled labor, perhaps as many as 13,000 Japanese—one in every three in the country—were working for the railroads. This probably was the peak, with employment dropping to 10,000 by 1909 and 4,300 in 1920. According to the Immigration Commission, one Seattle labor contracting firm, the Oriental Trading Company, supplied 15,000 Japanese laborers in the decade between 1898 and 1908. Most of these section hands drifted back to the West Coast. But out of these thousands a few remained in isolated pockets.

The first Japanese to work in the interior states probably were Union Pacific Railroad section hands hired in 1891, the year Japanese migration to the mainland topped one thousand. By the end of the following year about 400 Japanese were employed on the section of the Union Pacific between Granger, Wyoming, and Huntington, Oregon.[1]

Soon Japanese were working on maintenance and a few construction crews in all parts of the West except the Southwest where Mexicans, inured to the climate, were preferred.

Railway company records are no longer available to tell the story of Japanese employment, but the Immigration Commission's voluminous 1911 report includes detailed findings.[2] Even Yamato Ichihashi in preparing nearly a half century ago his pioneering study, *Japanese in the United States*, leaned heavily on the report.

The system by which Japanese labor was recruited and organized is described by the Immigration Commission in this manner: [3]

> These Japanese agents collect their men in various ways. Some apply directly to them for work, most have been obtained through boarding houses, while others are "recruited" through advertising and the more usual methods used with other races in Seattle, Portland, San Francisco, and Los Angeles. The most important of these methods has been the second, where the laborers have been collected through large boarding houses.
>
> Each of the large boarding houses in the coast cities has or has had affiliations with large Japanese contractors, or has been contacted by a contractor as a means of collecting laborers. The hotel keepers' organizations in San Francisco and Seattle establish the fee which the contractor shall pay the boarding house keeper for each man obtained through him—at $3 in the one city, at $1.50 in the other.
>
> Agents for Japanese labor invariably collect from each person employed as a railroad laborer an "office fee" or "interpreter's fee" of $1 per month and a second payment of so much per day or a given percentage of their earnings. Two of the largest of the contractors, and several of the smaller ones collect, in addition to the interpreter's fee, 5 cents for each day worked. One of these formerly collected 10 cents per day without an interpreter's fee, but in 1904 changed to the present rule in order to compete more sucessfully for laborers. Another agency collects an interpreter's fee of $1 per month and 5 cents for each day worked during the month up to 20, thus limiting the total deduction on account of the agency to $2 per month. Two agencies collect only 2 cents per day for each day worked, in addition to the interpreter's fee of $1 per month.
>
> It may be pointed out in passing that this arrangement is very much more satisfactory to the laborers than where each "job" is paid for in a lump sum commission. It, at any rate, protects the men from the graft sometimes practiced by foremen and agencies cooperating in collecting, hiring, and discharging laborers.
>
> As a second source of profit the contractors usually supply their men with most of the goods they consume, or else act through auxiliary organizations which do. Scarcely ever is the supply business absent. It is well worth the while, for the Japanese, for the most part, consume Japanese wares, and as the

laborers are far removed from towns, these can usually be had only from the contractor who finds employment for them. It is estimated that 30 per cent of the food used is American in its origin and 70 per cent Japanese. Most of this Japanese food and a small part of the clothing and miscellaneous goods purchased are supplied by the contractor.

If property accumulation is a good criterion, the commissions and profits from supplies sold have given the larger contractors a handsome profit. However, the contractor himself, or his interpreters through whom he usually acts, looks after all difficulties and disputes arising between laborers and foremen or other representatives of the company in regard to work, wages, bunk cars, and other matters. He does much more than find employment for laborers and supply them with goods at a profit.

As a general rule, the Japanese employed in railroad work are paid directly by the company, deductions to cover commissions and supply bills due being made, which sums are paid directly to the agency. However, the several railway companies supplied with laborers by two of the largest of the Japanese agents pay these agents for the men supplied, they in turn, paying the laborers after deducting commissions and sums due for supplies purchased.

Much of the foregoing applies to all labor contracting—in the mines, salmon canneries, sugar beet fields—involving Japanese. The Immigration Commission reported that: [4]

> The railroads with western terminals at Tacoma or Seattle began to employ Japanese as section hands in 1896 and 1898. On the railroads in the Southwest their employment dates from the close of the nineties, while on the railroads centering in San Francisco and Oakland and extending north to the Oregon line, east to Ogden, and south to Los Angeles, their employment began somewhat earlier. With these beginnings, when the Japanese in the country were comparatively few, the number employed increased with the expanding immigration from Japan and Hawaii until 1906.
>
> Three causes contributed to this increase in the number of Japanese engaged in railroad work. In the first place, they were made available through contractors at a time when industries were expanding and it was impossible to retain as section men (at the wages which obtained) the Americans, Irish, and north

Europeans, who had constituted the majority of such laborers previous to 1895, and when the number of Chinese available had become small as a result of the operation of the exclusion laws and the tendency of that race to seek agricultural employment or to withdraw to the cities. In the second place, they were willing to work for a lower wage than the Italians, Greeks, and Slavs, who were being steadily employed in large numbers. In the third place, except where Mexicans have been available, they have generally been regarded as satisfactory laborers.

A few Japanese rose to positions of some responsibility and made railroading their careers, but the great majority left as soon as better-paying opportunities became available. Railroad work was hard and living conditions at best were hardly acceptable. The Immigration Commission reported: [5]

> The Japanese, like other laborers employed as section hands, are usually provided with lodging in box cars "set" on the side-track. The men live in a cooperative group, purchasing much, if not most, of their supplies from the contractor under whose control they work. The limitations imposed upon them by these conditions are not the least important in explaining the strong tendency exhibited by thc Japanese to secure other employment. Their desire for better equipped and clean "bunk cars" was cited by one roadmaster as an important source of trouble with the Japanese. The Greeks and Italians were satisfied with less.

This helps lay to rest one of the canards employed by hostile forces who contended the Japanese were content with substandard living conditions and were undermining the advances the American working man had achieved.

While the Immigration Commission gives us an outline of what life was like for the Japanese, no one knows how many became casualties of the rough frontier conditions. The toll taken by disease and accidents may have reached several thousand. As early as 1892 a Japanese cemetery was established in Nampa, Idaho, probably by Tanaka Chushichi, a railroad labor contractor. The markers over the graves of nine Japanese are visible today. How many other young men were buried in unmarked graves along railroad rights of way in Montana, Wyoming, Colorado, Utah, and other western states must be a matter of conjecture. In Montana alone, where hundreds of Japanese worked on the Northern Pacific and Great Northern, at least 230 Japanese tombstones may be found. Most of them are believed to have been victims of Rocky Mountain spotted fever, a particularly lethal disease until medical researchers found it was transmitted by ticks and learned to control it.

Job opportunities in agriculture and mining were responsible for the Japanese leaving the railroads in large numbers. In both industries two factors helped the Japanese. First was the declining number and aging of Chinese laborers; the Chinese Exclusion Act prohibited new immigration. The other was the developing contract labor system which made Japanese workmen attractive to employers. Oddly enough, only Colorado, Utah, and Idaho attracted and retained the Japanese in substantial numbers.

The Japanese in Utah

At the turn of the century, census takers found 417 Japanese in Utah. Apparently most were contract laborers. By 1910, there were 2,110, primarily railroad and sugar beet workers who returned to Ogden and Salt Lake City between jobs. A stable urban population developed in these cities to serve the needs of the transients. In 1909 the Immigration Commission found forty-six Japanese business establishments in Salt Lake City and forty-three in Ogden. Of the total of eighty-nine, eleven were labor contracting offices and nineteen were boardinghouses and hotels.

Sugar beet cultivation had become important in Utah before the turn of the century. In 1903 a sugar company brought in forty Japanese laborers from California. Japanese moved rapidly into independent farming, and by 1909 they owned 157 acres and leased nearly 6,000. The Japanese were not harassed by anti-alien land legislation until World War II, but even so, they were slow to purchase land. Lack of capital was one factor. But more important, the Japanese were inclined to keep their assets liquid in anticipation of returning to the homeland.

Utah's Mormon environment did not subject the Japanese to the kind of hostility they encountered in California, but by the same token opportunities were limited for non-Mormons.

The Japanese also found employment in Utah's coal mines, mainly near Price and Helper, and the Bingham Canyon open-pit copper mine outside Salt Lake City.

The Japanese population was stable enough so that community organizations were established and a vernacular newspaper was founded in 1909. By 1930, the Japanese population had grown to 3,269, but

First Japanese diplomatic mission to the U.S. meets Secretary of State Lewis Cass in Washington, May 16, 1860. COURTESY, TOKYO UNIVERSITY

Grave of Okei near Gold Hill, California, as it appeared when "discovered" in the 1930's. A member of the Wakamatsu Colony, Okei arrived in California in 1869, died in 1871. TAK MURAKAMI COLLECTION

First Japanese plantation workers reached Hawaii in 1868. This woman probably was of a somewhat later era. TAK MURAKAMI COLLECTION

Thousands of Japanese immigrants helped keep U.S. railroads in repair during the first two decades of this century. DENVER PUBLIC LIBRARY WESTERN HISTORY COLLECTION

Coal and copper mines employed many Japanese who were caught up in labor disputes. These men are identified as survivors of the Ludlow Massacre in Colorado in 1915. DENVER PUBLIC LIBRARY WESTERN HISTORY COLLECTION

A few Japanese, such as this unidentified Wyoming cowboy, found jobs on cattle ranches.

Fred N. Kawamura learned to fly in Colorado and won his pilot's license in 1921. He took his Lozier runabout over Milner Pass in the Rockies in the winter of 1925. TOM MASAMORI COLLECTION

After railroad jobs ended, young Japanese took farm work. These men, some wearing ties, weeded sugar beets on the Kinoshita farm near Sedgwick, Colorado, in 1910. TOM MASAMORI COLLECTION

New immigrants and men returning from visits to Japan wait to go ashore at Angel Island U.S. Quarantine Station in San Francisco Bay about 1923.

NATIONAL ARCHIVES

Picture-brides arriving in San Francisco wait for immigration clearance before meeting husbands for the first time. VISUAL COMMUNICATIONS

New families eked out a living as sharecroppers or on leased farms. VISUAL COMMUNICATIONS

Those who settled in urban areas usually found homes in ghettoes such as "Jap Alley" in Fresno, California. BANCROFT LIBRARY, UNIVERSITY OF CALIFORNIA

Sugar beet harvest was a time when everyone worked, with the wife driving the wagon, husband and hired hands digging, topping, and loading beets. TOM MASAMORI COLLECTION

Japanese fishermen introduced technique of landing tuna with line and pole so fish were not damaged. TAK MURAKAMI COLLECTION

Issei women staff a Red Cross booth for World War I patriotic rally.
TOM MASAMORI COLLECTION

Many Issei pioneers were buried at Riverside Cemetery, Denver. This photo was taken in 1919. DENVER PUBLIC LIBRARY WESTERN HISTORY COL-LECTION

Early members of the Nisei generation. Their parents were "aliens ineligible to citizenship;" they were Americans by birth.

Racial discrimination plagued the Japanese. Signs in window say "Japs Keep Out," and "Member Hollywood Protective Association."

Willingness of Japanese farmers to work tirelessly led to laws prohibiting aliens from owning land. VISUAL COMMUNICATIONS

during the Depression decade that followed, their numbers dropped to 2,210.

The Japanese in Wyoming

Although the Immigration Commission reports that Japanese contract laborers began mining coal in Wyoming in 1900, a study entitled *The Intermountain Area and the Japanese* says they reached the state in 1898. According to this account a Salt Lake City labor contractor, Nishiyama Hajime, supplied workmen for the Union Pacific Coal Mine Company in Rock Springs.[6] Some time later the Japanese American Business Promotion Company of San Francisco became the most important source of contract labor in Wyoming mines, particularly around Hanna, Rock Springs, Green River, and Granger.

The United Mine Workers began unionization of coal miners in 1907. Traditionally, Orientals were regarded as enemies of the American working man. Japanese had been used as strikebreakers in Southern Colorado and Utah coal mines in 1903–04, in meat packing plants in Omaha, Nebraska, in 1904, and in Utah smelters in 1907. However, they appear to have been well thought of in Wyoming and were given an opportunity to join the union. The Immigration Commission found: [7]

> It is stated that the operators expected to be able to use the Orientals at lower rates than those fixed upon in the union agreement. However, a delegation of Japanese was sent to the convention of the union, which was held in Denver, to present their side of the case, with the result that a special dispensation was granted, and the Chinese and Japanese who were on the ground were allowed to become members of the union on an equal footing with other races. The Japanese now earn wages equal to those of other races—$3.10 per day for company men and the uniform piece rates for mining and loading. In this State the Japanese earn higher wages than in any of the other Western states where they are employed in coal mines. The difference is due to their participation in the results of union organization.

Wyoming mines were manned by workers from many ethnic backgrounds, most of them recent immigrants, and they seemed to get along quite well. The immigration report adds that the Japanese were "loyal members of the union and exhibit considerable pride in their connection with this organization."

The Japanese in Colorado

Census takers in 1900 counted forty-eight Japanese in Colorado. Ten years later, 2,300 were recorded. Jobs on the railroads, in coal mines, and sugar beet fields were largely responsible for this growth. An unknown number of Japanese arrived as strikebreakers in the Trinidad area. When the strike ended, many remained; sixty-five were reported in the region in 1909. A few Japanese are buried in a Trinidad cemetery. It was also in 1903 that a labor contractor, Hokazono Naoichi, brought seventy workers for sugar beet labor. By 1909, the number of Japanese in agriculture rose to 2,160, many of them farming for themselves.[8] Contractors in Southern Colorado who absconded with workmen's wages, together with competition from Mexican laborers, sped the movement to independent operations. In 1909 Japanese had leased or rented 14,000 acres in Northern Colorado and 4,400 acres in the southern part of the state. A few Japanese appear to have begun growing cantaloupes near Rocky Ford as early as 1902.

In 1904 approximately 100 Japanese were hired to help build the Moffat Road from Denver over Corona Pass on the Continental Divide to Steamboat Springs. Other Japanese went to work on the Rio Grande line. Hokazono soon expanded into contracting for railroad, highway, power line, and irrigation-dam construction, providing jobs for hundreds of young Japanese. At one time Hokazono is reputed to have had more than a thousand horses and mules. He suffered health problems and died, nearly destitute, in 1920. In 1976, Hokazono's role in the development of frontier Colorado was commemorated with dedication of a stained-glass window in his likeness in the state capitol. Hokazono shares the window with a Chinese pioneer, Chin Lin Soo, whose crews built railroads and mined gold at Central City.

The passing of the gang-labor period produced an urban settlement in Denver adjacent to a Chinatown which was founded some years earlier. Farmers from nearby areas came to this settlement to shop for Japanese provisions. In time the community became large enough to support Christian and Buddhist churches and two newspapers.

Aside from a brief anti-Japanese movement in 1908–09, the immigrants found Colorado a pleasant place in which to live and work. The population remained fairly constant from 1910 until the Depression years when the Japanese population in the entire United States declined. The entry of the U.S. into World War II saw a sudden influx of Japanese, directly from the West Coast at first, and later from the relocation camps. The abrupt rise in population created a number of problems which will be treated in another chapter.

Japanese in Other Mountain States

The story of the Japanese in Idaho differs little from that of other interior states. The railroads brought them in as contract laborers. They soon left this dreary work for the equally demanding chores of planting, thinning, cultivating, irrigating, and harvesting sugar beets. The more ambitious went into farming for themselves or established restaurants in towns while others returned to coastal states.

As we have seen, large numbers of Japanese worked in Montana but the cold winters there were not to their liking. When the Great Western Sugar Manufacturing Company began operations in the Billings area in 1906, it recruited a number of railroad workers. However, they were not destined to play an important part in Montana agriculture. A short growing season and the harsh climate discouraged all but the most hardy.

The first substantial group of Japanese to enter Nebraska were strikebreakers who were recruited in Colorado to work in the meat-packing plants in Omaha. In 1900 there had been only three Japanese in Nebraska; by 1910, there were 590. Many were former railroad workers who had gone into farming in the North Platte Valley.

Very few Japanese settled in New Mexico for reasons that are not entirely clear. Perhaps the dry climate that discouraged all but subsistence farming was a factor. Another was the competition for jobs from the native Hispano population.

The Japanese in Wisconsin

The good reputation Japanese farm laborers established in Colorado led to an anomalous situation. A small number of them were invited to move to Wisconsin. The report of the Immigration Commission states: [9]

> The Japanese . . . were brought from Colorado where the factory first began to operate in 1905. The manager of the factory had employed Japanese in the beetfields of Colorado, and because of the high degree of satisfaction experienced with this race brought 25 or 30 to the Wisconsin fields, where they have remained permanently, working as ice cutters or section hands on the railroad when not engaged in beet culture.

What happened to them over the years is not known. However, it
is apparent that in an area where Orientals were virtually unknown,
they faced none of the prejudice that was widespread on the Pacific
Coast. The Immigration Commission report noted: [10]

> The Japanese were spoken of in terms of unstinted praise,
> and, according to the manager of the factory which procured
> these laborers, it would be difficult to obtain more desirable
> immigrants. Their standards of living are said to compare favor-
> ably, in many respects, with those of skilled American laborers.
> In general character they rank much higher than the Belgians
> and Russians. As laborers they are efficient, energetic, sober,
> and tractable, and can be relied on not to waste their employer's
> time when working by the day, while as day laborers the Bel-
> gians will loaf on the job if not given constant supervision. The
> Japanese are appreciative of good treatment, but are intolerant
> of imposition or deceit. They are cleanly in personal habits and
> wear a good quality of ready-made clothing except when at
> work, when they put on the established garb of the farm laborer
> —overalls and shirt. Their food is of good quality, though it
> includes large quantities of rice. They are usually thrifty, and
> send their savings to a Japanese specie bank in California which
> issues receipts written in the Japanese language. The Japanese
> are manifesting a strong tendency to engage in agricultural pur-
> suits on their own account, and it is the ruling ambition of a
> great many of them to become independent farmers. Few have
> yet purchased land, but there are a number who have rented
> small tracts and are raising sugar beets, cucumbers, and other
> produce. Japanese are regarded at this factory as one of the
> most desirable class of immigrants ever admitted to the United
> States, and a desire was expressed for 100 additional laborers
> of this race.

The Japanese in Texas

The pattern of penetration and settlement noted in this chapter up
to this point does not apply to the Japanese in Texas. The pioneer
Japanese leaders who settled in the Lone Star State were not peasants,
nor were they "birds of passage" hoping to return home after accu-
mulating a little money. The labor contractor, therefore, played no
part in developments.[11]

These first settlers were, in the main, men of substance who came
well financed and often brought their own labor force. They inherited

no anti-Chinese tradition; Texas had its own form of racial prejudice but it did not affect the Oriental. In fact, since discrimination was directed at the blacks and Hispanos, the Japanese found themselves classified with the whites. Many of the Japanese came to develop rice culture which would help the economy, and they were welcomed in much the way the Wakamatsu Colony was welcomed in California in 1869.

It is likely that more than personal aspirations motivated some of these immigrants. They apparently saw an opportunity to serve Japan. A growing population had forced Japan to begin importing rice by 1890. By the time of the Russo-Japanese War in 1904, Japan was importing about 15 million bushels annually mostly from Korea and Taiwan. There seems to be little doubt that those who came to Texas had visions of a rice industry tied economically to their homeland. This view is supported by the fact that significant amounts of Japanese capital was poured into the Texas venture.

Rice had been grown in various parts of the South but the Houston Chamber of Commerce, seeking ways of building the local economy in 1902, got in touch with Consul-General Uchida Satatsuchi in New York City about the possibility of inviting Japanese rice-growers to farm in their area. At that time Saibara Seito was concluding two years of study at Hartford Theological Seminary. The consul-general invited Saibara to accompany him on an inspection trip to Houston en route to Japan. Saibara liked the possibilities, but unable to interest others in moving to Texas, he decided to undertake the venture himself. Although he had established a promising career in politics and education, Saibara liquidated his assets in Japan and began rice farming on a 120-acre tract near Houston in 1903.

The following year Arai Saburo came to St. Louis to assist in the Japanese exhibit at the Louisiana Purchase Exposition. On his way home he visited Texas. Back in Japan he borrowed $250,000 from the Mitsui Trading Company to finance a fruit orchard at Alvin midway between Houston and Galveston. Onishi Rihei was also a pioneer fruitgrower in Wharton County a short distance west of Houston. Other early rice growers arriving with substantial funds were Kishi Kichimatsu, Kobayashi Kotaro, and Mykawa Shinpei.

Each of these entrepreneurs brought his family and a few employees. Since their operations were fairly substantial, they hired many blacks and Mexicans. The Japanese population was never large, but about 100 attended a celebration in Houston celebrating the fall of Port Arthur in the Russo-Japanese War in 1905. Five years later census takers found only 340 Japanese in the entire state. Texas was an exception to the finding that Japanese usually took over menial jobs from the dwindling Chinese population. Black and Mexican workers were plentiful, and the Japanese found no labor vacuum to fill in Texas.

The first rice crops grown with Japanese seed were far larger than average. But continuous cultivation soon exhausted the land. Ironically, the fact the Japanese were free to purchase land, and had done so, worked against them. If they had been forced to lease land and move on to new leaseholds in a few years as in California, they might have prospered. Most Japanese turned from rice culture to truck gardening or cotton, or they left Texas. By 1920, only a few Japanese, including the Saibara and Kishi families, were still in the rice business.

Kishi was also in the oil business for a short time. A Japanese capitalist, Matsukata Kojiro, helped finance Kishi, probably with the needs of oil-poor Japan in mind, but the venture was unsuccessful.

The Japanese settled in two other sections of Texas; the lower Rio Grande Valley and the El Paso area at the state's westernmost point. The first Japanese to settle in the Rio Grande Valley is believed to have been Kiyamoto Heishiro who bought twenty acres and introduced citrus-fruit production to the area. However, Shimotsu Uichi is regarded as the pioneer in the development of Japanese agriculture. He married the first Japanese woman in the valley in 1917. The mild climate enabled the farmers to grow winter vegetables which were shipped to distant markets.

In 1919 a group of seven Japanese bought 400 acres from the Brulay Plantation near Brownsville and established what they called the Yamato Colony.[12] The timing was unfortunate. The postwar depression plus the inability of the members to cooperate caused its failure.

The lower Rio Grande Valley was the only part of Texas where the Japanese encountered racial hostility. A number of Japanese sought to settle there after California passed an alien land law in 1921. This led to a movement to expel those already there. The Texans agreed to let them stay provided no more Japanese came into the valley. In later years Nisei born and reared in the valley amused West Coast Nisei with their strong Texas accents.

Many members of the Japanese community at El Paso had been involved in mining and farming in Mexico and had fled across the border to escape one of the periodic revolutions. Some went into business in the city and others farmed nearby. Their numbers were augmented by Japanese from California. By 1915, there were enough of them to organize a Japanese Association in El Paso.

No one knows how many Japanese slipped across the Rio Grande from Mexico to become illegal immigrants. Eagle Pass, roughly midway between El Paso and Brownsville, is often cited as the most commonly used crossing point, and legend has it that at least some Japanese died in attempting to cross the wasteland in that part of Texas.

The Japanese in Florida

As in Texas, Florida was the site of a Yamato Colony. The Florida East Coast Railway, in a drive to develop land along its right of way in Palm Beach County, sought buyers. Two Japanese studying in New York learned of the opportunity and founded the colony in 1904. It did not prosper. Initial efforts to grow pineapples foundered because of Cuban competition. The colony did better with vegetables. In 1916 when a severe freeze damaged crops in other southern states, the Japanese made an enormous profit. Some returned immediately to Japan.

The opening of Miami Beach in 1925 inflated land values and most of the Japanese sold their farms at a great profit. By 1960, only one Japanese family was farming Yamato Colony land. Another who remained was George Sukeji Morikami, who had joined the colony two years after its founding. He never married, but made and lost a fortune as a vegetable wholesaler, then rebuilt that fortune in land investments. In 1973, three years before his death, he donated 140 acres to Palm Beach County for a park. He had bought the land for $15 to $17 per acre; it was worth more than $10,000 per acre when he gave it away. A museum of Japanese culture, called the Morikami Museum, has been built on the site.

Another ill-fated Japanese colony was established in 1913 at Middleburg in Clay County in Northeastern Florida. It was an ambitious venture involving some 60,000 acres. However, the heavy clay soils of the area and an impossible transportation problem doomed the project and many members soon left for California.

Japanese on the East Coast [13]

Railroading and mining had no part in Japanese settling in the eastern states. And only during World War II did Japanese go into agriculture, mostly at Seabrook, New Jersey, as part of the resettlement program.

However, students from Japan were attending universities on the East Coast long before Japanese settlement of the West began. Census takers in 1870 counted ten Japanese in Massachusetts and New Jersey, and one in Pennsylvania. These scholars—either government-supported or the scions of well-to-do families—were serious young men with a sense of mission who created a fine impression of the Japanese people. Virtually all of them returned to Japan to assume important posts in the developing government.

Those who arrived at a somewhat later period were not sojourners. Immigration companies and labor contractors had no part in their decision to seek opportunities in the new land. Many were compelled to accept menial positions at first, and some used these jobs as springboards to achieve distinguished careers and move easily into social circles. Still, these Japanese were handicapped by their status as "aliens ineligible to citizenship."

Largely overlooked in accounts of the Japanese in the United States is the story of three remarkable men who can be considered to be the "fathers" of today's vast U.S.-Japan trade, second only to trade between the United States and Canada. In the early days of U.S.-Japanese relations Japanese trading firms were no more than order-takers for American businessmen stationed in Yokohama or other port cities. Far-sighted Japanese merchants realized the need to establish direct trade ties. In March of 1876 six young Japanese arrived in New York to promote direct trade. They came to be known as the Oceanic group since they had crossed the Pacific to San Francisco on the liner *Oceanic*.

Only three of the six are important to the trade story. They are Sato Momotaro, Arai Ryoichiro and Morimura Toyo.* Sato opened a wholesale and retail business in silk goods, Japanese handicrafts, and tea. Arai, in collaboration with Sato, launched the raw silk trade which, up to World War II, became the single most important commodity Japan exported to the United States. Sato also was associated with Morimura in founding the Hinode Company, a trading firm. All three were Issei in the sense that they were long-term residents of the United States—as well as having to cope with prejudice based on race—but their experiences and problems were quite different from

* For persons most closely associated with Japan, the Japanese form is used —family name followed by given name. For Issei and others, the American form is used—given name followed by family name.

Issei who established a foothold on the West Coast by working on farms and railroads. Arai's son, Yoneo Arai, one of the earliest Nisei, is a prominent New York attorney.

The Japanese population remained small with the major concentration in New York City. Only after 1900 did their numbers exceed one thousand. Today, however, New York State ranks second in the continental United States in numbers of Japanese. This fact is misleading and requires explanation. Actually, the 1970 census shows 213,277 Japanese in California, 20,188 in Washington, and 19,794 in New York. Although precise figures are unavailable, it is believed the majority of those in New York are businessmen from Japan and their families who are in the United States only temporarily. Most of them are reassigned to other posts at intervals, usually four or five years. Although without doubt they are Japanese, they must be considered in a category different from that of United States citizens of Japanese origins and Japanese of whatever citizenship who are considered permanent residents. Since 1970, the number of businessmen from Japan, primarily employees of large trading companies, has increased dramatically in New York, justifying the assumption that the Japanese population has exceeded that of Washington. However, New York City also has attracted a substantial number of Japanese Americans, many of them in the professions.

Among the early Japanese on the East Coast, two achieved international distinction. Noguchi Hideyo, born to a peasant family in Northern Japan, became a world-known bacteriologist who played a key role in conquering yellow fever. Takamine Jokichi, of an elite family, was a pharmacologist credited with the discovery of adrenaline and diastase. The occupations of others ranged from importing and exporting to the academic positions, from restaurants to domestic service.

Although they were almost invisible in the multi-racial, polyglot populations of East Coast cities, Japanese immigrants and their offspring experienced a measure of discrimination which was the consequence of West Coast politics. And yet, it is probably correct to say that Japanese on the East Coast suffered fewer psychic wounds than was the lot of their peers on the West Coast.

VII ❧ The Chinese and Japanese

To most white Americans, Japanese and Chinese looked and acted very much alike. This is understandable in that they had certain characteristics in common. Many Caucasians professed to be unable to distinguish one Oriental from another. But anyone making the effort to look beneath surface similarities would have perceived significant differences. The story of how each group became established in the United States, and how they reacted to the American challenge, is also quite different.[1]

Both the push and the pull discussed in Chapter IV played a part in the earliest Chinese immigration. The push was economic depression that hit Kwangtung Province in South China after its chief city, Canton, lost its monopoly of trade with the Western World in the 1840's. The economic difficulties were compounded by flood and famine, creating a definite push to leave the area in search of something more promising. Thus it was that the earliest Chinese immigrants came to the United States from Canton Province, five districts in particular.[2]

The pull was the developing need for contract laborers in California, men to undertake the hard and menial work of a frontier region. In much the pattern that the Japanese were to follow a half century later, enterprising Chinese established urban footholds after periods of labor on farms and forests. By the 1850's, Chinese businesses of various kinds were to be found in several sections of San Francisco. The ghetto character of the San Francisco Chinatown developed later, partly as lonely immigrants were drawn together by common language and cultural heritage, and partly as a defensive reaction to white hostility.

The term "Chinatown" was in popular usage long before the Japanese appeared in significant numbers. Indeed, some of the earliest Japanese arrivals found the Chinatown atmosphere reassuring and worked and lived there until their own ethnic communities came into being.

Chinese, like many other immigrants, were generally of the lower socio-economic class. As a rule they came under indenture or the credit-ticket system, and were burdened with substantial debts which amounted to more than just the cost of passage from China. Out of this status developed a system of control which cost the individual much of his freedom until the debt was repaid.

The China that the immigrants left was more a culture than a nation-state. South China had never become fully reconciled to the Manchu dynasty in Peking and the imperial government exercised little influence over the Chinese in America. Thus, the attachment of the Chinese to their homeland was more in terms of cultural traditions than politics. They had come from a civilization that regarded outsiders as *fan kuei* (foreign devils) and it is understandable that they should respond in kind to the prejudices they encountered. It is also understandable that they should regard their Old World institutions as superior to that of the West. Thus, many preferred life in the ghetto, where they could retain their traditions. Though they worked "out," they liked to live "in." In Chinatown they reproduced Chinese institutions, continued to wear the queue until the overthrow of the Manchus who had imposed it on them as a sign of submission, continued to wear Chinese clothing, and made few compromises toward acculturation and integration.

Among the immigrants were a few members of revolutionary, anti-Manchu secret societies.[3] Not surprisingly, secret societies became a feature of Chinese life in America. In time they dominated the Chinatown underworld and lost their revolutionary character. They were conservative in the sense that, having won a measure of power, they became status quo oriented. Their activities centered largely around control of gambling and prostitution, charitable activities among members, or conflict with rival secret societies. (In this sense they were not unlike the gambling clubs that became a part of early Japanese American communities. In fact the Japanese justified their clubs as providing outlets so gamblers would not take their money to the Chinese.) Only occasionally did the secret societies show any interest in China's political problems, and never did they concern themselves with American politics aside from petty bribes to local police.

The Chinese in America also developed clan associations made up of persons bearing the same surname.[4] They functioned as a kind of immigrant aid society as well as an instrument of discipline. Marriage was not permitted between persons of the same surname. The clan association was likely to be the immigrant's first contact after arrival. It helped him find food and shelter and often, employment. The association also never permitted the immigrant to lose sight of his obligations to family and village in China. Associations of all who spoke a common dialect also came into being. They were called *wui kun* (*hui kuan* in Mandarin).

Associations of district, clan, language, and secret societies all were the support structure which maintained the overall authority of an umbrella organization popularly known as the Chinese Six Companies (*Chung Wah Wui Kun*), but officially titled Chinese Consolidated Benevolent Association. The extent of "benevolence" is difficult to determine; those in need were taken care of, those who died were given the traditional amenities. When in trouble the immigrant looked to the association, or one of its subsidiary groups, for help, protection, and guidance. But at least in the earlier years of his life as an immigrant, his debt was the overwhelming factor in his life. Collection of this debt was certain until 1880 since it was necessary for anyone returning to China to secure clearance from the Six Companies before steamship companies would sell him passage. (The United States enforces a somewhat similar regulation today: Resident aliens leaving the country must present an Internal Revenue document certifying they have paid income taxes due.) The Six Companies maintained order and discipline within the community and also dealt with the white man's world outside. And as the years passed, that became an increasingly hostile world.

The early Chinatowns were overcrowded, disease- and poverty-ridden slums marked by a terrible sexual imbalance. It was common practice for village elders to insist on the marriage of a young man about to go abroad. Since he lacked the means to take his bride with him, the husband went alone while his wife stayed with his parents, in many cases as a virtual servant. The presence of a wife in China tied the young man to his homeland and provided a lien on his earnings. The remitting of earnings to his family was often delayed until the immigrant had met his other obligations. Thus, few but merchants and the wealthy were able to bring their wives with them. The more successful immigrants could send for their wives or, as often happened, they returned home for periodic visits during which they sired a succession of children. The Chinese Exclusion Act of 1882 barred not only laborers but the wives of laborers already in this country, effectively sealing off even the small influx of women that existed. Thus, custom and law dictated that a sexual imbalance be perpetuated until contemporary times.

The United States had virtually no immigration policy when the Chinese initially came to the California gold fields. They were a largely helpless minority quicky brutalized in the raw frontier atmosphere of the American West. "John Chinaman" got the hardest, most menial, most undesirable jobs at the lowest pay. He was discriminated against legally; he was not permitted to testify on his own behalf in some courts when he stepped forward to accuse a white man of theft, fraud, or a physical beating. The harassment escalated to new heights after the transcontinental railroad was completed in 1869. Thousands of Chinese who had been employed by the Central Pacific were thrown on the labor market to compete with white men for jobs. Attempts to use the Chinese as strikebreakers in Massachusetts, New Jersey, and Pennsylvania, and on Southern plantations as a club to discipline recently freed blacks were unsuccessful.[5] These attempts served only to stir up anti-Chinese feeling. Organized movements against them were spawned, and in 1877, as noted earlier, an Irish immigrant, Dennis Kearney, founded the Workingmen's Party in California to agitate for exclusion of all Chinese.

Kearney and his associates soon found the Burlingame Treaty of 1868 made provisions for Chinese immigration. To stop immigration it was necessary to change the treaty. A diplomatic offensive would be required with the help of a rapidly forming anti-Chinese political coalition in Congress.

China would not agree to total exclusion, but in 1880 the imperial government accepted the right of the United States to suspend immigration of laborers. Congress quickly followed up with the Chinese Exclusion Act of 1882 which barred all immigration for ten years. The act was renewed in 1892 and 1902, and after that it was kept in effect until 1943 when Congress was made aware of the injustice of excluding as undesirable the citizens of an ally in the war against the Axis powers. It was the exclusion of Chinese laborers after 1882 that opened the doors of opportunity for the first Japanese immigrants.

At the end of World War II a substantial number of Chinese women began to enter the United States. Some were brides of American servicemen. But large numbers were elderly women joining husbands from whom they had been separated for decades. This influx alleviated the sexual imbalance somewhat. The 1970 federal census found 435,062 Chinese with only 22,068 more men than women.

Gradually, the influence of the Chinatown power elite weakened.[6] American-born Chinese were not inclined to submit to the authority which their parents had accepted. In many communities, as the numbers of unmarried Chinese males diminished and local hostility evaporated, the ethnic communities disappeared. Chinese restaurants, once largely confined to Chinatown, moved out to all parts of the cities.

Since the end of World War II, Chinese immigration—by way of Hong Kong and Taiwan—has been comprised of persons some of whom entered Chinatown and others who did not. Many who fled China when the Communists took over the country in 1949 were Mandarin-speaking, represented the elite class, and had no reason for accepting life in Chinatown. But others, primarily the Cantonese-speaking and the poor, concentrated in the Chinatowns of San Francisco, New York, Los Angeles, and Boston for the same reasons that drew their predecessors decades earlier. Life behind the neon facade of these communities was not always a happy one for these newcomers. The unskilled found the conditions for making a living little different from those of the sweatshops they left in Hong Kong. Youths, facing a high barrier of language standing between them and the good life, often gathered in gangs for protection and companionship.

The first Japanese community of substance, not surprisingly, also developed in San Francisco. They came from a nation in the throes of vast change caused by the impact of the West. They represented a culture which was in large part borrowed from China. Perhaps conscious of their cultural debt to the Asian Continent, the Japanese brought with them a resiliency and adaptability that was to serve them well in America. Yet they were keenly conscious of their identity as Japanese and possessed a pride which sustained them in times of trial.

The first Japanese usually settled close to Chinatowns. Separation into distinct communities seems to have been in part a consequence of developments in Asia. Japan's victory over China in their war of 1894–95 led to some hostility in San Francisco and Honolulu, particularly when the Japanese celebrated. The Chinese now had to accept the military superiority of a people they had long regarded as inferior.

Census takers in 1890 found enough Japanese to comprise an ethnic community only in San Francisco. In the next decade Japan towns developed in Sacramento, Fresno, Portland, Seattle, Tacoma, and Salt Lake City.

In contrast to Japanese in labor gangs, who were largely insulated from American society, the urban dwellers early came to grips with it. Many attended language schools, usually operated by Christian churches. Some established restaurants catering to Western or Japanese tastes or both. Inexpensive hotels and boardinghouses came under Japanese management, as did laundries, bathhouses, barbershops, and stores specializing in Japanese goods. The businesses that prospered were those that catered to the needs of other Japanese, services that were unobtainable for various reasons in the larger community. Just as Chinatown had been a service center for Chinese laborers entering the country or returning from seasonal employment, so Japan towns were sanctuaries for Japanese "birds of passage." [7]

As women arrived in increasing numbers during the first two decades of this century the original pattern of these urban Japanese communities changed. And with their coming, Japanese families were established and Nisei children became a growing and progressively more important part of the scene.

Governance in these communities within cities is not easy to discern. Unlike Chinatown, where power was exercised by the Six Companies, power within Japan town was diffuse. Priests and ministers, newspaper publishers, leaders of the local Japanese associations (*Beikoku Nihonjinkai*), heads of local prefectural associations (*Kenjinkai*), bankers and business leaders, and at least in the early period, Japanese consular officials—all these and perhaps others participated in determining proper Japanese behavior.

Out of this welter of forces emerged certain men who, as elder statesmen, became the accepted community leaders. Although they often quarreled among themselves, they nevertheless dominated the community and were responsible for policy and tactics in maintaining order within and dealing with the white community without. They prevailed, not through wealth or power or violence, but through general acquiescence by a people accustomed to status and order. They were the American counterpart of those who dominated comparable communities in Japan.

Unlike the Chinese, who paid little or no attention to Chinese government officials, the immigrant Japanese acknowledged the authority of Japanese consular representatives. So long as the immigrants lived in expectation of returning in time to Japan, they regarded consular officials as a tie to the homeland. This also was understandable in that the immigrants, being denied American citizenship, had to retain their Japanese nationality or become stateless.

The rise of hostility toward the Japanese caused them to organize against it. The triggering event was a bubonic plague scare in 1900 when, following the annexation of Hawaii to the United States, thousands of Japanese contract laborers left the sugar plantations to seek a better life on the mainland.[8] The sudden influx, which alarmed the West, coincided with the reported discovery of one case of plague in San Francisco's Chinatown. Mayor James D. Phelan ordered the Chinese and Japanese sections of the city quarantined. This was a totally uncalled-for medical precaution which the Japanese correctly read as anti-Oriental discrimination. To coordinate their efforts to combat it, the Japanese organized the *Zaibei Nihonjin Kyogikai* which was reorganized in 1905 as the Japanese Association of America (*Beikoku Nihonjinkai*).[9] It became a loose federation of regional organizations with relatively little actual power.

By 1924, approximately 12 percent of the immigrant Japanese were members. This was not a large membership, but it included the most influential segment of the population. In that year the Southern California region headquartered in Los Angeles had some twenty affiliates. The Northern California unit included thirty-eight locals in northern and central portions of the state. An office in Seattle was headquarters for units in Washington and Montana. Another office in Portland had affiliates in Oregon and Idaho. Affiliates also were organized in Colorado, Arizona, Utah, Texas, Illinois, and New York City. As the organization purporting to represent all Japanese, it tried to be a unifying force, but it had to contend with a certain amount of provincialism. The Japanese Association of America has been characterized as a coordinating rather than controlling group. It had five departments of concern—finance, social welfare, commerce, education, and young people's welfare. With none of the support structure such as underpinned the Six Companies, the Japanese associations exercised little social influence and none of the economic power that made the Chinese organization such a dominant force.

The precise nature of the Japanese associations has been the subject of some difference of opinion. Michinari Fujita, a young Japanese scholar, declared in 1929 that they were "practically a department of the Japanese government." Yamato Ichihashi in his pioneer study, *The Japanese in the United States,* dismissed Fujita contemptuously

as a "schoolboy author" and took him severely to task. In character-
izing the Japanese Association, Ichihashi asserted: [10]

> Certificate fees require a world of explanation, for it was this
> source of revenue to the organization that caused misunder-
> standing as regards its alleged connection with the Japanese gov-
> ernment. The military conscription law of Japan requires men
> between 20 and 37 years of age residing abroad to report annu-
> ally to the Japanese government through the local consulate in
> order to enjoy the privilege of nonmilitary service. The consulate,
> finding this work too cumbersome because of the scattered resi-
> dences of the Japanese in this country, delegated it to local Japa-
> nese associations along with the right to collect the customary
> fee of fifty cents each in issuing the certificate of notification.
> When the Gentlemen's Agreement went into effect, which,
> among other things, permitted the re-admission of those formerly
> domiciled here, those who desired to visit Japan temporarily
> usually secured from the consulate "the certificate of residence"
> needed to facilitate their re-admission into this country. This
> work, too, was turned over to the Japanese associations, which
> were better informed on their local personnel, and the organiza-
> tion, in turn, charged the regular fee in issuing the certificate.
> Beyond this there has been no official connection between the
> Japanese consulates and the Japanese associations.

Fujita's characterization may be too strong and Ichihashi's explanation too bland. The argument advanced by Professor Roger Daniels
is more persuasive: [11]

> While much ink has been spilled disputing the Association's
> connection with the Japanese government, it seems quite clear
> that this organization did in fact have very close ties with the
> Japanese government and should properly be designated as semi-
> official. There was nothing sinister or improper in its connections
> with Tokyo; after all, the Issei were, because of their status as
> "aliens ineligible to citizenship," still Japanese nationals despite
> their permanent residence here. They were, therefore, to a cer-
> tain extent, the responsibility of the home country—a responsi-
> bility that, through its consuls, Japan shouldered.

The Japanese Association remained the most influential organization in most Japanese American communities until Pearl Harbor

when most of its leaders were taken into custody. After that it disappeared, not to be revived at war's end.

The provincialism of the Japanese was expressed in the regional associations which they developed. *Kenjinkai*, or prefectural associations, appeared quite early in the history of migration to America. They expressed the deep affection of the Japanese for their home regions in Japan and were, in themselves, a measure of the problem faced by the leaders of Japan in producing a united people after centuries of feudal particularism. The Japanese in America did not develop clan associations or language associations, as did the Chinese. And it would be incorrect to draw a close comparison between the district associations of the Chinese and the prefectural associations of the Japanese. Unlike the district associations of the Chinese, the prefectural associations did not function as control groups. They were voluntary associations of people from the same regions of Japan.

Professor S. Frank Miyamoto of the University of Washington has characterized the *kenjinkai* in the following terms: [12]

Informally speaking, the organization is simply a social gathering of people from the same prefecture having, therefore, a common background of memories, speech, and customs that offer the members of the group an intimacy which they cannot feel with people from other *ken*. Formally speaking, the clubs function in the much more significant capacity of mutual aid, giving help to those members who are financially embarrassed by illness, death, or a lack of economic means. The financing of the organization is largely carried on by donations, but due to their somewhat obligatory character among Japanese, these donations take on the characteristics of dues.

It is perhaps more in the informal functions of the *kenjinkai* that we see their most characteristic solidifying effects. *Kenjin*, for example, are said to differ in their personality traits depending upon the *ken* from which they came. Common belief is that the Hiroshima people are sharp businessmen, the Gumma people are quiet, and so on. Throughout all these comparisons is a constant tendency to elevate one's own group. Parents desire their children to marry someone from their own *ken*, because, they say, it is then easier to trace the heredity of the other party. One always has a tendency to have more friends among one's own *kenjin,* and there is a tendency to favor a *kenjin* in any kind of relationship.

Professor Miyamoto has also commented upon the difficulties confronting a Japanese who came from a prefecture which produced few immigrants. Since the Japanese, as noted above, favored fellow *kenjin* in all relationships, an immigrant was at a severe competitive disadvantage if few of his own people were available as clients or customers. Though ethnic solidarity characterized the Japanese community in its confrontations with the white world, in many small ways the particularism expressed in the *kenjinkai* was a divisive influence within the community.

Since the *kenjinkai* were developed to meet the peculiar needs of the immigrant generation, and since the Nisei show little interest in perpetuating them, and the Sansei even less, the *kenjinkai* will probably pass from the scene in the not-too-distant future. Even the new quota immigration from Japan will probably have little influence on the *kenjinkai,* many of which have already disappeared, while others are moribund.[13]

Vast changes have come over the Chinatowns and Japan towns in the postwar years. The dispersion of the Chinese throughout the United States—the offspring of early immigrants as well as those newly arrived—has made traditional control impossible. The major areas of concentration—the San Francisco Bay region, New York City, Hawaii, Los Angeles-Long Beach—account for only 59 percent of the Chinese population in the nation. The others are scattered over the rest of the country.

The nature of Japan towns was extensively altered by the wartime Evacuation. Large numbers of former residents decided to remain in the friendlier environments they had found east of the Sierra Nevada. Those who returned found their old neighborhoods crowded with workers in war industries. Many of the immigrant generation were too old to begin again and rebuild what they had lost; economic, social, and political leadership flowed into Nisei hands. The losses sustained by the evacuees were so heavy that a resumption of life, as it had been, was impossible. And many had no desire to return to the old ways.

In Los Angeles, San Francisco, Seattle, and elsewhere the returning Japanese, after displacing the wartime residents, produced commercial communities which were not, as were the Chinatowns, the entire focus of life. Falling restrictive covenants enabled Nisei merchants, professionals, and businessmen to live elsewhere in the city.

Japan town in Los Angeles—the original Little Tokyo—today is an impressive collection of Japanese businesses, shops, and restaurants, many financed by an influx of capital from Japan. But it hardly does justice to the more than 200,000 Japanese Americans in Southern California. Many of them now live in clusters in several districts of the city—Gardena, Anaheim, and West Los Angeles, for example. A few service enterprises usually will be found in these areas to meet the specialty needs of style and appetite. But gradually, social class rather than ethnicity is influencing residential patterns, Japanese American families live where they can afford to without regard to the presence of their peers.

Both Chinese and Japanese ethnic enclaves were a response to the challenge of a hostile social environment. In different fashion, they remain as cultural and business centers as the social environment has changed.

VIII ❧ The Beginnings of Hostility

Oddly enough, West Coast hostility toward the Japanese began long before any substantial number of them reached these shores. Prejudice against them was not something which sprang suddenly into full flood after the turn of the century. In 1890, when the U.S. census counted only 2,039 Japanese in the entire nation, the Sailors' Union was voicing alarm over Japanese being employed as seamen aboard American ships.[1] The use of Japanese as strikebreakers in British Columbia coal mines in 1890–91 aggravated this concern.[2]

Some whites lumped the Japanese together with the Chinese, and as Orientals both were considered undesirable. Concerning the Japanese and their different appearance, one newspaper commented: "Cutting the hair and tucking in the shirt tail is not enough."

Apparently, the San Francisco *Bulletin* had raised its editorial voice in alarm as early as 1889. Writing in 1892, the editor said: [3] "It is now some three years ago that the *Bulletin* first called attention to the influx of Japanese into this state, and stated that in time their immigration threatened to rival that of the Chinese, with dire disaster to laboring interests in California."

The Oriental question was receiving a great deal of attention at this time because of the impending expiration of the Chinese Exclusion Act of 1882. As we have seen, the act was renewed, but not before much public agitation.

On April 25, 1891, Japanese Consul Chinda Sutemi submitted a confidential memorandum to Tokyo which was knowledgeable and prophetic.[4] He reminded his superiors that the United States in 1885 had passed legislation prohibiting the entry of contract laborers. Enforcement had been lenient, he reported, but the "climate of opinion" was changing with a sharp rise in immigration from Europe and "only desirable foreigners" were likely to be admitted in the future. Chinda predicted Japanese prostitutes and indigent or unhealthy persons would be denied admission and added: "In my opinion, such cases of refusal will, regardless of their nationalities or race, be numerous in the future."

Chinda observed that earlier Japanese migrants were predominantly students, but recent arrivals engaged in menial labor. He warned that U.S. authorities would be inclined to view Japanese as probable contract laborers because they usually arrived in small groups from the same village or prefecture. In the five weeks prior to writing his memorandum, Chinda said, approximately 140 "Japanese laborers" arrived in four ships and among them were many who "could be regarded as paupers or persons likely to become public charges." Even so, he said, all had proper passports and were admitted.

Chinda added that his staff had helped find Americans who would act as sureties for those detained, but predicted that if the trend continued "the consulate will eventually be unable to render any assistance to these unfortunate, penniless Japanese." Chinda went on to the climate in America stating: [5]

> . . . even if all the Japanese passengers arriving at this port do in fact possess the required amount of money, the continuation of the mass migration of lower class Japanese in the future will undoubtedly create a grave situation in the relationship between Japanese and Americans in this country which, sooner or later, will adversely affect the honor and reputation not only of the Japanese in this country but also of those in Japan.
>
> . . . An unrestricted mass migration of lower class Japanese . . . will, without doubt, arouse and aggravate suspicion among the working class in this country. In addition, some among the politicians in America who are only interested in manipulating public opinion will indeed take advantage of the resultant situation and try to agitate the working class to launch anti-Japanese drives for their own benefit. . . . Furthermore, some publishers of local newspapers have also sensed the trend of public opinion and begun placing in their newspapers rather exaggerated accounts of the recent arrivals of lower class Japanese at this port . . .
>
> It goes without saying that the city of San Francisco is one of the contact points where the Orientals and the Occidentals can meet. It is in this city, therefore, that we can endeavor to uphold our national prestige. For this reason, these Japanese who come to this city must be the true representatives of the Japanese

people who can indeed maintain Japan's national honor. In recent years, nevertheless, it is the poor and needy, prostitutes and outlandishly dressed fellows who have landed in ever increasing numbers at this important port. The sheer presence of these undesirable Japanese in this city will, I am afraid, inevitably incite detestation of and resentment against the Japanese as a whole in the minds of many Americans. And, the increasing arrival of lower class Japanese will unavoidably provide a pretext to the American working class and pseudo-politicians for their drive to exclude the Japanese from this country.

Such serious eventualities can, in my opinion, be prevented. The Chinese in general are now detested and discriminated against wherever they migrate, simply because they failed to grasp the seriousness of the situation at the outset. Their failure must be a lesson to us Japanese. In view of this, I beg your excellency to pay immediate and particular attention to this matter and instruct the respective government officials to adopt appropriate measures so as to prevent the departure of these undesirable Japanese to this country in the future.

Chinda's communication reflects a certain elite snobbishness toward the peasantry, which also was to be exhibited in later years by representatives of Japanese trading firms and banks stationed in the United States. However, another factor is involved in Chinda's concern. Japan at the time was not a fully sovereign nation, having lost control of her tariffs and legal jurisdiction over foreign residents in the initial treaties with Western powers. One of the dominant themes in Japan's foreign relations during the Meiji Period was recovery of these rights. Her officials abroad naturally were sensitive to anything which seemed to put Japan in an unfavorable light.

The archives show that Chinda about a year later forwarded several newspaper articles to Tokyo.[6] Some of them expressed concern about the number of Japanese women being imported for immoral purposes. Generally, the comment was mild. The San Francisco *Call* on May 4, 1892, said:

Every steamer from Yokohama brings a full cargo of the pleasant little people from the Mikado's realm. They are picturesque people, as well as pleasant. They are polite, courteous, smiling, and nobody ever has occasion to kick or cuff them, or even to upbraid them. They rarely get into the police courts and there are a few if any in San Quentin. But they are taking work away from our boys and girls and away from our men and women.

Perhaps the first overt discriminatory action took place about a year later, on June 14, 1893. The San Francisco Board of Education passed a resolution that required "all persons of the Japanese race seeking entrance to the public schools must attend what is known as the Chinese school."

This was a segregated school which had been established after a ruling in 1860 that Chinese were not admissible to the public schools. There were fewer than fifty Japanese children in San Francisco schools. The Japanese had no wish to be associated with the Chinese either in the schools or in the public mind. Leading Japanese citizens protested to the school board in writing.[7] Consul Chinda also made an eloquent plea in person. Under this kind of pressure the board rescinded the resolution.[8] Segregation of Japanese children was not attempted again until 1905, and by that time the political and social climate had worsened materially.

The history of the anti-Japanese movement in the Pacific Northwest is marked by a particular irony. Following statehood for Washington in 1889, the Northern Pacific Railroad and the Great Northern raced to link Tacoma and Seattle with the East. Laborers were needed, but the Alaska gold rush (1897–99) drained the state of manpower. The railroads looked to Japan for workmen. It was this sudden influx of laborers, however, that led to hostility.

Sometani Nariaki, who headed the branch consulate in Seattle (the main consulate at the time was in Tacoma), reported that 2,333 Japanese had been admitted in 1898 at Puget Sound ports, Portland, or had transferred from British Columbia.[9] An even larger number entered in 1899, and in 1900 the influx was boosted still further by plantation workers from Hawaii moving to the mainland. Consul Sometani in a lengthy dispatch to Tokyo in 1899 reported: [10]

> . . . the companies welcomed Japanese workers with open arms in spite of the fact that they had to offer higher wages than they paid to Chinese workers; Japanese workers have been paid five cents more per day than Chinese workers were. And, the Northern Pacific Railroad Company, which is constructing a transcontinental line connecting with Tacoma, began its hiring of the Japanese in May of last year, and the Great Northern Railway Company which is also constructing a transcontinental line from Seattle began in July of last year . . .

Since the number of Japanese railroad workers varies considerably from month to month at one locality, it is difficult for me to estimate their total accurately. According to a reliable source, however, a total of about 500 Japanese are currently employed in the states of Idaho and Wyoming, 800 to 900 in the state of Oregon, about 350 by the Great Northern Railway Company, and about 20 by the Seattle and International Railway . . . Furthermore, I am informed that each of those two large railroad companies, the Great Northern and the Northern Pacific, still need to hire an additional 1,000 workers. I anticipate, therefore, that the number of Japanese railroad workers in the Pacific Northwest region will increase considerably in the near future.

An insight into the way the demand for labor was met is provided in a book, *Ayumi no Ato*, by Shiro Fujioka. He writes that Ototake Yamaoka organized the Oriental Trading Company (*Toyo Boeki Kaisha*) in Seattle in 1898 to recruit Japanese workmen. On one of his recruiting trips he returned to the native Shizuoka Prefecture and issued a number of forged passports, later extending his operations to Niigata Prefecture. Fujioka alleges the forgeries were unchallenged in Japan, perhaps because of bribery of officials.[11] Unfortunately, Fujioka does not say how many Japanese entered the United States with these fraudulent passports, or when this took place.

A newspaper report on April 24, 1900, may be in reference to some of Yamaoka's recruits, although there is nothing to indicate this is so: [12]

> One by one the tangled threads of illegality in the admission of the hordes of contract Japanese immigrants are being untangled. As announced in the Star yesterday, those who came to Victoria on the Milos, and from there to Seattle on the Utopia, were found by Inspector Snyder not entitled to admission. They will be deported to Victoria on the Utopia with the exception of two men who were able to pass a satisfactory examination.
>
> These men had forged and irregular passports, and were cross-questioned very closely. The passports produced by them were not numbered, which is a fatally suspicious irregularity, and the names of the bondsmen were not given.
>
> Besides this, a great many of the passports were from one district—Niigata. In the examination it was developed that Nii-

gata is a small district with a population of a few hundred. Yet, despite the fact that the Japanese government only allows five men a month from each district to come to America, over 600 Japanese have recently come to this country from Niigata.

The return of these men to Victoria on Vancouver Island meant they later would enter surreptitiously by small boat. Those who arrived in Vancouver could slip across the border. Japanese denied admission at American ports were subject to deportation to Japan. But those who arrived first at a Canadian port could be returned by U.S. authorities only to Canada. The arrival of so many Japanese in Victoria and Vancouver indicates it was a carefully devised tactic.

West Coast newspapers paid a great deal of attention to Japanese immigration and the activities of various organizations opposing it. Much attention also was focused on the general subject of Oriental immigration since the Chinese Exclusion Act would lapse if it were not renewed in 1902. The anti-Japanese agitation has been aptly described as a tail to the anti-Chinese kite, but Japanese immigration was stirring up plenty of hostility on its own as this report in a Seattle newspaper in 1900 illustrates: [13]

> The denunciatory resolutions of the Western Central Labor Union last Wednesday night, and their action in appointing committees to investigate the matter, was only the beginning. Friday night of last week the King County Republican Club followed up with resolutions petitioning congress to pass a Japanese exclusion act. Monday the state delegates to the national Republican convention met in Tacoma and decided to use every effort to secure the insertion of an anti-Japanese clause in the national Republican platform. . . . Last night another set of ringing resolutions were adopted by the McKinley Republican Club at its regular meeting. Not only were resolutions passed against the Japs, but a resolution was added requesting all Republican papers to publish the resolutions. The resolutions follow. They are the strongest yet adopted on the question.
>
> "Whereas, During the past few months a large number of Japanese laborers have migrated or have been imported to the Pacific coast of the United States, and his majesty, the Emperor of Japan, is pleased to cooperate in restricting such migration and importation, and,
>
> "Whereas, Said laborers consist of a class who live and subsist

at so small a cost that they unfairly enter directly into competition with intelligent American workmen, and,

"Whereas, The American workman is compelled to maintain his family and provide for the education and improvement of his children and the maintenance of his home at a cost not to be compared with the expense of the living of people of other races, and,

"Whereas, Said Japanese laborers are a menace to the conditions which make it possible for the intelligent American working man to maintain himself, his family and his home, and,

"Whereas, The immigration and importation of said Japanese laborers to the Pacific coast will speedily produce the conditions which now exist in the Southern states, with all of its race controversies and race horrors, and,

"Whereas, The people of the Eastern states are not informed in respect to the gravity of the harm arising from such importation and immigration, and are in a large measure indifferent to its consequences; therefore, be it

"Resolved, That the further importation and immigration of said Japanese should be limited and restricted; and be it further

"Resolved, That the act of Congress entitled, 'An act to prohibit the coming of Chinese laborers to the United States,' approved September 13, 1888, should be amended by inserting the words 'and Japanese' after the word 'Chinese' in each place in said act where the word Chinese occurs; and be it further

"Resolved, That a copy of these resolutions be forthwith transmitted by the secretary of the club to all senators and members of Congress; and be it further

"Resolved, That all Republican newspapers be requested to publish these resolutions."

Although organized labor and many elements of the Republican party appeared to be united in their hostility toward Orientals, there were others, notably ranchers and large-scale farmers, who were interested in maintaining an adequate floating labor supply. To them it did not matter who the laborers were—Chinese, Japanese, or whatever. Thus, there were two pressure groups at work—one seeking to keep costs low with an inexpensive labor supply, the other expressing concern that continued immigration would force down the American working man's standard of living. California, where most of the Orientals were concentrated, was the center of the agitation which, strangely enough, was over a relatively small number of persons. The census of 1900 revealed there were fewer than 115,000 Orientals in the entire United States—89,863 Chinese and 24,326 Japanese. The move to lump Chinese and Japanese together as undesirable Asiatics is revealed in a resolution passed by the San Francisco Building Trades Council on April 12, 1900. The San Francisco *Examiner* the following day reported passage of this resolution:

> "Whereas, Measures have been taken and a movement set on foot for the purpose of breaking down the present barriers against Chinese immigration, and thus robbing white labor of its protection as embodied in the provisions of the Exclusion Act; and,
>
> "Whereas, We are satisfied after a careful and thorough investigation of the matter that there are already too many loopholes in the present law, known as the Exclusion Act; and,
>
> "Whereas, Judging by what experience and the past decade has taught us, that the present open-door policy toward Japanese immigration is injurious to labor and detrimental to the best interests of the country, therefore be it
>
> "Resolved, That the Building Trades Council of the City and County of San Francisco does hereby most emphatically protest against any modification of the Chinese Exclusion Act whatever. On the other hand it is our sincere hope that the law will be preserved and strictly enforced.
>
> "Be it further resolved, That we respectfully petition our Senators and Representatives in Congress to use their best efforts to enact a similar law or secure such international agreement as will secure this Coast against any further Japanese immigration, and thus forever settle the mooted Mongolian labor problem."

The anti-Japanese campaign in San Francisco was now heating up. On May 7, 1900—two months after the bubonic plague scare and less than a month after the Building Trades Council resolution— various labor groups called a meeting in Metropolitan Hall. (Their Western Labor Council meeting in Seattle preceded the San Francisco labor rally by several weeks. However, since the anti-Japanese movement was dominated by developments in California, the San Francisco meeting should be considered the more significant.) San Francisco Mayor James D. Phelan, the principal political speaker, declared: [14]

The Japanese are starting the same tide of immigration which we thought had been checked twenty years ago . . . The Chinese and Japanese are not bona fide citizens. They are not the stuff of which American citizens can be made . . . Personally we have nothing against Japanese, but as they will not assimilate with us and their social life is so different from ours, let them keep at a respectful distance.

The union men then dutifully passed a resolution urging that Japanese as well as Chinese be excluded from the United States. Organized labor was clearly spearheading the anti-Japanese movement and politicians were sensitive to its voting strength. California Governor Henry T. Gage soon joined those demanding Japanese be included among the undesirables when the Chinese Exclusion Act was renewed.

As Congress prepared to take up the issue, a convention was called in San Francisco to make California's feelings known. The delegates, mostly union men, met November 21, 1901. As the meeting opened, a number of Japanese stood outside the entrance and distributed literature opposing, not Chinese exclusion, but the inclusion of Japanese in the restriction. Whether this effort had any effect is not known, but the fact is the Japanese were exempted after lengthy argument. A newspaper report says: [15]

> The committee . . . held a protracted meeting . . . on the question whether the convention should recommend the exclusion of Japanese as well as Chinese. The Labor union members strongly advocated an amplification of the present law so as to include the Japanese. . . . but this was opposed by other members on the ground that such a recommendation might endanger the success of the whole movement. It was also urged that as the convention was called merely to secure reenactment of the present law, the committee would be transcending its power if it should seek to embrace the Japanese in the proposed exclusion. These arguments finally prevailed, and a resolution was adopted providing that the memorial to be presented by the convention to Congress shall be devoted entirely to the exclusion of the Chinese, as provided in the Geary law.
>
> There was an understanding, however, that while the memorial was to be thus limited in its scope, resolutions might be presented on the floor of the convention, that the same restrictions should be placed upon Japanese as upon Chinese immigration.

As a consequence, a supplementary report was filed:

> Whereas, We recognize the character and rapidly increasing numbers of Japanese and other Asiatic immigrants a menace to the industrial interests of our people,
>
> And Whereas, We believe that the time has arrived when cognizance should be taken; therefore be it
>
> Resolved, by the California Chinese Exclusion Convention, That the question of Japanese and other Asiatic immigration be referred to the executive committee of this convention, with instructions to devise and pursue such steps as may be necessary and advisable to secure all possible protection from the evils herein set forth.

The Chinese Exclusion Law was duly extended in 1902, but nothing substantive came of the anti-Japanese resolution. The outbreak of the Russo-Japanese War revealed Japan as a significant military power. Japan's ultimate victory added to anxieties in some quarters. They suggested that Japan, flushed with victory, might try to seize the Philippines. Others argued that Japanese war veterans might well seek to avoid the problems of a nearly exhausted nation and rush to America in increasing numbers. That these viewpoints were contradictory did not seem to be of much concern.

Now, political charges were added to the various economic grievances advanced by spokesmen for white working men. It was contended that the Japanese would never divest themselves of allegiance to the Emperor, and that the immigrant laborers were busily gathering intelligence about American coastal defenses in preparation for a military invasion. Bay area churchmen spoke out vigorously from time to time in defense of the Japanese immigrants, but were without real effect.

On March 10, 1905, the San Francisco Labor Council, with the support of Mayor Eugene E. Schmitz, a corrupt, ineffective political hack, launched a new offensive against the Japanese. The Chinese, apparently, were no longer an important factor. Boycotts were started against Japanese merchants and whites who employed Japanese. Two months later, on May 7, the Japanese and Korean Exclusion League was organized at a mass meeting at Metropolitan Hall. Labor leaders were the instigators, but in time, the league was to lose its labor coloration and become dominated by a cross section of California's elite who gave the movement leadership and continuity. The league's objections to Japanese immigration were expressed at the organization meeting in these words: [16]

> We have been accustomed to regard the Japanese as an inferior race, but are now suddenly aroused to our danger. They are not window cleaners and house servants. The Japanese can think, can learn, can invent. We have suddenly awakened to the fact that they are gaining a foothold in every skilled industry in our country. They are our equal in intellect; their ability to labor is equal to ours. They are proud, valiant and courageous, but they can underlive us . . . We are here today to prevent that very competition.

The racist nature of the Exclusion League is betrayed in these words, based on the belief that Anglo-Saxon and Teutonic culture must be supreme in the development of American culture. Nowhere was it suggested that the Japanese, with many admirable characteristics, should be given an opportunity to become assimilated into American life.

The new Exclusion League recruited members of California's congressional delegation and laid plans for introducing bills to bar further Japanese immigration. President Theodore Roosevelt learned of this and lectured California congressmen on the sensitive international implications of what they were proposing. Intimidated by Roosevelt's bullying, the congressmen drew back. Then nature, in the form of an earthquake, took a hand on April 18, 1906. Fire swept Japan town, and the residents, in search of any kind of accommodations, moved into "white districts." It was a move bound to stir hostility. That summer and autumn the Japanese were made the target of personal abuse and economic boycott.

As we have seen, on October 11, 1906, the San Francisco school board ordered all Japanese and Korean children in the public schools transferred to the segregated Oriental school in Chinatown. The children attended schools all over the city and it was virtually impossible for them to comply with the order. After protesting without satisfaction to the school board, Japanese community leaders sent word of developments to Tokyo newspapers. The Japanese government expressed its displeasure, and shortly Roosevelt's secretary of commerce and labor, Victor H. Metcalf, a Californian, was sent to San Francisco to investigate.

In a message to Congress on December 3, Roosevelt characterized the San Francisco school board action as a "wicked absurdity." A month later the federal government filed two suits against the school board in an effort to force a reversal of the segregation order. But Roosevelt had miscalculated badly. Federal pressure only hardened the San Francisco community's resolve. The California state legislature took up a number of bills and resolutions aimed at the Japanese and the congressional delegation introduced new proposals for Japanese exclusion. One scholar reports Roosevelt's reaction in this manner: [17]

> When Roosevelt found that he had underestimated the temper of the Californians, and that his message was resulting in more rather than less agitation in California, he and [Secretary of State Elihu] Root revamped their plans. Three things had to be accomplished before the restriction of Japanese immigration could be effected: The San Francisco segregation order had to be revoked by one means or another; the California legislature had to be restrained from passing further discriminatory legislation; and a bill had to be passed by Congress giving the president power to restrict Japanese immigration from intermediate points such as Hawaii, Mexico and Canada. All these preconditions were related; the executive order limiting intermediary immigration was to be offered to the Californians as a sort of prize for good behavior, and it would not be proclaimed until the segregation order was revoked and all anti-Japanese measures in the California legislature were killed.

Roosevelt summoned the entire California delegation to the White House on January 3, 1907, to reveal his proposal. As a consequence the delegation wired the governor of California asking that action on anti-Japanese legislation be deferred. The delegation also asked the San Francisco mayor to come to Washington. Mayor Schmitz went along.[18] He was under grand jury indictment for various irregularities and apparently he hoped to ease the pressure by distinguishing himself in some fashion on this junket.

After a week of discussions with presidential aides, the school board agreed that only older Japanese students and those with little facility in English, would be placed in special schools. All other Japanese children would return to their regular schools. In return, President Roosevelt promised to find ways to limit Japanese immigration and drop the suits which had been filed against the school board.

Congress at the time was considering the immigration bill discussed earlier in this volume. An amendment to this bill gave the President power to deal with secondary immigration. The Act of February 20, 1907, contained this paragraph which had been drafted in the State Department: [19]

> . . . Whenever the President shall be satisfied that passports issued by any foreign government to its citizens to go to any country other than the United States or to any insular possession of the United States or to the Canal Zone are being used for the purpose of enabling holders to come to the continental territory of the United States to the detriment of labor conditions therein, the President may refuse to permit such citizens of the country issuing such passports to enter the continental territory of the United States.

On this authority the President by executive order of March 14, 1907, barred immigration by Japanese from Hawaii, Canada, and Mexico—which had become a serious issue. Other aspects of the immigration problem were met by patient negotiation with the Japanese government. In late 1907 and early 1908 a series of notes was exchanged between the two governments, but these notes were not published until 1939. The notes contained the essence of a significant development known as the Gentlemen's Agreement. In deference to American wishes, Japan agreed not to issue passports to laborers, skilled or unskilled, and the categories "Laborers" and "Craftsmen" disappeared from Japanese passport records. However, it was agreed that Japan could issue passports to laborers resuming residence in the United States, or persons who were parents, wives, and children of laborers already American residents. The evidence indicates Japan honored the agreement. Unquestionably, some who came under student passports did become laborers, but such students once in the United States were beyond the authority of the Japanese government. In effect, the Gentlemen's Agreement constituted a major Japanese accommodation to the American concerns.

The Japanese public knew, of course, that drastic immigration restrictions were being negotiated. In an effort to enter the United States before the ban went into effect, the influx leapt from 14,243 in 1906 to 30,824 in 1907. Another 16,418 Japanese entered the United States in 1908 before the barriers took effect. In 1909, immigration dropped to 3,275.

After 1908, Japanese immigration topped 10,000 in only two years, 1918 and 1919. In every year between 1908 until all immigration was halted in 1924, women outnumbered male immigrants, often by a two-to-one margin as efforts were made to adjust the sexual imbalance.

No explanation has been found as to why the details of the Gentlemen's Agreement were kept secret for more than thirty years. Perhaps there was a desire to spare Japan the embarrassment of having it known that she had accepted a discriminatory pact. Be that as it may, in later years foes of any kind of accommodation with Japan charged that the Gentlemen's Agreement was a secret understanding and demanded that it be made public. This led to the unfortunate Hanihara incident, which will be discussed in a later chapter. It is sufficient to say here that the incident triggered the furor that resulted in the total exclusion of the Japanese.

As for California, the anti-Japanese mood was such that neither the school board compromise nor the Gentlemen's Agreement brought much satisfaction. A partial ban on immigration did not accomplish California's purposes, which were to rid the state of all Japanese and prohibit all further Japanese immigration. The Exclusion League became moribund by 1909, but it had served labor's goals by making life difficult for Japanese in the cities and justice almost impossible for them in the courts.

The arrival of the thousands of Japanese women—66,926 between 1908 and 1924 to Hawaii and the mainland—led to a development that the anti-Japanese forces had not anticipated: Families were started and children were born. And the children were American citizens by being born on United States soil.

The founding of families had two effects:

—They gave the Japanese a stability that would delay, if not preclude, their departure from the United States.

—Men moved out of the contract labor force to enter agriculture and farm on their own on leased or purchased land, and into semi-permanent endeavors in the cities. California ranchers, who had been happy with Japanese seasonal laborers, began to take another look when they became competitors.

Following the Gentlemen's Agreement, legislation hostile to the Japanese was presented regularly in the California legislature. However, Republican President Roosevelt and William Howard Taft were able to exert a moderating influence on the Republican majority in Sacramento. This is not to say the pressure was willingly accepted. Rather, it was endured until 1913 when Woodrow Wilson, a Democrat, entered the White House.

Wilson, no less than his predecessors, urged moderation on the California extremists lest they complicate the conduct of foreign policy. The Progressives who came into power in California in the 1912 election were hardly liberals on the Japanese question and the legislature quickly adopted a land law aimed at them. In a sense, it was a distillation of more than thirty bills that had been proposed. It was drafted jointly by California Attorney General U. S. Webb and Senator Francis J. Heney. Curiously, it avoided the phrase "aliens ineligible to citizenship," but limited alien ownership of land "to the extent and in the manner provided by the respective treaties then existing" between the United States and the homeland of the alien immigrant. This language enabled British interests, which had extensive investments in California land, to retain their foothold while eliminating the Japanese.

Count Chinda Sutemi, by then Japan's ambassador in Washington, fully aware of the discriminatory intent of the legislation, expressed "earnest hope" to Secretary of State William Jennings Bryan that the President would head off the Heney-Webb Bill. Nonetheless, the measure became law and went into effect August 10, 1913. In a speech before the Commonwealth Club of San Francisco three days later, Webb left no question about the intent of the legislation:

> It is unimportant and foreign to the question, whether a particular race is inferior. The simple and single question is, is the race desirable . . . It [the law] seeks to limit their presence by curtailing their privileges which they may enjoy here; for they will not come in large numbers and long abide with us if they may not acquire land. And it seeks to limit the numbers who will come by limiting the opportunities for their activity here when they arrive.

The law specified that aliens "eligible to citizenship" could acquire land just like American citizens, but others could not own property and could lease land for a maximum of three years. There was, however, a significant loophole. A Japanese immigrant with citizen-children could purchase land in the minor child's name and then secure court appointment as the child's guardian. In addition, the intent of the law was circumvented by setting up corporations, in which Japanese held substantial minority interests, to purchase and operate land. In these efforts the Japanese were assisted by attorneys who saw the unfairness of the alien land law. This caused the State Board of Control to complain: "It is a source of deep regret that there are attorneys in the state who despite their oath to support the constitution and the laws of the state, nevertheless sell their legal talent in aiding this breach of the spirit and purpose of the Alien Land Law."

Hostility against Japanese immigrants tapered off during World War I when Japan joined the Allies in the war against Germany and the Central powers. By 1920, however, the Alien Land Law once more was a hot political issue, stimulated in considerable part by U.S. Senator James D. Phelan, a Democrat fighting for his political life. Phelan had been mayor of San Francisco in 1900 when anti-Japanese sentiment began to intensify. Now he based his campaign on attacks against the Japanese and arranged for a series of hearings by the Committee on Immigration and Naturalization. It proved to be a sounding board for hysterical charges against the alleged danger to the United States posed by Japanese immigrants.

Partly as a consequence, a more restrictive Alien Land Law was presented to voters as an initiated measure. Its sponsors confidently predicted a ten-to-one victory margin. The measure was approved in every county but the vote was only 668,483 to 222,086; those who voted for the law numbered fewer than half the total of registered voters. At the time Japanese owned fewer than 75,000 of California's 28 million acres of agricultural land.

The furor in California spread to other areas and similar alien land laws were adopted during this period by Washington, Oregon, Idaho, Nevada, Arizona, New Mexico, Texas, Nebraska, and several other states.

The campaign to pass the 1920 Alien Land Law initiative, aside from the outcome, is significant for the appearance of a new element in the anti-Japanese coalition. The old Exclusion League was joined by such conservative organizations as the newly formed American Legion and the Native Sons and Daughters of the Golden West, aided and abetted by the then-powerful Hearst Press. A Harvard professor writing in the *Political Science Quarterly* indicts the American Legion for its role: [20]

> The latter organization not only entered vigorously into a political campaign, but it used methods which cannot be too strongly condemned. It sponsored one of the most vicious examples of propaganda ever witnessed in the state—a moving picture, entitled *Shadows of the West*. Graphically illustrating every charge made against the Japanese, this picture depicted a ridiculously mysterious room fitted up with a wireless apparatus by which

a head Japanese ticked out prices which controlled a state-wide vegetable market! It showed Japanese dumping fish and vegetables into harbors in order to keep prices high. Worse still, it invented a Japanese spy system, and it "exposed" the headquarters of a secret government. It did not hesitate to appeal to the deepest instincts of racial prejudice by picturing the abduction of two white girls by Japanese; an attempted assault and a melodramatic rescue by the "Legion boys" after a bloody race war.

It is a measure of changing times that many Japanese American veterans of World War II and the Korean War are members today of American Legion posts.

IX ❦ The Road to Exclusion

To understand the virulence and stubborn persistence of anti-Orientalism on the West Coast, it is necessary to review the long and checkered history of American racism. At various periods, American discrimination was focused on Indians, Africans, Asians, and whites from various parts of Europe. The record makes it difficult to refute a black American militant's contention that "violence is as American as apple pie."

In a sense, it can be said that for the most part Americans in other parts of this huge nation accepted, tolerated, or ignored the West Coast's prejudices against the Orientals as a regional aberration, for which there were many precedents. Only on the issue of black slavery, which had become so repugnant to a large segment of Northerners, did the residents of one part of the nation attempt to impose their standards on the people of another.

The cynicism with which Americans could voice ideals while practicing something entirely contradictory can be illustrated by the Statue of Liberty on Bedloe's Island (now Liberty Island) in New York harbor. Graven on a tablet within the pedestal on which the statue stands is Emma Lazarus' poem, *The New Colossus*:

> Not like the brazen giant of Greek fame,
> With conquering limbs astride from land to land;
> Here at our sea-washed, sunset gates shall stand
> A mighty woman with a torch, whose flame
> Is the imprisoned lightning, and her name
> Mother of Exiles. From her beacon-hand
> Glows world-wide welcome; her mild eyes command
> The air-bridged harbor that twin cities frame.
> "Keep ancient lands, your storied pomp!" cries she
> With silent lips. "Give me your tired, your poor,

Your huddled masses yearning to breathe free,
The wretched refuse of your teeming shore.
Send these, the homeless, tempest-tost to me,
I lift my lamp beside the golden door!"

Noble sentiments and ringing words. Yet in 1882, four years before the statue was dedicated, the golden door had been slammed shut across the Golden Gate for the Chinese, one of the world's tempest-tost, by an immigration ban that singled them out as an undesirable race.

It is admittedly conjectural, but arguable nonetheless, that the wellsprings of American racism can be found in what is often called "the expansion of Europe." Beginning in the sixteenth century, the British, French, and Dutch created vast empires in Asia and the Western Hemisphere for commercial and political gain. These empires were developed rapidly in the seventeenth and eighteenth centuries, and Africa came under their influence in the nineteenth century. The West Europeans were troubled by few doubts about the propriety of what they were doing. They were taking the benefits of superior civilization to inferior peoples—in Kipling's phrase, "lesser breeds without the law." And if the empire-builders profited, that was right and proper. Missionaries accompanied traders and soldiers. This reduced any remaining doubts since the heathen were to be blessed with the true faith. It was inconceivable that lesser breeds might possess souls equal to that of the white man before the Christian God. (In America learned clerics were to debate the question as to whether black slaves possessed "souls.")

The peopling of America proceeded in the same spirit. The seizure of Indian lands and destruction of their culture troubled few white men.[1] When the Civil War was concluded, the blacks freed in that struggle were brutalized in both North and South. The westward movement across the plains wiped out many tribal nations. In Texas and the Pacific Southwest the Spanish traditions were so heavily overlaid with Anglo–Saxon-Teutonic practices that Spanish and Indian cultures remain only as charming reminders of an older way of life.

The coming of the Chinese to the American West Coast opened another degrading chapter in American race relations, producing allies for the racism of the white American South. The thrust was given additional impetus by the concepts of Manifest Destiny, the White Man's Burden, etc., which were advanced by the Spanish-

American War and America's first steps in overseas empire-building. The patronizing expression, "little brown brother," for Filipinos enhanced a sense of white superiority.

Meanwhile, a new type of immigrant was arriving from Europe. These were the unskilled, sometimes unwashed, migrants from Southern and Eastern European ghettoes and peasant villages. They crowded into city tenements and broke the sod of the high plains. Often they were used as strikebreakers.[2] Soon regional political balances were being upset as hitherto dominant groups found themselves overwhelmed by immigrant voting blocs.

Not surprisingly, misgivings among intellectuals in New England produced a reaction which resulted in the formation of the Immigration Restriction League in 1894.[3] Basic to their thinking was the theory that heredity was more important than environment, postulating a position that was very close to the idea of "Nordic supremacy." These men were, organizationally at least, the prototypes of those who much later were to be stereotyped as Wasps (White, Anglo-Saxon, Protestants). As we shall see later in this chapter, one of these New England elitists was to have an enormously influential part in bringing about the ultimate goal of West Coast racists—total exclusion of Japanese.

While the league originally was reluctant to put immigration on a forthrightly racial basis, it found a workable device in literacy tests. Senator Henry Cabot Lodge, a Massachusetts Republican, introduced a bill in 1896 which would deny entry to any immigrant who could not read a passage of some forty words in any language. Its supporters believed the measure would reduce undesirable immigration from Eastern and Southern Europe. The bill was passed by Congress but President Grover Cleveland vetoed it.

The New Englanders, who had based their efforts on little more than pure prejudice toward those unlike themselves, could not support simple xenophobia because they were not opposed to further immigration from Western and Northern Europe. To establish their position, they turned to relatively new fields of study—anthropology and eugenics—to come up with a distorted theory that went like this:

Anthropologists divided the Caucasian race into the Nordic, Alpine, and Mediterranean subgroups. Only Nordics were considered acceptable, but the bulk of immigration was coming from Alpine and Mediterranean groups. Eugenics held that racial differences are established genetically and are relatively unchanging. Therefore, the influx of non-Nordics was dangerous to the racial purity of the original

American stock; interbreeding with this inferior stock was tantamount to "race suicide."

There is, of course, a disturbing similarity between this line of thinking and that propounded by a man named Adolf Hitler a generation later.

Three academicians stand out among those who pushed racist theories. Edward A. Ross, while a sociologist at Stanford University, in 1900 had supported restriction of Japanese immigration on economic grounds. By 1906, he was on the faculty of the University of Wisconsin where, together with the noted labor historian John R. Commons, he directed his attention to immigration from Europe. Both were strongly influenced by William Z. Ripley who had gained a reputation as an anthropologist with his work titled *The Races of Europe*. Ripley found the Alpine and Mediterranean groups undesirable "beaten members of beaten breeds." Commons argued that not even the American environment would enable immigrants from Eastern and Southern Europe to overcome their "inherently undesirable" qualities. On the eve of American entry into World War I these theorists found support from Madison Grant in a book called *The Passing of the Great Race in America*. Grant argued that America was in the process of "mongrelization," that American institutions and the American environment could not improve the hereditarily inferior peoples pouring into America from Eastern and Southern Europe, and that they inevitably would produce a decline and degradation of the United States.

This line of thinking was carried another step farther by Lothrop Stoddard who in 1920 published *The Rising Tide of Color Against White World Supremacy*, and two years later, *Revolt Against Civilization: The Menace of the Under Man*. Grant and Stoddard were not alone in advancing the new racism, but they clearly were the most influential.[4] They were widely read in the United States (as well as Germany) and, beyond question, contributed to the political climate which led to drastic immigration legislation in 1924.

Fortunately, even the relatively moderate proposal for a literary test was a long time in becoming law. The primary barrier to enactment of such legislation was the opposition of recent immigrants or those who could trace their origins to recent immigrants. They felt that if certain types of immigrants were to be branded as unlikely to become good citizens, the criticism would be based on the assumption that those already here had not in fact become good citizens. And they were not prepared to accept this.

Both major political parties were aware of the vast pool of potential political support within immigrant groups. Until the end of the nineteenth century the Democrats had been more successful in winning the support of immigrants. Maldwyn Allen Jones observes: [5]

> Up to about 1900 the immigrant, and especially the Irish, associations of the Democratic party had enabled nativists to use the G.O.P. as a vehicle of restrictionism. But as increasing numbers of Italian, Slavic and Jewish voters became attracted to Republicanism, that party was forced to take their wishes into account.

Therein lies the explanation for the fact that on two occasions when Congress passed literacy tests, Taft (a Republican), and Wilson (a Democrat), vetoed the measures.

Congress finally had its way in 1917. The Dillingham Commission, established in 1907 by Congress to investigate and recommend reforms in immigration policy, finally completed a forty-one-volume report which, among other things, supported a literacy test. Congress voted such a provision and overrode President Wilson's second veto.

The new law also provided for a barred zone from which no further immigration would be accepted, thus extending limitations first imposed by the Chinese Exclusion Act in 1882. A step-by-step review of the gradual tightening of restrictions is enlightening. Following the law barring Chinese, a measure was passed in 1891 prohibiting entry of polygamists and individuals suffering from "loathesome diseases," and paupers. In 1903, a year after the Chinese Exclusion Act had been extended for the second time, anarchists, epileptics, prostitutes, and professional beggars were barred. In 1907 the prohibition was expanded to those convicted of moral turpitude, imbeciles, and victims of tuberculosis.

These, of course, were not unreasonable limitations and had nothing to do with the new racism which was developing. However, 1907 was also the year during which the United States persuaded Japan to accept the Gentlemen's Agreement under which Japan undertook to issue no more passports to common laborers. Gradually, the West's hostility toward Orientals and the East's concern over allegedly inferior immigrants from Europe began to interact upon each other, and in concert with the traditional attitudes of the white South produced a climate in which a restrictive immigration policy could thrive.

The barred zone was described in terms of latitude and longitude.

It did not include Japan, but affected most of China, all of India, Burma, Siam (now Thailand), the Malay states and the rest of Southeast Asia, the Asian part of Russia, part of Arabia, part of Afghanistan, and most of the Polynesian islands and the East Indies. The Chinese, of course, were already excluded by law and the Japanese restricted by the Gentlemen's Agreement. The law was a calculated blow against all Asians and an affront to many nations which, unlike China and Japan, had never sent significant numbers of immigrants to the United States. The legislation was welcomed on the West Coast, but as time demonstrated, it was not enough.

Immigration, which had slowed during World War I, resumed with the return of peace, particularly from the most devastated areas. Growing American disenchantment with the European adventure, the collapse of Wilsonian idealism, and the Senate's rejection of membership in the new League of Nations heightened nativist temper. This feeling was fed by concern over the alleged menace of "Bolshevism" and the deportation of alien radicals accused of instigating labor strikes.

More and more the expression "Yellow Peril" was being heard on the Pacific Coast. The idea of Western nations being inundated by hordes of Orientals had been part of the anti-Chinese movement, and the barred zone provided by the 1917 law failed to quiet these fears. Oddly, a German autocrat, Kaiser Wilhelm II, is credited with coining the catch phrase that articulated this fear. He used the expression "Yellow Peril" (*gelbe gefahr*) to stir the fear of Russians about the possibility of a new Mongol invasion from the East.[6] If he could thus divert Russian attention away from Europe, Imperial Germany would be free to pursue her own aspirations without worrying about her eastern frontier. No doubt the fears planted by Wilhelm had more than a little to do with the outbreak of the Russo-Japanese War.

Late in 1906 the Hearst Press began what one scholar has described as a thirty-five-year war with Japan [7] and "Yellow Peril" became part of the American lexicon. A book by Homer Lea titled *The Valor of Ignorance,* published in 1909 (and reissued after Pearl Harbor), fed fears about Japanese military expansionism. Lea, who had been an associate of Sun Yat-sen, the Chinese revolutionary leader, predicted a war in which Japan would seize the Philippines and invade the Pacific Coast. Lea's book became the bible of tens of thousands of Californians who found in it justification for their persecution of Japanese immigrants. At the time there were some 72,000 Japanese in the United States.

After war erupted in Europe in 1914, German agents attempted to divert the attention of Americans toward Japan which was pictured as poised to attack the United States. The Hearst Press, which strongly opposed the entry of America into the war, echoed German propagandists in stepping up its attacks on the Japanese in the United States.

By the end of the war, hostility toward the Japanese had become almost a conditioned reflex on the West Coast. Japan itself was partly to blame. Tokyo had exploited the wartime situation to make its infamous Twenty-one Demands for special concessions in China. After Russia surrendered to Germany, various Allied powers joined in sending an expeditionary force into Siberia. Japan kept her troops there long after other nations withdrew and came under severe international criticism.

In California, the anti-Japanese movement was expressed in the stronger alien land law of 1920. But this was only an intermediate step. The real goal was for Japanese exclusion—some even advocated ultimate deportation of all Japanese—which, in their view, had not been achieved by the Gentlemen's Agreement. The coming of the picture-brides meant a new generation of this "lesser breed" was establishing a foothold. The diehards were not appeased even when the Japanese government in 1921 ceased issuing passports to picture-brides.

That same year Congress enacted the first of several restrictive immigration measures aimed primarily at Eastern and Southern Europeans. President Wilson, who was about to leave office, disposed of this bill by pocket veto. When the Warren G. Harding administration took office, both houses of Congress quickly passed the immigration bill again. Its main provision was to limit immigration for one year, but it exempted the Japanese.[8] In 1922 the bill was passed again to run for two years. It was restrictive in that immigration in any one year from a specific nation was limited to 3 percent of the foreign-born persons of that nationality found to be resident in the United States in 1910. Theoretically, the use of the 1910 census would be disadvantageous to Eastern and Southern Europeans, who were among the late arrivals, but in reality the allowable number was still substantial.

Californians at this time made no effort to inject the Japanese issue into the debate. They were marshaling forces for a major campaign when Congress would take up a complete revision of immigration policy. They realized the time was near when the Supreme Court, in a landmark decision in 1922, ruled that Japanese were "aliens ineligible to citizenship." The suit had been brought by Takao Ozawa, born in Japan but a graduate of high school in Berkeley, California, and a former student at the University of California. Ozawa contended that since Orientals were not specifically named as ineligible to citizenship, they had the right to become naturalized. This contention was rejected on the grounds that Congress had limited naturalization to free "white" persons and those of "African nativity." Since Ozawa was neither white nor African, he was left in limbo.

Two years later, Congressman Albert Johnson of Washington, chairman of the House Committee on Immigration and Naturalization, introduced a sweeping immigration bill. It set 1890 as the base year for setting national origins quotas, a move that discriminated sharply against Eastern and Southern Europe. Further, the percentage was reduced from three to two. Johnson's bill also prohibited all further immigration of "aliens ineligible to citizenship." The Supreme Court decision in the Ozawa case had firmly locked the Japanese into this category.

The bill easily passed the House. It was in for difficulty in the Senate, traditionally more concerned with international relations which in this case would involve Japanese resentment.

As Senate hearings opened, three implacable foes of Japanese immigration went to Washington to testify. They were V. S. McClatchy, the power behind the reorganized Japanese Exclusion League; former Senator Phelan; and California Attorney General Ulysses S. Webb. They had no disagreement with provisions of the bill concerning European immigration, but they dredged up all the old racist arguments against the Japanese. McClatchy did everything but characterize the Japanese as a "lesser breed"; he argued forcefully that the Japanese were different from whites, therefore undesirable, and could never become good American citizens.

Despite the Californians' efforts, the committee rejected the House bill and reported out a substantially different measure. It left the matter of Japanese immigration under the Gentlemen's Agreement. Some senators indicated Japan should have an immigrant quota. The Coolidge administration through Secretary of State Charles Evans Hughes supported the idea of a quota within the limitations of the Gentlemen's Agreement.

During debate, complaints were heard that the Gentlemen's Agreement was a secret document. As a matter of fact, while its text had not been published, its operative provisions had been well known for years. But Hughes was persuaded that the air must be cleared. Strangely, instead of providing the Senate with the necessary documents, he asked the Japanese ambassador, Masanao Hanihara, for a summation of the agreement. Hanihara complied with the request but went one step farther. He commented on the pending immigration bill, remarking that retention of the provisions for Japanese exclusion would have "grave consequences" on relations between the two countries.

No notice was taken of Hanihara's comment for several days. Then Senator Lodge, the aristocratic Boston Brahmin who hitherto had remained out of the Japanese issue, suddenly stepped in to seize upon the two words. Referring to Hanihara's letter, Lodge declared: "It contains, I regret much to say, a veiled threat . . . The United States cannot legislate by the exercise by any other country of veiled threats." Hanihara quickly denied any threat was intended, but Lodge's speech stampeded his colleagues into acceptance of Japanese exclusion.

The accelerated deterioration of U.S.-Japanese relations can be dated from this single incident. Congress by its action had classified the Japanese as undesirable, and the proud Japanese nation found it an intolerable insult. Before long, Japan's civilian leaders, who had cooperated in every possible way with the United States, yielded power to militarists and a course that was to result in the collision at Pearl Harbor was laid.

Just why Lodge, who was less than seven months away from his grave, took this needlessly offensive action is a mystery. He undoubtedly shared the nativist views which arose initially in New England, but he was also chairman of the Senate Committee on Foreign Affairs and knew the consequences of the step he took. Despite his long service to his country, Lodge's last major act as a senator must be judged a tragic error. Had he not taken this wanton action, there is good reason to believe Japan would have received an immigration quota of 100. It would have been only a token, but it would have avoided the sting of total exclusion. Undoubtedly, the course of history that followed would have been very different.

X ꙮ Hawaiian Success Story

There are both strong parallels and sharp differences in the experience of the Japanese in Hawaii and those on the mainland United States. In addition, although the main Hawaiian Islands are separated from North America by more than two thousand miles of ocean, the story of the Japanese there is closely linked to that of the contiguous forty-eight states. For these reasons, and because Hawaii's membership in the Union was both retarded and advanced by the Japanese portion of its population, it is desirable to include the experience of the Japanese there in this study.

Hawaii was still an independent kingdom when thousands of Japanese were welcomed to its shores as contract laborers on sugarcane plantations. As we have seen, the first of these workers—fewer than 150—known as the *Gannen Mono,* arrived in 1868. Although this initial experience was not satisfactory to either Japan or the Hawaiian planters, no insurmountable problems troubled relations of the two peoples. Indeed, on August 19, 1871, only a few weeks after expiration of the labor contracts of the *Gannen Mono,* a treaty of friendship and commerce was concluded between Hawaii and Japan.

Article Five of the treaty seemed to give promise of further contingents of Japanese laborers for plantation work: [1]

> The Japanese government will place no restrictions whatever upon the employment by Hawaiian subjects of Japanese in any lawful capacity. Japanese in the employ of foreigners may obtain passports to go abroad, on application to the Governor of any open port.

However, no contract laborers were received from Japan for more than a decade. This was in part the result of the fact that the American minister to Japan, Charles De Long, was also acting for Hawaii. Since the United States was opposed to "coolie labor," he frowned on the use of Japanese contract workers.

139

In 1875, a treaty between Hawaii and the United States ended the tariff on sugar. Hawaiian planters anticipated huge profits and expanded their fields, turning again to Chinese for labor. Some white elements in Hawaii viewed this development with concern since the Chinese were inclined to leave the plantations at the expiration of their contracts. They sought independent livelihoods as farmers or small shopkeepers. One estimate made in 1882 showed 13,000 Chinese in Hawaii, with only 38 percent still on plantations.[2] The majority, thus, were already playing roles not envisioned for them by the economically dominant white population. Continued importation of Chinese laborers, many whites feared, would in time lead to a kind of Sinicization of Hawaii with all kinds of attendant problems.[3] For a time South Pacific islanders and Portuguese were tried as substitutes, but neither proved satisfactory.

The few Japanese who had remained in Hawaii at the end of their labor contracts in 1871 disappeared into Hawaiian society. It has been suggested that being too few to produce a Japanese community, they simply assimilated to survive.[4]

In Japan itself, there was no great interest at first in meeting Hawaii's needs. Population pressure was not yet a problem. The government was preoccupied with internal matters and revision of unequal treaties with the major powers. Further, Japan was fearful of any special arrangement with Hawaii that might affect negotiations over those treaties. Then, an internal problem changed the situation. As a necessary precondition to the creation of a modern state, Japan terminated the feudal rights of lords and their samurai retainers who were paid off with bonds and great amounts of paper currency. This led inevitably to rapid inflation of prices and financial instability. In the deflationary program of 1881, large amounts of paper money were retired. Many small businessmen and peasants were bankrupted and unemployment became serious. Spreading opposition to the policies of a growing oligarchy and demands for a more representative system of government produced almost revolutionary conditions. Unrest reached a peak in 1884; the press was muzzled and uprisings were put down by force.

Although order was restored, the building social and political pressure made emigration an attractive means of reducing unemployment and unrest.[5] Two shiploads of contract laborers left for Hawaii in 1885 while negotiations for a labor convention were still in progress. By the time that convention was concluded on January 28, 1886, more than 1,900 Japanese were already at work on Hawaii plantations. In the nine-year period between 1885 and 1894 during which the convention-contract system was in effect, 28,691 men, women, and children migrated to Hawaii. The great majority were single men, women comprising only 5,487 of the total.[6]

Although plantation labor was grueling, the majority of Japanese remained in Hawaii after completion of their labor contracts. The figures at the end of 1894 show 717 left for the American mainland, 7,454 returned to Japan, and 19,232 were still in the Islands. In addition, 1,422 Japanese were born in Hawaii during these years and 1,671 died.

In contrast to the First Year People, the contract laborers were experienced farmers inured to grinding toil. It is well that they were. The normal contract was for three years and specified twenty-six days of labor each month, a ten-hour work day in the fields and twelve hours in the mills. Pride was one reason that so many remained in Hawaii after their contracts expired. It was difficult to save any substantial sum and the Japanese were reluctant to return home without the monetary evidence of their successful sojourn abroad. And so the decision to return was delayed and the years passed.

The labor convention contained a provision for termination of the agreement, but neither Japan nor Hawaii invoked it. However, by 1894, private emigration companies were operating and Japan took the view that government involvement was no longer required. The plantation experience has been described in these words: [7]

> The Hawaiian plantation was a Japanese frontier, but it was not like the great western frontier of the United States, which Americans have come to think of as synonymous with the word "frontier." It had some of the ingredients, the roughness, the crudeness, and the drabness, but none of the freedom, and little of the opportunity. The Japanese frontier was one controlled by other men.
>
> Each of the contract immigrants had to spend three years on this frontier and, as in any frontier situation, life was harsh. Work was hard, and long, and hot. Housing was bad, food was poor, quarrels were frequent. It was a male society, with just enough women to give the men something to fight about.
>
> There was many a rough-and-tumble incident on this frontier, but everything considered, the most important thing that happened during the three-year contract period was a change of mind among the immigrants. Somewhere in the long process of

cutting row upon row of sugarcane or in the hours of labor in
the sugar house a majority of these people lost sight of the
original reason for their coming to Hawai. Although figures on
the earliest shipment reveal that perhaps 75 per cent of the immigrants returned to Japan after the contract period, by the
fifteenth shipment only 25 per cent were returning. More and
more people forgot that they had come to Hawaii for a three-
year hitch only to return and make a better life in Japan. After
this, negative loss of purpose had the effect of a positive decision;
they made up their minds to stay on in Hawaii.

Some qualification of the above is required. Most workers retained
the hope and, indeed the expectation, of returning to Japan. Few in
Hawaii or on the mainland made an irrevocable decision to live out
their lives abroad, for they were not in any sense alienated from
Japan. Indeed, they were virtually forced to retain legal as well as
sentimental ties with the homeland by the denial of any real status
in Hawaii and the mainland. Many were trapped, in a sense, by
marriage and the arrival, and in time, the maturing of citizen-children who knew little of Japan and were at home only in the land of
their birth.

Plantation life provided few of the traditional Japanese social and
cultural amenities. Long absence from Japan weakened family ties
and obligations.[8] Many years were to pass before urban communities
developed to create a somewhat more orthodox Japanese society. But
Japanese norms were modified by the environment. A benign climate,
a relaxed social atmosphere in the larger community, and the seduc-
tive influence of a more casual way of life prevented the creation of
a completely orthodox Japanese subculture. In many respects the
society the Japanese created on the mainland was much closer to the
social norms of the homeland. Ironically, however, the situation in
the judgment of many scholars is now reversed with mainland Japanese Americans more Americanized and less traditional than their
peers in Hawaii.

Because of the harsh living and working conditions on the plantations, the Japanese government maintained an interest in the welfare
of its citizens by regulating the operation of emigration companies.
Since young men most anxious to go to Hawaii or the mainland
United States to work were least likely to be able to meet the cost
of travel, the emigration companies stepped in to provide services
for a price.[9] In Japan, eager young men were recruited, housed and

fed until departure. On arrival, temporary board and room had to be provided until the workers could be sent off to their jobs.

Such a system, if uncontrolled, provided many opportunities for exploitation. To protect the workers, a measure known as Imperial Ordinance No. 42, Law to Protect Emigrants, was promulgated in June, 1894. In 1896 and again in 1907 other laws regulating emigration companies were passed.[10] The companies were required to provide medical assistance when needed and passage back to Japan if the worker became ill or was injured. Workers also were protected against having to pay charges other than those agreed upon in the original contract.

However, these measures applied only to emigration companies in Japan. Since planters in Hawaii and independent Japanese labor contractors on the mainland were beyond Japanese-government regulation, harsh treatment and penalties for failing to meet work quotas were common. In fact, the Japanese in Hawaii had no genuine civil rights until the Islands became a United States Territory in 1900. Until then the Japanese were a minority suffering discrimination at the hands of an even smaller but politically and economically dominant white minority and their Japanese agents.

The Hawaiian census of 1896 revealed the total Japanese population, including Hawaiian-born children, to be 24,407.[11] With annexation of Hawaii by the United States being widely discussed, planters feared that the mainland's Chinese Exclusion Law would be applied to the Islands. The planters also feared that the mainland's ban on importation of contract laborers would be applied, and rushed to bring in thousands of Japanese workmen. In 1899, after annexation but before congressional legislation creating the Territory of Hawaii, 26,103 Japanese contract laborers arrived in the Islands. It was the largest number ever admitted in a single year. By 1900, the U. S. census counted 61,111 persons of Japanese stock in Hawaii.

The planters had expected that the Organic Act establishing the Territory of Hawaii would not apply retroactively and contract laborers would be permitted to work out their agreements. However, contracts were outlawed immediately and the laborers were freed of their obligations.[12] That led to the departure of thousands of liberated Japanese for the mainland, a movement discussed in an earlier chapter. Others returned to Japan. Those who remained in Hawaii could now strike for better conditions and improved wages, and they frequently did. Some plantations instituted a form of sharecropping that provided an opportunity to make more money than simple wages. Still, trade unionism lay far in the future. The first strikes were isolated efforts, plantation by plantation, and only small successes were recorded. Nonetheless, the Organic Act, which was to be Hawaii's constitution for more than a half century, brought a new period in the history of the Japanese in Hawaii.

In 1890, five years after Japanese immigration to the Islands was resumed, only 286 Japanese were in classifications other than laborer. The Chinese, who had been there somewhat longer, were the importers and shopkeepers who met Japanese needs. By the end of the century the Japanese business community had grown substantially, although it remained smaller than the Chinese.

Most of these businessmen were from an element different from the plantation laborers—they had come to Hawaii with the intention of going into commerce. It was this urban group that provided the necessary sophisticated leadership that produced the sense of community which ultimately emerged.

The orderly organization of the Japanese community was not easy. Its members had come from various districts of the Old Country, bringing with them diverse dialects and customs. Provincialism was a barrier to unity in Hawaii as well as on the mainland.

One large Hawaii element not well known on the mainland was the group of workmen from Okinawa. By 1907, there were several thousand Okinawans on the plantations, filling the jobs vacated by those who had left for the States. Ultimately, an estimated 30,000 Okinawans settled in Hawaii. Though accepted and respected today, the Okinawans for a long time were considered inferior and the victims of discrimination by other Japanese. The Okinawan language, though related to Japanese, was different enough that a substantial communications gap existed.

Bubonic plague appeared in Honolulu in December, 1899. While the outbreak seemed to be focused within the twenty-square-block Oriental quarter, deaths occurred in various parts of the area.[13] In desperation the authorities ordered the affected buildings burned. Fires were set on January 20, 1900. They quickly went out of control and twelve entire blocks were destroyed. The Chinese business community filed claims for losses at $1,761,112. In one of their first efforts at cooperative action, the Japanese formed an organization called *Rinji Nihonjinkai* (Special Japanese Society) which drew up claims for $639,742. Congress appropriated $1 million to help the territorial government meet the claims, and they were finally settled in 1903 for about fifty cents on the dollar—$845,480 to the Chinese and $333,730 to the Japanese. The Special Japanese Society was dissolved after the claims were paid, but before then another minor crisis led to formation of still another *ad hoc* group.

That was in 1901 when concern about bubonic plague was still strong. A Japanese ship arrived in Honolulu with a passenger suspected of having the plague. All passengers were subjected to medical examinations, the quarantine officer compelling the Japanese women to submit to excessively intimate scrutiny. One of the women was the wife of a diplomat and two were students en route to mainland colleges. This incident occurred at a time when many Japanese believed the Chinatown fire had been no accident. When the Japanese consul-general hesitated to protest the affront to the women, businessmen organized the Hawaii *Nihonjinkai* (Japanese Association) and forwarded complaints to President Roosevelt, Congress, and the Japanese embassy in Washington. Consequently, the quarantine officer was discharged and authorities promised to employ a woman doctor for future examinations. With the incident resolved, the *Nihonjinkai* was allowed to lapse.

The Honolulu fire had another effect on the Japanese community, which had been plagued by a serious vice problem. That story is told by a recent publication in this manner: [14]

> The seeds of social evils continued to flourish, however, and by 1900, gambling, prostitution, and extortion had come to have a strong grip on the Japanese community. An area bounded by Pauahi, Maunakea, and King Streets was commonly known as the "devil's den" where the gangsters reigned supreme, flaunted government authority and extorted money from merchants.

> On pay days they infiltrated into plantation camps in twos and threes in order to avoid detection by the camp police and enticed restless youth to take part in all night gambling sessions.

> Professional gamblers in all numbered about 200, who in turn manipulated about 300 prostitutes; some of the women were engaged in this business of their own free will, but there were many others who had unsuspectingly fallen into the clutches of the gangsters during a period of loneliness and weakness when they had had disagreements with their husbands. A Christian home, founded in 1896, extended many a helping hand to these unfortunate women, gave them sanctuary and assisted them in starting new lives. There were some incorrigibles, however, who

rebuffed all efforts to reform them, (sic) "Even an able-bodied
man is earning only $15 a month. But we are sending home
$150 to $200 each month. You should commend us for doing
our patriotic duty!"

The gangsters were strongly organized. They had their own
organ newspaper and were capable of raising two to three thousand dollars on a minute's notice to fight off any attempt to curb
their activities.

However, the 1900 fire sounded the death knell for their activities. When the gamblers were quarantined along with the
other residents after the fire, strong efforts were made by community leaders to deport about thirty ringleaders. The case col-
lapsed, however, when witnesses refused to testify in fear of
future reprisals. With no headquarters to return to, however,
the gamblers dispersed after being released from quarantine in
April, 1900. Some reformed to take up gainful occupations,
while others left for the other islands and the city was cleansed
of its vice dens as a result of the disastrous fire.

Vice was dispersed, not ended, by the fire. Gambling and prostitution remained facts of life for a large segment of single males, much
as was the case on the mainland.

Oddly enough, the movement of Japanese laborers from Hawaii to
the mainland—bitterly opposed by powerful elements at both ends
—was facilitated by the Organic Act. With Hawaii a Territory of the
United States, such travel was considered a coastwise voyage and the
Japanese were not subjected to immigration procedures.

In response to growing hostility on the West Coast toward Japanese immigration, the Japanese government on August 2, 1900, ordered prefectural governors to stop issuing passports to the U.S.
mainland. However, passports to Hawaii continued to be issued. As
a result many of the new immigrants simply made Hawaii a temporary stopover before proceeding to the mainland.

West Coast labor contractors, seeking workmen for an expanding
economy, defied public opinion and encouraged Japanese in Hawaii
to move to the mainland. This, of course, aroused the ire of Hawaiian
planters and disturbed Japanese businessmen and shopkeepers as well
as consular officials. The adverse effect of the exodus on Hawaii's
economy led to reports that the anti-Japanese movement on the mainland was nourished in part by Hawaiian money, the logic being that
hostility in California would discourage plantation hands from leav-

ing for the higher wages available there. This allegation cannot be proved, but it was widely believed.

So substantial was the movement of Japanese—mostly young single men—to the mainland that although the total Japanese population in Hawaii increased more than 18,000 between 1900 and 1910, the number of adult males rose by only about three hundred. The growth is accounted for by some 5,000 women and 13,000 children under fifteen years of age. U.S. census data present the following picture: [15]

Year	Male	Female	Children Under 15	Total
1900	44,341	10,684	6,086	61,111
1910	44,652	15,200	19,823	79,675
1920	41,751	26,596	40,937	109,284

After the first two short-lived attempts at organization, the Japanese in Hawaii in 1903 pooled their resources to attack not exploitation by Hawaiian planters, but the Japanese emigration companies. The first organization was the Central Japanese League. It accomplished little and was succeeded by the Reform Association in 1905.[16] Their target was a situation made possible by an 1894 law which required all Japanese immigrants to have at least $50 or a written employment contract before being permitted to enter Hawaii. To comply with this law, the immigrants turned over 100 yen to the steamship company providing passage in return for a certificate of deposit.

On reaching the Islands the laborers surrendered these certificates to agents of the emigration companies who deposited them in the Keihin Bank. Workers found that at the end of their terms of labor they could not collect these deposits in Honolulu but must apply for reimbursement in Tokyo. Further, the deposits were subject to many charges which reduced the amount returned. The Reform Association finally persuaded the Japanese government to outlaw these practices. The commission which the emigration companies collected from workers was cut in half, and other improvements were put into effect. The Keihin Bank and agents of the emigration companies then left the Islands, and the Reform Association, its work completed, dissolved in 1906.

Soon afterward, the Gentlemen's Agreement between the United States and Japan came into being. Ironically, the heavy movement of Japanese from Hawaii to the mainland had helped to stir West Coast hostility which led ultimately to Japan volunteering to halt

further emigration of laborers. Passports to Hawaii were included in
the ban. President Theodore Roosevelt then issued a proclamation
on March 14, 1907, excluding from the continental United States all
Japanese and Chinese seeking to enter the country on passports issued
for Hawaii, Mexico, or Canada.

With that, free movement of Japanese from Hawaii to the mainland came to an end. In time, the citizen-children of Japanese immigrants would go to the mainland, but the immigrants themselves were
limited in their movement. Their only alternatives were to return to
Japan or remain in Hawaii indefinitely.

But the Japan to which they could return was changing rapidly.
The financial stake which workers had in mind when they left home
would no longer buy them security in Japan. One of them noted: [17]

> The standard of life in Japan has risen more than in any other
> place. Ten years ago Japanese laborers who saved a few hun-
> dred dollars could maintain their families in comfort for the
> remainder of life in Japan. But now a few hundred dollars will
> not suffice to keep them for two years. Therefore we have de-
> cided to permanently settle here, to incorporate ourselves with
> the body politic of Hawaii—to unite our destiny with that of
> Hawaii, sharing the prosperity and adversity of Hawaii with
> other citizens of Hawaii.

Despite such brave talk, it is probable that few made an irrevocable
decision to remain. For the time being, however, Hawaii offered
prospects for a good life. A benign climate, opportunities to fight
one's way off the plantations, and citizenship for locally born children
swung the balance against hurried return to Japan. Many felt, perhaps with justification, that they had been offered up as a sacrifice
to West Coast racists. In any event, it is true that after 1907 the
Japanese government paid scant attention to the Hawaiian scene.

With the arrival of more and more women, family life became possible. By 1910, 25 percent of the Japanese population in the Islands
was native-born; two decades later the ratio was 65 percent native-
born, 35 percent foreign-born.

By 1907 the institutional foundations for a Japanese community
were in place. Japanese-language newspapers were fairly well established. A Buddhist temple had been established in Honolulu in 1898.
Christian churches operated Japanese-language schools for the Hawaiian-born children.

So long as the majority of immigrants regarded themselves as transients in Hawaii only until they could save a certain amount of money, they were resigned to enduring a rigorous life with few amenities. They had been little inclined to come to grips with the culture about them. Few had bothered to learn English or the customs of the majority. But once the Issei saw that their stay might be permanent, they began seriously to accommodate themselves to the Hawaiian setting. Saving for the future yielded somewhat to the appetites of the present—better food, more comfort, a family. As on the mainland, women in most cases were picture-brides. The importance of this development can hardly be exaggerated.

The Japanese press in Hawaii began its halting development in 1892 with a mimeographed paper called the *Nippon Shuho*. The newspaper destined to endure, however, began as the *Yamato* in 1895. In 1906 it became the *Nippu Jiji* which was published continuously until the Pearl Harbor attack. It resumed publication a month later. In November of 1942 its name was changed to Hawaii *Times*, and it continues to be published as a bilingual daily. The Hawaii *Hochi*, founded in 1912, was the *Nippu Jiji*'s principal competition. It, too, was suspended briefly immediately after Pearl Harbor and is also published bilingually. One writer has characterized the role of the Japanese press in Hawaii as follows: [18]

In the early Japanese community the press was almost the sole medium of education of the people. Generally speaking, the intellectual and cultural level of these working classes as a whole was low. Therefore, the press always had to take the lead for the promotion of intellectual interests and the protection of the laborers' legitimate rights and in helping them solve various trying problems confronting them in their attempt to adapt themselves to the strange environment. The simple-minded industrious laborers were, from time to time, made the victims of reckless exploitation by the capitalists as well as by some of their own greedy parasitic countrymen. On these occasions, the Japanese press often rendered valuable service in remedying and coping with these situations.

The press has always shown its particular interest in the welfare of the Japanese laborers on the plantations. It has been said that had it not been for the initiative taken by the Japanese press in calling, from time to time, the attention of the sugar planters to the unsanitary, inhuman living conditions on the plantation camps and extremely low wages for long hours of hard labor, the status of semislavery of the laborers of the early days might have remained undisturbed even to this day.

This characterization of the Japanese press in Hawaii is also applicable to that on the mainland with one qualification. The Hawaiian plantation economy limited work opportunities in sharp contrast to the diverse labor market open to Japanese on the West Coast. The mainland press, therefore, was able to focus on a broad range of immigrant problems.

The Hawaiian Japanese press played a major role in a critical test of strength between planters and laborers which came to a head in 1908. Japanese workers contended that their accommodations were poorer and pay lower than those provided for Portuguese and Puerto Ricans. Rapidly rising living costs—up 20 percent in three years—worsened the problem. On December 1, 1908, an *ad hoc* organization, the *Zokyo Kisei Kai* (Higher Wage Committee) was formed and its leaders requested a conference with the Planters Association.[19] The Japanese newspapers were split on the issue of labor militancy. Unlike the *Hochi*, the *Nippu Jiji* strongly supported the workers and public opinion generally endorsed its position. On February 26, 1909, the *Nippu Jiji*'s editor was arrested on charges of inciting unrest in a raw demonstration of the power the planters held over the Territorial government. Intimidation of this kind failed. On May 8, workers at Aiea plantation on Oahu struck, followed four days later by workers at Waipahu.

The strikers were evicted from their quarters, but shelter was found for them in Honolulu and food provided by Japanese from all parts of Oahu. Financial support came from other islands where workers sympathized with the strike but remained on the job. A number of strike leaders were jailed as violence flared, but the dispute ended only after the workers had exhausted their resources. The strike had cost the workers and their supporters an estimated $40,000, a relatively large sum for the laborers. But the strike, which had lasted three months, resulted in a $2-million loss for the planters. Within a few months the Japanese imprisoned for strike activity were freed. Although it did not appear the workers had "won" the dispute, the Planters Association soon agreed to provide improved housing, a merit system of wages, and a bonus. Payments to Japanese cane growers on contract were also increased. Additional gains were made by the workers in 1912.

Meanwhile, the planters were looking for another source of labor that would be more tractable. Beginning in 1910, Filipinos were imported in significant numbers and by 1922 they outnumbered the Japanese on the plantations.[20]

The record of the Japanese in Hawaii during World War I was exemplary. Hawaii oversubscribed its quota for war bonds and the Japanese made a substantial contribution. Prior to American entry into the war, Japanese had been discouraged from joining the National Guard. However, more than 11,000 Japanese, most of them noncitizens, registered under the draft and a Japanese company was organized in the National Guard for domestic duty.

The war years saw a rapid deterioration in the economic position of all plantation workers. Wage gains were wiped out by inflation. With the support of the Japanese-language press, the Federation of Japanese Laborers was organized in 1919 to demand more pay.[21]

The Filipinos struck on January 17, 1920. Two weeks later the Japanese joined them. The white press attacked the Federation of Japanese Laborers as an agent of Japanese nationalism, and to counter this charge the name was changed to Hawaiian Laborers' Association. The Filipinos returned to work in June, and the Japanese, realizing further resistance was useless, ended their walkout a few weeks later. Again, neither side could say it had "won" the strike. However, the dispute was damaging in that the entire Japanese population fell victim to the postwar Americanism fever. The social consequences of the strike have been described in these terms: [22]

> During the six months of the labor controversy, a deep gulf between capital and labor and between the American and Japanese communities in Hawaii was created. This fact was clearly shown by the subsequent enactment of the foreign-language school supervision bill and the so-called foreign-language press control bill by the Territorial Legislature in the fall of 1920 and the spring of 1921, respectively. Prior to and during the strike the Japanese press and the Japanese language schools of the territory had been made the targets of constant and severe attacks by the Americanizers and the plantation interests and their adherents as the propelling force of labor troubles and as effective instruments for Japanizing of the Islands. The Japanese newspaper editors and the language school teachers were often called "agitators" and "conspirators" who were looking forward to the control of labor and industry and even of the political destiny of Hawaii. It was natural, therefore, that vigorous efforts

were made by this group of Americans to suppress the "alien agitators and conspirators" and to preserve "Americanism in Hawaii."

The language-school issue involved classes set up to teach Japanese reading, writing, and often, ethics, to the American-born children of the immigrants. The Nisei attended these classes after regular school hours and on Saturdays. Because wives had accompanied many of the earlier immigrants to Hawaii, there were more than 6,000 Nisei under fifteen years of age in Hawaii in 1900. By contrast, there were only a handful on the mainland. By 1910, one fourth of the Japanese in Hawaii, nearly 20,000, were American-born and under age fifteen. On the mainland, there were only 4,502 Nisei. Indeed, by 1910, there were many citizen-Nisei in Hawaii who were older than Issei arriving from Japan. In 1920, 16 percent of the enrollment in the University of Hawaii was Japanese.

The Territorial legislature in 1920 brought foreign-language schools under control of the Department of Public Instruction. It was a mild measure and provoked little reaction in the Japanese community. However, it failed to satisfy the more militant leaders of the Americanization movement and more stringent regulations were adopted two years later. Among its provisions, it assessed students a dollar per student per year to pay language-school inspectors. The Japanese challenged this measure and lost in the Territorial courts. However, the United States Supreme Court, which had taken its position on language schools in *Meyer* v. *Nebraska* and other cases, ruled in favor of the Japanese litigants.[23] The Japanese then sought to reassure the Hawaiian community by passing a resolution urging suggestions "from the Department of Public Instruction, which we will give careful attention, to the end that our schools may become of greater value to our children and to the community of which we consider ourselves a part . . ."[24]

By 1930, Hawaii's total population had reached 368,336, of which 139,631—nearly 38 percent—were Japanese immigrants and their citizen-children. Approximately one third of the Japanese, aliens and citizens, were in Honolulu. The movement off the plantation had continued through the previous decade, many entering the crafts and trades as well as commerce.

The 1930's were not an easy time for the Japanese in Hawaii. The steady growth in their numbers, plus their economic gains, created increasing concern that the Japanese would dominate Hawaii. As on the mainland, statistics were misused against the Japanese. A 1920 Department of the Interior study predicted that because of their high birth rate Japanese Americans would comprise 47 percent of Hawaii's voting population by 1940.[25] What the figures failed to show was that the birth rate climbed during the period in which young Japanese couples were in their prime childbearing years, and that the birth rate would drop steadily after 1925. There was also much apprehension about the dual citizenship of some Hawaiian-born Japanese and their possible disloyalty to the United States in event of war.

The politically dominant white minority in the Islands always had remained aloof from the Japanese as well as from all other ethnic groups. Most young Hawaiians of Asian ancestry, bearing psychic wounds from slurs and slights by their white peers, also preferred to move in their own circles. Still, relations between the races in Hawaii were much better than on the mainland.

On February 17, 1935, the Japanese community celebrated the fiftieth anniversary of the arrival of contract laborers in 1885.[26] Caucasian civic leaders took part in the observation and their addresses betrayed little evidence that anyone had doubts about the worth of the Japanese element in the polyglot population. Twenty-seven of the original arrivals were feted.

Although their parents could not become citizens, the Nisei had no doubts about their own Americanism. By sheer persistence and ability more and more of them earned places in municipal and Territorial government, became schoolteachers and administrators, practiced law and medicine, and staffed the businesses owned by old line Caucasian families. Yet there was mounting concern about war clouds over the Pacific as Japan pursued a policy of aggression in China, and American opposition to Tokyo militarists appeared to put the two nations on a collision course. Particularly notable is the fact that while the Issei viewed the future with apprehension, only a few (mostly those with no strong ties in Hawaii) chose to return to Japan.

When Congress instituted Selective Service in the autumn of 1940, 42,706 Japanese Americans registered. Of the 701 men inducted in the first draft call in Hawaii, 479 were Japanese Americans.[27] At the outbreak of war, 1,543 Americans of Japanese ancestry, about one third of them volunteers, were in the armed forces in Hawaii.

Pearl Harbor Day was without doubt the most traumatic day ever experienced by Hawaii's Japanese Americans. The quiet of a Honolulu Sunday morning was blasted by the attack of Japanese naval bombers. Among Nisei, in that instant, sentimental ties with Japan were shattered. Issei who had lived in Hawaii a half century or more suddenly were enemy aliens. Nisei faced the prospect of fighting cousins, even brothers, in Japanese uniform.

In the hysteria that followed the attack, the conduct of Japanese Americans in Hawaii was unfairly maligned, particularly by Navy Secretary Frank Knox who, after a hurried inspection of Pearl Harbor and Hawaii, was quoted as saying: "I think the most effective fifth column work of the entire war was done in Hawaii, with the possible exception of Norway." Most of the mainland press promptly interpreted Knox's report as confirming earlier reports of treachery on the part of Japanese Americans. Only months and years later was it confirmed that Japanese Americans, citizens and alien alike, had comported themselves in a most exemplary manner. Bill Hosokawa writes in his book, *Nisei*:

> In addition to nearly 4,000 military casualties, more than 300 civilians—most of them of Japanese ancestry—were killed or wounded by bombs and shells. Japanese Americans manned guns to repel the enemy, staffed medical stations and operated on the wounded in hospitals, fought fires, directed traffic, patrolled the beaches, transported sailors and soldiers from the city back to their battle stations. Thousands of Issei and Nisei stood in line to donate blood. When it was rumored (falsely, it turned out) that two regiments of Japanese paratroops had landed in the hills, the University of Hawaii R.O.T.C. battalion —most of whom were Nisei—were deployed to engage them and delay their advance into Honolulu. In this emergency no one hesitated about sending them out to oppose the enemy. The Japanese Americans distinguished themselves in Hawaii that black day, but in the confusion and hysteria of the attack and its aftermath, dispatches to the mainland created a totally false impression of sabotage and disloyalty.

Other insights are provided by Dr. Dennis M. Ogawa, associate professor in the Department of American Studies at the University of Hawaii, in his English language book *Kodomo no Tame ni* (For the Sake of the Children), undoubtedly the most complete volume on the Japanese American experience in Hawaii:

> On December 7, approximately 200 Nisei were serving in engineering units, later known as the 1399th Engineering Construction Battalion, involved in the construction of bridges, water

systems, defense enforcements, airfields, and training camps for combat soldiers. Eventually 900 Nisei comprised the total strength of the battalion, doing important defense work for which they received the Meritorious Unit Plaque.

Another all-Nisei group which performed important construction and military defense duties was a unit known as the Varsity Victory Volunteers (VVV). The VVV was made up of young Nisei who were formerly with the University of Hawaii's Reserve Officer's Training Corps (ROTC) and the Hawaii Territorial Guard (HTG). On January 19, 1942, the HTG was given orders from Washington that all men of Japanese ancestry were released from duty since their "services were no longer needed." Since the Nisei members of the HTG were associated racially with the enemy and involved in the vital defense of Hawaii, some military authorities had viewed them with suspicion. Anxious to volunteer their services in any capacity, to prove that the rebuke of their loyalty was unfounded, the HTG Nisei petitioned the military governor of Hawaii, Lieutenant General Delos C. Emmons, to accept them unconditionally in the war effort:

"We, the undersigned, were members of the Hawaii Territorial Guard until its recent inactivation. We joined the Guard voluntarily with the hope that this was one way to serve our country in her time of need. Needless to say, we were deeply disappointed when we were told that our services in the Guard were no longer needed. Hawaii is our home; the United States, our country. We know but one Loyalty and that is to the Stars and Stripes. We wish to do our part as loyal Americans in every way possible and we hereby offer ourselves for whatever service you may see fit to use us."

The military governor accepted the Nisei's request and on February 23, 1942, the Corps of Engineers Auxiliary—the Varsity Victory Volunteers, as they were commonly known—was activated as a part of the 34th Combat Engineers Regiment. For nearly eleven months the 150 Nisei who made up the VVV lived at Schofield Barracks and labored on Oahu quarrying rock, building military installations, roads, warehouses, and dumps.

Other military units comprised partly of Nisei recruits before December 7 were the 298th and 299th Infantry Regiments. About 1,500 Nisei served in these units, guarding shore lines and military installations. Incoming mainland recruits however looked with disfavor upon working with "Jap" soldiers, and the military was uneasy about integrating Japanese with other servicemen. Consequently, in June of 1942, all Nisei military personnel, except those in the Engineering units, were gathered to form the Hawaii Provisional Battalion (Separate). Later called the 100th Infantry Battalion, these Nisei were sent to the mainland for training at Camp McCoy, Wisconsin.

Hawaii had been subjected to intensive intelligence scrutiny before Pearl Harbor. When war broke out, 1,440 among the approximately 160,000 Issei and Nisei in the Islands were taken into custody. Many were released after appearances before special hearing boards. Approximately 981 were sent to internment camps or War Relocation Authority Centers on the mainland. Hawaii's Japanese population, in and out of service, behaved in exemplary fashion during the course of the war.

After the war Hawaii's various nonwhite ethnic components seized on the idea of political action to bring about change. Nisei war veterans, who had demonstrated their loyalty beyond challenge, were in the forefront of the movement.

The Republican party, long the instrument of the dominant white elite in the Islands, was committed to the preservation of the status quo and had done little to encourage support of the nonwhites. It was natural the veterans should turn to the Democratic party. But other advocates of change also sought control of the party and a struggle ensued between the International Longshoremen's and Warehousemen's Union (ILWU) leadership on one hand, and on the other, John Burns, a Honolulu police captain at the time of Pearl Harbor who had worked his way up party ranks. Most of the veterans supported Burns. Burns ultimately won control and forged a strong political organization with important support from Nisei, Chinese, and part-Hawaiian components of the electorate. By 1950, Nisei voters, who had become an urban people, numbered slightly more than one third the total.

The election of 1954 was the turning point. Japanese Americans were in the thick of political campaigns, most of them as Democrats. The Democratic party captured control of the Territorial legislature and numerous city and county offices throughout the Islands. Nisei candidates won nearly half the seats in the legislature.

The next step was statehood, a status denied Hawaii because of racist fears in many quarters—in Hawaii as well as on the mainland

—for the future of a state dominated politically by Japanese Americans. Fortunately, times had changed. The "Yellow Peril" had been laid to rest. Japanese Americans had distinguished themselves as Hawaii's political, civic, and business leaders, and all but the most biased were ready to accept them as loyal Americans.

In March, 1959, Congress approved admission of Hawaii as the fiftieth state in the Union. It was a time of great rejoicing in Hawaii. In Hawaii's first election as a state, Daniel K. Inouye, son and grandson of Japanese immigrants and a wounded and decorated veteran of World War II, was elected to serve in the House of Representatives. When Inouye moved up in 1962 to the Senate, his House seat was filled by another decorated Nisei veteran, Spark Masayuki Matsunaga. And when Hawaii was given a second representative in 1964, the new district elected Patsy Takemoto Mink, the state's first Nisei woman attorney. For a dozen years from 1964 until 1976, all four of Hawaii's delegation in Congress were persons of Asian extraction —Mrs. Mink and Matsunaga in the House, and in the Senate, Inouye and Hiram L. Fong, a Republican of Chinese origin.

In 1976, Fong retired. Mrs. Mink and Matsunaga both declared for the Senate seat. Matsunaga won after a spirited primary battle that put to rest for all time—even though it wasn't necessary—the canard that Japanese Americans vote in solid blocs. Periodically, the racial issue arises—"Hawaii should have an ethnically balanced delegation," the argument goes—but no one suggests the Japanese Americans represent less than the entire state of Hawaii. Dr. Ogawa describes the new Hawaii in these terms:

By 1974 the descendants of Japanese immigrants to Hawaii had come to occupy influential and powerful positions in Island society. As a result of the state election in that year, Japanese American men and women not only occupied Hawaii's top political offices of governor and lieutenant governor but also sat in significant numbers in the state House and Senate. In the economic life of Hawaii, Japanese had become major business figures helping to guide Hawaii's financial destiny. In public education, in civil service jobs, and in the statewide adminstration, Japanese could be found exercising a significant degree of power . . . There were no anguished cries over a Japanese "takeover." When the people of Hawaii elevated Japanese Americans to their highest state offices, the bugaboo of the "Yellow Menace" was not resurrected. Obviously, in the decades between the Thirties

and the Seventies significant changes had occurred in the status
of Japanese in Hawaii. During World War II, Japanese Americans had proved their loyalty to America, dispelling doubts over
their national affiliation and their degree of adaptation to American ways . . .

Political change had come to Hawaii and with it the end of white
political domination. Even the governorship went to a Nisei, George
Ariyoshi. But social change proceeded more slowly. An anthropologist who studied postwar changes in Hawaii in 1971 describes a
process which has continued: [28]

> Today . . . barriers to inter-ethnic contact are disappearing.
> Many Japanese can afford private schools and the restrictive
> admission policies at such schools as Punahou are slowly dis-
> appearing. Income levels, as measured by the census, are less
> disparate. Furthermore the Japanese are dominant politically,
> representing 54 percent of the state legislators. Today the Big
> Five companies must employ Japanese lobbyists to promote
> their causes at the capitol. Few Caucasian politicians can ad-
> vance without speaking pidgin in the capitol cloakroom. In fact,
> many important positions in both the private and public sector
> are occupied by Japanese.
>   Yet attempts to integrate community institutions are largely
> unsuccessful. The Japanese Chamber of Commerce persists even
> though the original function (to protect the interests of the
> Japanese businessman) is no longer required. There remains a
> Japanese Christian church alongside separate Chinese, Hawaiian
> and Caucasian churches, although the policy of the church board
> espouses integration and the elimination of these ethnic labels.
> The Caucasians, on the other hand, are slowly lowering restric-
> tions on memberships to their exclusive clubs, permitting a few
> successful Orientals to join them.

These observations about contemporary Hawaii are, of necessity,
superficial judgments about an extremely complex and dynamic society that has fascinated scholars and has been the subject of many
in-depth studies. On the surface, it appears that Hawaii has developed
a special way of life based on cultural pluralism. Yet, how deep does
this pluralism go?

As Dr. Ogawa points out, one cannot simply build a shopping center with Hawaiian, American, Chinese, Japanese, or Filipino goods

and foods and say complacently that Hawaii is perpetuating cultural pluralism. He adds: "Cultural pluralism involves not just the cohabitation of artifacts and customs but the free interaction of behaviorally diverse people. Not merely the creation of a smorgasbord of cultural embellishments but human beings with different backgrounds intermingling peacefully, rewardingly, and equitably in the same community is the gist of cultural pluralism."

As a group, the Japanese in Hawaii have adjusted remarkably well to the American economic and political system, aggressively taking leadership roles once the opportunity became available. There is no doubt that they have achieved success in both the American and Japanese sense of the word.

XI ❦ Nisei and Kibei

Scholars frequently refer to the children of immigrants as members of a transitional generation. Usually—particularly when those involved were from a culture quite different from the Anglo-Teutonic background of the American majority—the immigrants were so thoroughly immersed in the problems of making a livelihood that they had little time to adapt to American ways. It was the children of these immigrants, exposed to the powerful influence of the American public school system, who bridged the gap between their parents and the customs, mores, and values of the majority society.

Naturally, the children of European immigrants who brought with them variants of Western culture would find the transition to American life somewhat easier than those whose parents represented non-Western cultures. In the case of the Chinese and Japanese, these difficulties were compounded by the racist hostility outlined in previous chapters.

Put another way, Nisei shared many problems in common with the second generation of all immigrant groups in America. But some of their problems were unique, and some they shared with all those who would forever be physically visible as members of minority groups.

For their immigrant parents, the challenge of the American environment involved political, economic, social, and psychic stresses and strains. These the Nisei shared in great measure. The hostility the Orientals faced affected them in at least two important ways. It hindered Chinese and Japanese efforts to move out and become assimilated into the larger community. At the same time, it forced them to look inward into their own society for physical and emotional support, which in turn inhibited their Americanization. Illogically, they were to be criticized and their loyalty held suspect because of their alleged unassimilability.

Thus, while the Nisei were exposed to the American language, history, customs, ideals, and aspirations in the schools, in most instances

160

they had to seek their gratification in the ethnic communities, making their private accommodation between what might be and what could be.

Two noted scholars have recently published assessments of the Japanese American community. One, Dr. Harry H. L. Kitano, a Nisei, characterizes it as a subculture. The other, Professor William Petersen, a Caucasian, refers to it as a subnation.[1] These judgments would seem to suggest that the transitional stage continues and that Japanese Americans are a distinct and, in some ways, separate entity in the American community.

Generalizations about the Nisei are difficult because, as in all groups, the individuals vary widely as to outlook, malleability, degree of aggressiveness, or docility. In addition there is a wide divergence of experience between those of the mainland, a tiny minority, and those of Hawaii, who comprise a large fraction of the total population. The latter also enjoyed the more serene social climate in the midst of a polyglot, ethnically diverse population. (This lays the stage for an interesting but unanswerable question: How would mainland Nisei have fared if the West Coast atmosphere had been as accommodating as that of Hawaii?) In reality, however, the difference in attitude toward Orientals was a matter of degree. The white man dominated Hawaii economically, and the mainland economically and numerically. For Oriental Americans, growing up was not easy in either environment.

Leaving the admittedly critical matter of economics for the moment, Nisei like many other second generation children received their pre-school training from parents who were insecure in the new environment. Issei mothers were rarely competent in English and virtually everything the child learned at the mother's knee was couched in the Japanese language, traditions, and values. Childhood fairy tales had to do with Momotaro, the Peach Boy, and the Tongue-cut Sparrow rather than Jack-and-the-Beanstalk. Many Nisei spoke virtually no English until they were enrolled in the first grade; there was no one to teach them other than Japanese. These early years were a kind of uterine extension in which the child was spared the harsh realities of prejudice and discrimination which would come when he ventured outside the confines of the family. Monica Sone in her charming biography, *Nisei Daughter*, alludes to this protected period when she begins with, "The first five years of my life I lived in amoebic bliss, not knowing whether I was plant or animal . . ." Of course, it can be argued that this is not an uncommon experience in any protected family atmosphere.

Leaving the sanctuary of family and home, the young Nisei encountered new problems of language and adjustment. Few entered school with a command of English the equal of their white peers. They encountered schools that were segregated both *de facto* and legally, as in Sacramento County in the 1920's.[2] *De facto* school segregation came about as a result of segregated housing patterns. A prime example is the old Bailey Gatzert grade school in Seattle's Oriental quarter which had few pupils other than Japanese. It has been established that while Nisei rarely caused a deportment problem and excelled in mathematics and art, their skill in English in the segregated schools was inferior to that of Nisei in integrated schools. In segregated schools with only Nisei peers about them, many children never became entirely fluent in English. Few of them became entirely fluent in Japanese either, particularly in reading and writing, despite attendance at Japanese-language schools after public school hours.

At home they also had difficulty communicating. As their English vocabulary grew and their interests broadened, they had trouble carrying on serious discussions with their parents since their Japanese vocabulary did not expand at anywhere near the same pace. This was particularly true between mothers and their sons. The Nisei girl fared somewhat better, being closer to the mother and keeping up with her Japanese in order to maintain the intimacy. In general, because the father needed some understanding of English to make a living, he did a little better with the language than his wife who was largely confined to her home. Even so, as the Nisei progressed in school the opportunity for family discussions of significant matters was negligible in most families. Some scholars have suggested that the difficulty many Nisei experience in articulating their thoughts can be traced to the absence during their formative years of dinner table conversation about abstract ideas, politics, and similar subjects requiring thought and expression of opinion. The Issei took great pride in their children's facility with English, but their own inability to converse in that language contributed substantially to the gap between the two generations.

The cruelty of children presented the young Nisei with some of their most difficult emotional problems, particularly when they were shy and lacked the support of other Nisei in unsegregated schools. On the playgrounds children of a minority race—any minority—were often subjected to torment and abuse. From the outset of their schooling, young Nisei learned the harsh facts of racial intolerance and dealt with it in diverse ways. Some confronted their tormentors and many a playground altercation ensued.[3] Others avoided discrimination and humiliation, a technique perhaps learned from their parents. One example of this "dodging" has to do with a Japanese golfer in Los Angeles who said he never encountered discrimination on the public links. Later it was revealed he played only early in the mornings and never on Sundays or holidays.

Despite difficulty in communicating, a strong sense of family supported the Nisei during occasional periods of discouragement and helped him maintain his self-respect. One of the products of discrimination for some minorities is a measure of self-hate and resignation to the status to which white racists would relegate them. It is likely that many Issei helped their children avoid a sense of inferiority by emphasizing their "Japanese-ness"—urging them to take pride in Japan's long history and rich culture and the swift progress the Old Country was making as an industrial and military power. One distinguished sociologist contends: [4]

> One important reason that Japanese Americans overcame their extraordinary hardships is that they truly believe (as do Jews) that they are innately superior, that others are inferior.

However, the Nisei generation ranges over a wide span of years and their experiences differ substantially as a result of changing times and different customs in various locales. There were Nisei among the children whom the San Francisco School Board segregated for a time in 1906. Yet in 1942, at the time of the relocation, the median age of the Nisei was only seventeen.[5] Thus, many of them reached maturity in the postwar years when the social climate was quite different from that of the prewar period. The diverse experiences of the members of this generation have inevitably influenced their self-image, and while some fit the image projected in the quotation above, many others do not.

If there is one thing a large number of Nisei had in common, it was scholastic achievement. They seemed to sense that in a competitive society in which they operated at a disadvantage, they would need to be superior to compete even equally. To be sure, not all Nisei were strongly motivated, but the best of them were brilliant. Parents took great pride in their children's accomplishments and encouraged them to excel. In schools where there were large numbers of Nisei, the competition for grades often was with other Japanese Americans and not the white community. Thus, the strength of the Japanese family system supported and motivated Nisei students.

Although Nisei enjoyed great freedom in infancy and early child-hood in accordance with Japanese tradition, family control over their behavior was asserted at adolescence when they came under more rigorous family restraints than their white peers. The father exercised full authority, relieved only by devices mothers might employ to soften apparent harshness although never to the extent of undermining the father's authority. Because most families were of limited means, the power of the purse was decisive and over this the father exercised rigid control. But here we are dealing in stereotypes, for the degree of tradi-tionalism varied from family to family and the parent-child relation-ships in many differed little from those of Caucasian families of the same socio-economic status.

It was inevitable that the American environment should have a moderating influence on the Japanese family system. As Nisei grew older, their command of English and ability to cope with the pressures of a hostile or indifferent society won them a status within their fami-lies different from the lot of children in Japan. Yamato Ichihashi in his pioneering study, *Japanese in the United States*, describes the situ-ation in the early 1930's: [6]

> The Japanese . . . recognized the advantage of the American citizenship accorded to their native-born offspring. In fact in some instances they tried to get around the alien land laws . . . by utilizing the legal status of their children . . . Older chil-dren now recognized their advantage, and parents began to lose control over their children more and more.

Late-arriving Issei as well as visitors from Japan often commented on the difference between families in the Old Country and the United States, usually deploring the "decadence" and lack of discipline among Americanized Japanese. One observer noted that while there seemed to be much affection by Nisei toward their parents, they failed to show much respect. He may well have been misled by the decline in the forms and symbols that are part of expressing respect in Japan.

Though the Nisei of the 1920's and 1930's often chafed at parental restrictions, they seldom rebelled. Family discipline was an accepted part of life, and inevitably the usual economic difficulties exacerbated by the great Depression only tightened family bonds.

For the most part, friendships with white students in school with-ered after graduation. Their horizons limited by discrimination, the Nisei withdrew into the Japanese community. Where numbers per-mitted, a self-contained Japanese community had developed which provided opportunities for a varied social life. Ethnic churches, Christian and Buddhist, were the focus of much social activity, and to a lesser extent, the prefectural associations which were primarily vehicles for the Issei. Sports leagues abounded. Nisei took naturally to sports of all kinds, but usually their slight physiques made it difficult to compete against Caucasians even at the high school level. Thus, they played baseball, football, and basketball against each other and developed some vigorous rivalries.

The various professional and service organizations which contributed to the social life of their white peers played no part in the lives of the Nisei. Much of this was the result of the prejudice; the Nisei knew they were not wanted and rarely tried to push their way into these organizations. Another reason was tacit or legal discrimination which kept Issei out of certain professions and therefore denied Nisei the privilege of association with those groups. Even the Young Men's Christian Association subjected them to some discrimination.

Facing closed doors outside of their communities, Nisei for the most part had to look to their friends and neighbors for a livelihood. An education alone was no guarantee of economic opportunity. Few Nisei in this period were permitted to reach their potential, and college-trained men and women were forced into the most menial of occupations to survive. The Nisei of the 1930's had the misfortune of reaching maturity at the time of the economic Depression. Vast unemployment meant even greater white discrimination against the Nisei, forcing them still more firmly within the Japanese community.

It is pertinent to ask why, when they apparently faced only a dead-end future, so many Nisei persisted in getting college educations. One key answer is to be found in Confucian traditions which placed great value on learning. The Issei, usually of limited education, blamed their inability to get ahead on their lack of formal schooling. They saw education as the key to breaking through American discrimination. It is likely that many of them saw the future day when opportunities for the Nisei would become available, and they wanted their children fully qualified to meet the new responsibilities. In any event, they encouraged their children to go on to college even though a diploma was no passport to a job, and made great personal sacrifices to help pay for tuition and books.

Frustrated in their native country, it was inevitable that some Nisei should look to Japan for opportunity. A few found employment of sorts in the American offices of Japanese banks and trading firms. But responsible jobs were reserved for Japanese nationals, the so-called

Kaisha people (Japanese company personnel), and Nisei had little or no prospects of advancement. A small number went to Japan, usually at the urging of parents who felt knowledge of English was a salable asset. Most were disappointed. Japan also was caught in the Depression. The rigid hierarchical system with its emphasis on graduation from prestigious universities blocked the Nisei, who were looked upon as outsiders. Their American education and acculturation made them what sociologists called "marginal" people even in the homeland of their parents.

Other Nisei, usually at a younger age, were sent to Japan by their parents for one or more of several reasons. A few were entrusted to grandparents or uncles and aunts because of the death of the mother, or because of difficult economic circumstances in the States. In some instances a child who had become a discipline problem was shipped off to relatives where, it was hoped, a stricter society would help the youngster straighten out. By far the largest number were sent to Japan for their educations in the expectation that that was the key to future success. Those who eventually returned to the United States were known as *Kibei*, and they added a new and somewhat different dimension to the Japanese American picture. Dr. Kitano makes this observation: [7]

> The Kibei are technically Nisei—born in the United States—but differ in having spent their early years in Japan, usually with grandparents. Because members of this group differ in regard to sex, particular experiences in Japan and length of expatriation, it is difficult to arrive at meaningful generalizations about them.

The attitude of the Kibei and their readjustment to American life depended on a number of factors, among them the age and therefore the impressionability of the individual when he was sent to Japan, the length of the period of school, and the period in time when the schooling occurred. Obviously, the younger the child, the greater would be the impact of Japanese culture. Indeed, some Nisei who were sent to Japan at an older age, after graduation from an American high school for instance, reacted adversely to the experience. A brief stay in Japan would hardly counteract the influence America had impressed on the young Nisei. And finally, the rise of Japanese nationalism after about 1928 made the ensuing years a time during which the youngster would be subjected to a militant, authoritarian education.

As a result, while some Kibei returned to their families and settled down easily among their peers, others displayed strongly pro-Japanese and anti-American attitudes. Thus, long before the eruption of World War II, a sharp dialogue developed between extremist Kibei and Nisei concerning the role Japan was playing in the Far East and the merits of Japanese culture compared with the American scene. Sometimes the Kibei were closer to their parents and other Issei than to brothers and sisters who had never been to Japan, although occasionally some Kibei were so strongly pro-Japanese as to alienate even some Issei. To put this in different terms, the generation gap was narrower in many cases between Issei parents and Kibei children, even though they had been separated for years, than between the parents and Nisei who had never been to Japan. However, the Japan the Kibei experienced was in many ways no longer the Japan which the Issei had left. What the Kibei brought back with them as invisible baggage was not identical with that which the Issei had brought with them a generation earlier. In this regard, Japanese culture in America was static, reflecting a Japan and its values that had disappeared.

The one characteristic common to the Kibei who had spent their formative years in Japan was a deficiency in English. Uncomfortable in communicating with Nisei, many Kibei sought out one another for companionship and reinforcement, thus further retarding their readjustment to American life. However, much of their seeming pro-Japanese outlook was cultural rather than political and based on a sense of inability to fit into the American scene. When war came, hundreds of Kibei provided an invaluable service as instructors in military language-training programs, as interpreters and translators in the Pacific theater, and psychological warfare specialists.

As a group the Nisei seem to have faced far more than their share of problems and dilemmas not of their making. Not least among these was the matter of dual citizenship. Under American law, persons born in the United States are citizens by birth. Under Japanese law prior to 1924, the offspring of Japanese citizens, regardless of the place of birth, were recognized as subjects of Japan. Technically, then, Nisei were dual citizens although many of them were ignorant of their status. Anti-Japanese forces had often used the fact of dual citizenship to discredit the loyalty of Nisei. A congressional committee investigating statehood for Hawaii studied the dual citizenship matter thoroughly in 1938. Its statement explaining the situation is a clear review of the facts and it is quoted here at length: [8]

Under American law all persons born in the United States and subject to the jurisdiction thereof are American citizens. But

Japan likewise formerly recognized the children of their nationals, wherever born, as subjects of Japan. This provision is, as has been pointed out, not peculiar to Japan. It is well-nigh a universal practice among the nations of the world. The United States follows the same principle by conferring American citizenship upon children born of American parents in foreign countries, in some of which such children may also exercise the privilege of citizenship, thus becoming American dual citizens.

The Japanese government, by a law adopted in 1924, went further to meet America's position on the question of citizenship than any other foreign government appears to have done. Since that year no claim to jurisdiction to any American-born child of Japanese parents is made by Japan unless the parents register such a child at a Japanese consulate within 14 days after its birth. Dual citizenship is prevented at the beginning instead of being left to possible termination after the individual comes of age. For those born prior to 1924 and even those who were born after that date and were registered as Japanese by their parents, a procedure for complete expatriation from Japan is provided, which was simplified and made easier by the act of 1924. From testimony before the committee it appears that over half of the citizens of Japanese ancestry in Hawaii were born after 1924, and as only a negligible number were registered with the Japanese consulate the question of dual citizenship does not arise with these children. Of those still considered subjects of Japan by the Japanese government a fair number have expatriated themselves.

After all, the issue of dual citizenship, both for the Japanese in Hawaii and on the mainland, and for the many more thousands of Europeans, can only become a live one if the persons involved visit the country of their parents' origin and subject themselves to its jurisdiction. Otherwise the claims of some foreign government in no way affect their ordinary way of life or their rights and obligations as American citizens.

In view of the Nisei's many knotty problems, their belief in their future as Americans, the reluctance of vast numbers of whites to recognize them as Americans, and the drive and perceptiveness of individual Nisei, it is not surprising that at an early time in their history some of them sought to pool their talents and energies in an organization dedicated to establishing and protecting Nisei rights. Two entirely

Hundreds of Nisei were serving in the U.S. Army at the time of Pearl Harbor and no one thought anything of it. But soon afterward many were discharged "at the convenience of the government." INTERNATIONAL NEWS

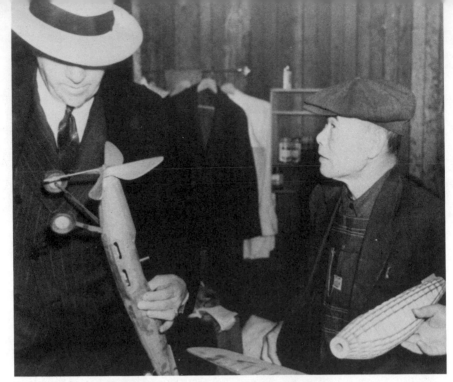

After war's outbreak even an Issei's model-plane hobby became a reason to seize him as a security risk. INTERNATIONAL NEWS

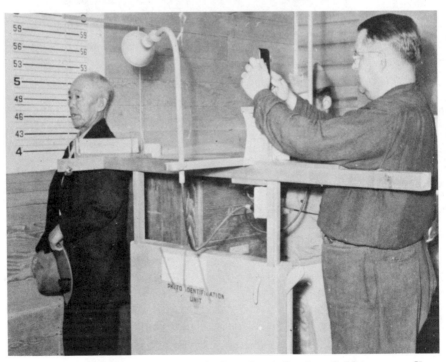

Issei community leaders were picked up by federal authorities regardless of age or length of time they had been in the United States. TAK MURAKAMI COLLECTION

After President Roosevelt signed Executive Order 9066 the Army quickly posted notices requiring "all Japanese" to register preparatory to Evacuation. INTERNATIONAL NEWS

One of the first areas to be evacuated was Bainbridge Island in Puget Sound. Men, women, and children under armed guard prepare to board a ferryboat on the first leg of their trip to Manzanar camp in California. PACIFIC CITIZEN

WESTERN DEFENSE COMMAND AND FOURTH ARMY
WARTIME CIVIL CONTROL ADMINISTRATION
Presidio of San Francisco, California
May 3, 1942

INSTRUCTIONS
TO ALL PERSONS OF
JAPANESE
ANCESTRY
Living in the Following Area:

All of that portion of the City of Los Angeles, State of California, within that boundary beginning at the point at which North Figueroa Street meets a line following the middle of the Los Angeles River; thence southerly and following the said line to East First Street; thence westerly on East First Street to Alameda Street; thence southerly on Alameda Street to East Third Street; thence northwesterly on East Third Street to Main Street; thence northerly on Main Street to First Street; thence northwesterly on First Street to Figueroa Street; thence northeasterly on Figueroa Street to the point of beginning.

Pursuant to the provisions of Civilian Exclusion Order No. 33, this Headquarters, dated May 3, 1942, all persons of Japanese ancestry, both alien and non-alien, will be evacuated from the above area by 12 o'clock noon, P. W. T., Saturday, May 9, 1942.

No Japanese person living in the above area will be permitted to change residence after 12 o'clock noon, P. W. T., Sunday, May 3, 1942, without obtaining special permission from the representative of the Commanding General, Southern California Sector, at the Civil Control Station located at:

Japanese Union Church,
120 North San Pedro Street,
Los Angeles, California.

Such permits will only be granted for the purpose of uniting members of a family, or in cases of grave emergency.

The Civil Control Station is equipped to assist the Japanese population affected by this evacuation in the following ways:

1. Give advice and instructions on the evacuation.
2. Provide services with respect to the management, leasing, sale, storage or other disposition of most kinds of property, such as real estate, business and professional equipment, household goods, boats, automobiles and livestock.
3. Provide temporary residence elsewhere for all Japanese in family groups.
4. Transport persons and a limited amount of clothing and equipment to their new residence.

The Following Instructions Must Be Observed:

1. A responsible member of each family, preferably the head of the family, or the person in whose name most of the property is held, and each individual living alone, will report to the Civil Control Station to receive further instructions. This must be done between 8:00 A. M. and 5:00 P. M. on Monday, May 4, 1942, or between 8:00 A. M. and 5:00 P. M. on Tuesday, May 5, 1942.
2. Evacuees must carry with them on departure for the Assembly Center, the following property:
   (a) Bedding and linens (no mattress) for each member of the family;
   (b) Toilet articles for each member of the family;
   (c) Extra clothing for each member of the family;
   (d) Sufficient knives, forks, spoons, plates, bowls and cups for each member of the family;
   (e) Essential personal effects for each member of the family.

All items carried will be securely packaged, tied and plainly marked with the name of the owner and numbered in accordance with instructions obtained at the Civil Control Station. The size and number of packages is limited to that which can be carried by the individual or family group.

3. No pets of any kind will be permitted.
4. No personal items and no household goods will be shipped to the Assembly Center.
5. The United States Government through its agencies will provide for the storage, at the sole risk of the owner, of the more substantial household items, such as iceboxes, washing machines, pianos and other heavy furniture. Cooking utensils and other small items will be accepted for storage if crated, packed and plainly marked with the name and address of the owner. Only one name and address will be used by a given family.
6. Each family, and individual living alone, will be furnished transportation to the Assembly Center or will be authorized to travel by private automobile in a supervised group. All instructions pertaining to the movement will be obtained at the Civil Control Station.

**Go to the Civil Control Station between the hours of 8:00 A. M. and 5:00 P. M.,
Monday, May 4, 1942, or between the hours of 8:00 A. M. and 5:00 P. M.,
Tuesday, May 5, 1942, to receive further instructions.**

J. L. DeWITT
Lieutenant General, U. S. Army
Commanding

SEE CIVILIAN EXCLUSION ORDER NO. 33.

Detailed instructions were contained in Evacuation orders. This notice was dated May 3, 1942, nearly five months after Pearl Harbor, and Evacuation date was May 9.

Federal authorities cited need to protect Japanese Americans from violence as one reason for evacuating them. Nisei charged authorities had an obligation to protect them from vandals. VISUAL COMMUNICATIONS

Merchants who had stocked up for the Christmas business were badly hurt when Evacuation made it necessary to liquidate their stock hurriedly. VISUAL COMMUNI-CATIONS

Some farmers were able to lease their land to tenants. Those who did not own land had to sell furniture and equipment for whatever they could get. LIBRARY OF CONGRESS COLLECTION

Heavy losses were sustained by San Pedro fishermen. Boats and nets purchased with life savings were disposed of at distress prices. NATIONAL ARCHIVES

The Evacuation order affected everyone of Japanese extraction. LIBRARY OF CONGRESS COLLECTION

On the way to a concentration camp; what lay ahead, no one could say.
BANCROFT LIBRARY, UNIVERSITY OF CALIFORNIA

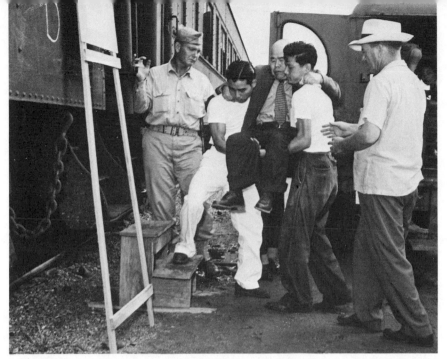

Only the critically ill were allowed to remain behind in hospitals and tuberculosis sanatoriums. WAR RELOCATION AUTHORITY

The Evacuation was conducted peacefully but armed troops stood by to make sure of compliance. NATIONAL ARCHIVES

Evacuees arriving at Santa Anita reception center have luggage inspected for contraband. LIBRARY OF CONGRESS COLLECTION

An elderly evacuee numbly contemplates the future. NATIONAL ARCHIVES

Camps were not fully prepared for the evacuees, but straw was available for mattresses. TAK MURAKAMI COLLECTION

Mess hall fare was usually plentiful, frequently monotonous, seldom pala-table. TAK MURAKAMI COLLECTION

Slow Motion

Federal authorities were unprepared for the involved task of preparing, filling, and operating concentration camps. The California press was impatient with the pace of Evacuation. TAK MURAKAMI COLLECTION

War Relocation Camps at first were enclosed by barbed-wire fences but intense evacuee resentment caused them to be removed after it was determined they weren't needed. Signs later marked the boundaries, but armed sentries remained. TAK MURAKAMI COLLECTION

When the Supreme Court ruled in 1944 that evacuees could not be kept in the camps once their loyalty was determined, West Coast was reopened to Japanese Americans. By war's end, several hundred had returned to their homes. ASSOCIATED PRESS

independent movements developed in the years immediately after World War I, one in San Francisco and the other in Seattle. The leaders in both instances were Nisei who had recently reached maturity and sought to promote their welfare and status as citizens. One of the prime movers in San Francisco was a young dentist, Dr. Thomas T. Yatabe, who in 1906 had been among the children the San Francisco School Board had segregated.

The San Francisco organization was called the American Loyalty League. In Seattle it was named the Progressive Citizens' League. Neither achieved much vitality. Objectives and programs were poorly conceived because of inexperience and the members had little time to spare after a day at their jobs. When Dr. Yatabe moved his practice to Fresno, that community became the most active center of Nisei citizen activity.

Near the end of the 1920's, with increasing numbers of Nisei reaching adulthood, the citizen movement was revitalized. Meetings between California and Washington Nisei leaders led to proposals for a national organization. Considerable debate ensued over its name. Some Nisei wanted no reference to Japan or Japanese. The name finally chosen was Japanese American Citizens League (JACL), the *Japanese* being employed as an adjective to define the origin of these Americans, rather than to signify a hyphenated organization. Each local chapter was permitted to employ its own name as a member of the national Japanese American Citizens League. Dr. Yatabe's chapter in Fresno continued to call itself the American Loyalty League.

The first national meeting was held in Seattle in 1930. It was attended by Nisei from the three coastal states with a small scattering of others from various parts of the nation. After endorsing the idea of a national organization, the delegates passed resolutions underscoring the importance they placed on their citizenship. They petitioned Congress to change the Cable Act, and urged naturalization rights for Orientals who had served in the U.S. armed forces in World War I. Both eventually were enacted into law.

The Cable Act, passed in 1922, stipulated that any American woman who married an alien ineligible to citizenship would lose her U.S. citizenship. If the marriage ended, the woman could apply to regain citizenship. However, this provision did not apply to a Nisei woman marrying a Japanese alien. Because she was of a race ineligible to naturalization, once she lost her citizenship she could not regain it. The veterans' measure ultimately enabled some 700 Issei to become citizens.

For the first few years JACL's goals were poorly articulated. In 1936 Jimmie Sakamoto, the blind Seattle newspaper publisher, was elected president and he laid out an ambitious if somewhat vague program that called for Nisei to become good American citizens by: [9]

1—Contributing to the social life of the nation, living with other citizens in a common community of interests and activities to promote the national welfare.

2—Contributing to the economic welfare of the nation by taking key roles in agriculture, industry, and commerce.

3—Contributing to the civil welfare as intelligent voters and public-spirited citizens.

In his book *Nisei*, Bill Hosokawa comments as follows:

> The goals, like motherhood, were beyond challenge and controversy, but no one quite knew how to achieve them, particularly when the economic and social hostility against the Nisei was intensified by the pressures of the Depression. How could one contribute to the social life of the nation when one was not accepted into that life? How could one contribute to the economic welfare when one couldn't get a job? The JACL, which had established the goals, was no more effective than anyone else in showing how those goals could be reached.

Sociologist Frank Miyamoto recalls most JACL chapter meetings dealt with upcoming national and sectional conventions and a variety of social functions. "For the majority of Nisei who participated in the functions of the group," he has written, "it fulfilled a social purpose and meant little else. To be sure, the JACL constantly tried to stimulate political interest among the Nisei . . . The significant fact is that despite the dissatisfaction among the membership, there was little understanding of how to change the organization for the better . . ."

Political ideals were fine, but the grim reality was that almost every mature Nisei was preoccupied with the necessity to survive.

One other factor must be mentioned in understanding the plight of the Japanese American communities during this period. Japan had launched its military push to control the Asian mainland with an invasion of Manchuria in 1931. A few years later the aggression spread to North and Central China. Many Issei supported Japanese policy, much as immigrants from Germany and Italy applauded Hitler and Mussolini before World War II. These Issei bought Tokyo's propaganda line that Japan was seeking to establish an Asian "co-prosperity sphere" and combating Chinese "bandits." There is little doubt that some Issei, weary of being discriminated against because of race and scorned as inferiors, were pleased to see the homeland asserting its strength militarily just as the white nations had done in their years of imperialism.

Many Nisei were uneasy about Japan's aggression but they hesitated to speak out against what was pleasing their parents. Others boldly criticized Japanese militarism. Still others remained apolitical. The political development of the Nisei suffered during this period because of the generational split in Japanese American communities over something that was going on thousands of miles away.

Despite its shortcomings, JACL was about all the Nisei had in the way of an organization to look after their interests and seek to improve their social and economic status. There was relatively little Nisei interest in Issei organizations such as the Japanese Association and prefectural clubs, partly because of the language gap, partly because their mutual concerns such as finding a better job were not addressed by the Issei groups, partly because the Nisei outlook was American rather than Japanese.

In some communities there was an element of rivalry between JACL and the Issei organizations. The Nisei were anxious to assert themselves; the Issei were reluctant to yield community leadership roles. No doubt the situation was complicated by the fact that many Issei married so late in life there was a missing generation in the Japanese American community. It was not unusual for a man in his sixties to have an eldest son in his twenties, and this wide difference in ages may have contributed to Issei feeling that Nisei were too young to assume responsibility and authority.

This was the disquieting internal situation within the Japanese American communities in the late 1930's as Japan, firmly in the grip of a military clique, embarked on a course of armed expansion that was to lead inevitably to war with the United States.

XII ☙ The Winter of '41–'42

In the late 1930's and up until Pearl Harbor Japanese Americans viewed the growing record of Japanese aggression in Asia with a mixture of apprehension and wishful thinking. The apprehension was based on the fear that Japan and the United States were headed for a collision, and who could say what that might lead to? The wishful thinking was based in the case of the Issei on the hope that Japan soon would get all that she wanted—or rather needed—in China, peace would return, and the United States would back off; in the case of the Nisei it was focused on the forlorn hope that since war was unthinkable, somehow it would be averted.

Thus, while the events of Sunday, December 7, 1941, came as a tremendous shock to the American people, the most shaken of all were the Japanese Americans and their immigrant parents. Abruptly, they faced a new and unknown dimension in their relationships with those around them. Not only war itself, but also the manner of its coming produced for them special problems. In the years before the war, hostility toward them had begun to subside, but it was only dormant, not dead. When the shooting started, they quickly realized they were as easily identifiable as the German Americans and Italian Americans were not.

Diversity inevitably characterized the reaction of Japanese Americans, ranging from shame and anger that the country of their ancestors had perpetrated the "day of infamy" to a sense of relief among some militant anti-fascists that the issue was finally joined. There were also mixed feelings among the Issei who had both profited from and suffered in the American environment, and it is very likely that many did not really know their own minds.

This much, however, is incontrovertible from the record; the overt behavior of the group left nothing to be desired. The immediate reaction of the Japanese American community on that fateful Sunday was a momentary retirement into itself; in a sense its members seemed to be anxiously awaiting the reaction of the larger community. They did not have long to wait. The Federal Bureau of Investigation quickly took into custody Issei leaders believed to have strong pro-Japanese sentiments. These were men who had been under surveillance for long periods of time. For the most part they had positions of influence in the Japanese communities, and when they were seized there was left a leadership vacuum into which untested and relatively inexperienced Nisei leaders soon moved.

On December 8 the funds of Issei were frozen. Families of Issei taken into custody faced serious problems without resources. Japanese were discharged from jobs, creditors demanded immediate payment of bills, automobile insurance policies were canceled, and checks sent out the previous weeks were not honored by banks.

Both Hawaii and the mainland quickly became rife with rumors concerning roles allegedly played by Japanese prior to, during, and after the attack on Pearl Harbor. Preposterous stories spread on the mainland—arrows cut in the cane fields had guided Japanese bombers to Pearl Harbor, Japanese Americans had blocked traffic and delayed servicemen trying to return to their posts, enemy pilots wearing American college rings had been shot down—and these were widely believed. The authorities did nothing to dispel them and their silence seemed to give these rumors a validity.

Even so, immediately after Pearl Harbor the voice of sanity was heard from many quarters, including editorials in leading Pacific Coast newspapers. The American attitude at first was not antagonistic toward Japanese Americans. The climate which ultimately prevailed had to be created, and as December wore on, forces were at work to bring into being the suspicion, fear, and hate which characterized the West Coast scene by late winter. The early days of the war produced disaster after disaster for the Allied forces, and this added to the hostility.

It is the fashion of historians in studying cause and effect relationships to assign credit and assess blame for what comes to pass. In analyzing the events that led to the mass expulsion of Japanese Americans from their homes and confinement in inland camps, the tendency is to blame the machinations of misguided or even evil groups and individuals. But it can be argued that even though the "devil theory of history" is beguiling, it is simplistic. The real explanation is to be found, instead, in a broad spectrum of attitudes comprised of racism, the pursuit of narrow self-interest, inertia when the rights of others were under attack, and the fear and hatred engendered by the manner in which the Pacific war had begun. All these, interacting in a kind of multiple causation, produced a climate which men of little vision or imagination could exploit and produce what is today often referred to as America's greatest wartime mistake.

If, as historians insist, the past is prologue, the United States on the eve of Pearl Harbor was sharply conditioned by its recent history. Clearly, Americans at that time were not of one mind regarding the European war. America Firsters, German-American Bundists, members of the American Legion, and others held disparate opinions about the world at large and America's role in it.

Perhaps even more important was the impact of the Depression years. Many Americans had lost confidence in their society and its institutions. An economic system which seemed to condemn large numbers of people to periodic misery was felt by many to be of questionable value. Many flirted with socialism, communism, and even some of the premises of fascism.

Only the federal government had proved capable of providing much relief from the trials of the Depression and there had gradually developed among the people the inclination to turn to Washington for relief from, or solution of, all major problems. Little was expected of government at state and local levels. Despite philosophical objections which were usually voiced in terms of nineteenth-century maxims, the American people placed their hopes in that Big Government which was anathema to conservatives of that period.

Thus, when war came, the American people were predisposed to acquiesce to decisions taken at the national level on virtually all questions by a government suddenly faced with the direction of a national military effort.

It is also important to understand that a new expression which came into widespread use after World War II related to a very old human phenomenon. "Guilt by association" was a burden which German Americans had borne during World War I, and which many feared they must shoulder again during World War II. For Japanese Americans, guilt by association was compounded by easily identifiable race, and the fact that the immigrant generation, being ineligible to naturalization, automatically became "enemy aliens" on the outbreak of hostilities.

Under these conditions, business competitors and commercial vultures saw an opportunity for a quick takeover from the Japanese Americans in various fields. Many kinds of organizations, public and private, now wrapped themselves in the American flag which they quickly soiled. Pundits and politicians broadcast emotional views which were eagerly seized upon by military leaders as justification enough for what some of them wished to do from the beginning—get rid of the Japs. It was a time of fear and irrationality, a time when the American people as a whole demonstrated their lack of confidence in themselves and their own institutions.

The campaign of hate and vilification, which politicians and newspapers fostered, influenced military minds but did not produce any great popular outcry for the evacuation of the Japanese. Most of the violence from which the Japanese suffered was produced by a few Filipinos whose homeland was under Japanese attack. The argument sometimes advanced that the Japanese must be removed from the West Coast for their own safety was patently false. There was no blood bath in being or in prospect. Genuine civil restraints impartially applied would have been sufficient to protect Japanese Americans.

On December 11 the Western Defense Command was established. The West Coast was declared a theater of war although martial law was never declared. Named commander was Lieutenant General John L. DeWitt who had spent virtually his entire career as an administrative officer and was unfamiliar with combat, politics, and public relations. He was retired before the end of the war.

He served, however, during the critical period when fateful decisions regarding the Japanese Americans were made. One scholar has said DeWitt tended to echo the views of the last strong personality he had encountered. After Pearl Harbor he was surrounded by powerful civilian forces and strong personalities on his own staff. He clearly was unable to cope with them, even if he had wanted to, but there is much evidence he sided with the racists. Even before the war he had complained about Nisei in uniform "going around taking pictures." After the war began he protested that his superiors expected him to protect the West Coast with black troops.

The Japanese American communities gradually came out of their shock but normalcy did not return. In all, while only about 1,500 Issei were taken into custody by the Federal Bureau of Investigation, they were the community leaders and Issei organizations were virtually destroyed. Only one organized group remained viable, the Japanese American Citizens League. It could exercise no real authority but in community after community the people in the absence of any alternative turned to JACL for help, guidance, and comfort.

Despite various allegations that some mysterious command authority could marshal the Japanese Americans as a fifth column, federal officials found no group other than JACL to serve as their channel for reaching the people. Emergency JACL committees were set up in various communities and were manned by volunteers who had lost their jobs or had been forced to close their businesses. The membership of the JACL—in fact the entire adult Nisei generation—brought very limited resources and experience, but boundless energy and goodwill to the task confronting them. It was just as well, for the problems of the communities probably would have overtaxed the skills and certainly the linguistic ability of the Issei leaders had they remained in authority.

During the first weeks after Pearl Harbor, hostility toward Japanese Americans was mild to moderate. Presently, various forces generated a chorus of hate and intense political pressures on the authorities. The federal government did little to discourage hostility. In fact, great damage was done to the Japanese American cause by Secretary of the Navy Frank Knox. After a quick inspection of the damage at Pearl Harbor, Knox said in a Los Angeles press conference that the Japanese attack had been accompanied by "the most effective fifth column work that's come out of this war, except in Norway." This was a ridiculous lie, and the most charitable explanation for it is the possibility that he was misled in Hawaii by military personnel trying to explain away their shortcomings. Another view, which cannot be substantiated, is that Knox deliberately misinformed the American public in a calculated effort to stir up war fever. In any event, this charge of treachery by the Japanese population of Hawaii was never refuted in the weeks that preceded the Japanese evacuation from the West Coast.

On January 2, 1942, Assistant Attorney General James Rowe, Jr., began a series of conferences in San Francisco with General DeWitt and Major Karl R. Bendetsen, chief of the aliens division of the Provost Marshal General's office headed by Major General Allen W. Gullion. Gullion was seeking transfer of authority over all enemy aliens from the Justice Department to his office. In this ploy to expand his empire Gullion arranged with DeWitt that communications concerning aliens between the West Coast Command and Washington be sent directly to his office. As a consequence, Stetson Conn, official Army historian, has made clear "the responsible Army command headquarters in Washington had little to do during January and February 1942 with the plans and decision for Japanese evacuation."

In the Justice Department there was a quite proper concern by

Attorney General Francis Biddle and his staff over the question of
civil rights as well as national security. Because of this concern Justice
was reluctant to move against the Japanese Americans as vigorously
as the military wished. Only under intense pressure did the Justice
Department finally agree to reregister enemy aliens, to authorize FBI
spot raids on Japanese homes on a large scale, and to declare numerous restricted zones around military and defense installations from
which aliens would be excluded.

On December 30, more than three weeks after the outbreak of war,
Biddle authorized search warrants for any home of an enemy alien
for suspected contraband. Contraband was defined as anything which
might be used as a weapon, explosives, radio transmitters, receivers
with short-wave bands, and cameras. Thousands of families were subjected to search all hours of the day and night. Contraband was, of
course, found. Some Japanese farmers had dynamite for clearing
land. Others operated sporting goods stores with stocks of sporting
rifles, shotguns, and ammunition. Cameras were normal possessions
of most families. Reports of the contraband seized were magnified
out of all proportion in press reports, adding to the growing suspicion
and hostility against Japanese Americans.

Meanwhile, the clamor in the press was growing for stringent restrictions against the Japanese. Continuing bad news from the battle
zones and allegations in the Roberts Report on Pearl Harbor all contributed to the increasing public frustration and anger. The Roberts
Report, compiled by Supreme Court Justice Owen Roberts, probed
the reasons for the Pearl Harbor disaster. It was vague and inconclusive on the role of the Japanese American population. It charged
that "espionage in Hawaii had centered in the Japanese consulate,
and that through its intelligence service the Japanese had obtained
complete information on Pearl Harbor." In the absence of refutations
of rumors concerning treachery among Japanese Americans, it further
heightened suspicions concerning mainland Japanese.

While the press and politicians had no qualms about demanding
forthright action against Japanese Americans, Washington officials
harbored many doubts for various reasons. Agriculture Department
agents on the West Coast were reporting their concern about food
shortages if anything should happen to Japanese American farmers.
Ultimately, Agriculture Secretary Claude Wickard supported the idea
of large agricultural reservations where the Japanese would be confined and put to work.

The Army itself was divided. The two men who remained stubbornly committed to complete removal of Japanese Americans from the West Coast were Gullion and Bendetsen, both civilian lawyers in uniform. Career officers were dubious about the necessity, practicality, or desirability of an evacuation. In fact, Mark Clark, a still-junior general on the staff of General George C. Marshall, wrote a report recommending against any mass evacuation just a week before a contrary decision was reached. In the Justice Department, Biddle remained opposed to evacuation to the end, but one of his subordinates, Tom C. Clark, later a Supreme Court Justice, was won over.

On the West Coast, members of Congress, governors, mayors, newspaper commentators, and many others, almost without exception supported removal of the Japanese Americans. The opinion of these civilian leaders plus the personal force of Gullion and Bendetsen held General DeWitt in line. The assistant secretary of war, John J. McCloy, was won over and through him Secretary of War Henry Stimson was persuaded.

February 11, 1942, was the fateful day although no Japanese Americans realized it. On that day Stimson talked with President Franklin Delano Roosevelt by phone and won his approval for removing Japanese Americans en masse from the West Coast. If the illegality of arbitrarily suspending the civil rights of American citizens entered Roosevelt's mind, he made no mention of it. His only admonition to Stimson was to be reasonable. Executive Order 9066, which gave the Army blank check authority to move civilians out of the Western Defense Command, was not signed until February 19, but DeWitt and those around him knew that mass evacuation was authorized by the President. While the order was directed against "any or all persons" its practical effect was to permit DeWitt to declare the entire West Coast a military zone and remove all persons of Japanese blood from it.

The Japanese American communities were unaware of behind-scenes developments. They understood only that Executive Order 9066 was an enabling directive to be used at the discretion of the military commander on the West Coast. They could not know how, or when, he intended to use that authority. They could not know that the day after Executive Order 9066 was signed, DeWitt had received a directive from Stimson in effect ordering him to proceed with the removal of certain classes of West Coast residents.

Stimson's letter was backed up by a memo from McCloy to DeWitt classifying West Coast residents into five categories: [1]

Class 1   Japanese aliens
Class 2   American citizens of Japanese lineage
Class 3   German aliens
Class 4   Italian aliens
Class 5   Any persons, whether citizens or aliens, who are sus-
          pected for any reason by you or your responsible sub-
          ordinates of being actually or potentially dangerous
          either as saboteurs, espionage agents, fifth-columnists
          or subversive persons.
Class 6   All other persons who are, or who may be within the
          Western Defense Command.

McCloy's memo added: "I suggest the advisability" of designating military areas "in which you will provide (a) for the exclusion of all persons in Classes 1, 2 and 5, and where in your judgment it is essential and (b) for the exclusion of persons in Class 3 . . ."

In McCloy's estimation, then, American citizens of Japanese ancestry were potentially more dangerous than German aliens. As for the Italians, Stimson had written: [2]

> In carrying out your duties under this delegation, I desire, so far as military requirements permit, that you do not disturb, for the time being at least, Italian aliens and persons of Italian lineage except where they are, in your judgment, undesirable or constitute a definite danger to the performance of your mission to defend the West Coast. I ask that you take this action in respect to Italians for the reason that I consider such persons to be less dangerous, as a whole, than those of other nationalities. Because of the size of the Italian population and the number of troops and facilities which would have to be employed to deal with them, their inclusion in the general plan would greatly overtax our strength.

When the evacuation decision was finally made public, it was a sweeping order directed at "all persons of Japanese ancestry, both alien and non-alien." Somehow, it seems, the expression "non-alien" was a little more palatable to the government than recognizing the Nisei as United States citizens. The government justified the evacuation as a "military necessity" and that phrase, along with "national security," popped up at frequent intervals. Few among the general public sought to question the constitutional implications of the evacuation—the Fifth Amendment providing that no person could be deprived of his liberty without due process of law, and the Fourteenth Amendment providing for equal protection under the law for all citizens. In fact, by this time much sentiment supported columnist Westbrook Pegler who wrote: "'The Japanese in California should be under armed guard to the last man and woman right now—and to hell with habeas corpus." [3]

It must be noted, however, that the constitutionality of mass evacuation had concerned top civilians in government in addition to Biddle. A transcript of a telephone conversation in the National Archives has General Gullion saying to General Clark: [4]

> ". . . yesterday Secretary Stimson, McCloy, Bendetsen and I talked for an hour and a half on the situation and I can tell you that the two Secretaries are against any mass movement. They are pretty much against it. And they are also pretty much against interfering with citizens unless it can be done legally. Well, I think McCloy did say this to Biddle—you are putting a Wall Street lawyer in a helluva box, but if it is a question of the safety of the country (and) the Constitution . . . why the Constitution is just a scrap of paper to me. That is what McCloy said. But they are just a little afraid DeWitt hasn't enough grounds to justify any movements of that kind."

Meanwhile, Congressman John H. Tolan, a California Democrat, added to the confusion by announcing a congressional committee would hold hearings on the "problems of evacuation of enemy aliens and others from prohibited military zones." Presumably, it would provide a forum for discussion of basic Evacuation issues, although it was never made clear why civilian input was necessary for what was being trumpeted as a purely military matter. The hearings began in San Francisco on February 21, 1942, two days after Roosevelt had signed Executive Order 9066 and one day after General DeWitt had been designated to carry it out. For national security purposes the Tolan Committee's hearings were a total waste of time, particularly after it became evident they merely provided a podium for politicians to air their prejudices. The first two witnesses set the tone for the hearings, which moved up and down the coast like a dog and pony show.

San Francisco Mayor Angelo J. Rossi, the first to speak, contended German and Italian aliens were no real problem and they "should be considered separately from those of the Japanese.[5] The Japanese situ-

ation should be given immediate attention." The implication was clear
—Italians and Germans are white, the Japanese of another race,
which raised the level of their potential danger.

Rossi was followed on the stand by Earl Warren, then California's
attorney general and later to become Chief Justice of the United
States Supreme Court. He charged that Japanese were clustered
around aircraft plants, airports, highways, dams, bridges, power stations, and other strategic points and interpreted this as a sinister
pattern of land ownership. Warren also interpreted the fact that there
had been no fifth-column activity in California as proof that the
Japanese Americans would be responsible for a wave of sabotage as
soon as an "invisible deadline" approached, presumably to be set by
Tokyo.

The most serious canard Warren voiced was unabashedly racist.
After charging that the Nisei, born in the United States, posed a
greater danger than alien Japanese, Warren was asked if there were
any way of distinguishing the loyal from the disloyal. He replied:
"We believe that when we are dealing with the Caucasian race we
have methods that will test the loyalty of them, and we believe that
we can, in dealing with the German and Italians, arrive at some fairly
sound conclusions because of our knowledge of the way they live in
the community and have lived for many years. But when we deal
with the Japanese we are in an entirely different field and we cannot
form any opinion that we believe to be sound."

Despite the preponderance of hostile, and often irrelevant testimony, the Japanese Americans approached the Tolan hearings hoping that they might influence government policies in favor of their
people. The die, however, had been cast. The hearings were merely
an exercise in futility. But they did put a great many people on record
regarding the Japanese Americans, something which many of them
lived to regret. The testimony of the Japanese Americans themselves
was without effect. The gist of their statements was a strong asser-
tion of their loyalty, a plea for justice, and an expression of willingness to accept an evacuation order as a patriotic duty if it were a
military necessity. But many of them expressed strong doubt as to
whether military necessity was really involved. The false and misleading reports from Hawaii, undenied by federal officials, plus the War
Department's failure to provide a clear-cut assessment of the possibility of a Japanese attack on the West Coast, left the impression
that an invasion was a viable hazard even though history shows such
a plan was never a part of Japanese strategy. In fact, early in Febru-

ary when the Evacuation decision was still being debated, General Clark and Admiral Harold R. Stark agreed in a congressional briefing that the chance of any sustained attack or of any invasion was—as General Clark put it—nil.[6] This estimate of the military position was ignored by both members of Congress and the DeWitt-Gullion-Bendetsen faction who evidently wanted to believe the worst.

The Tolan Committee testimony of Mike M. Masaoka, the young national executive secretary of JACL, expressed the position of most Japanese Americans. He declared.[7]

> If in the judgment of military and federal authorities evacuation of Japanese residents from the West Coast is a primary step toward assuring the safety of this nation, we will have no hesitation in complying with the necessities implicit in that judgment. But if, on the other hand, such evacuation is primarily a measure whose surface urgency cloaks the desires of political or other pressure groups who want us to leave merely for motives of self-interest, we feel that we have every right to protest and to demand equitable judgment on our merits as American citizens.

Some days earlier, a recently released transcript of telephone conversations shows DeWitt was telling Bendetsen:[8] "There are going to be a lot of Japs who are going to say, 'Oh, yes, we want to go, we're good Americans and we want to do everything you say,' but those are the fellows I suspect the most." And Bendetsen's reply was: "Definitely. The ones who are giving you only lip service are the ones always to be suspected."

The reasoning behind JACL's decision to accept evacuation—to cooperate in their own incarceration, as it were—needs exploration, particularly since it came under angry criticism in later years. Roger Daniels observes:[9]

> Masaoka and the other JACL leaders stressed that they wanted federal responsibility for the evacuation. They understood that if they opposed the evacuation, it would merely add to the disloyal stereotype that already existed. It is easier to criticize this accommodationist policy than to construct viable alternatives for a responsible leadership to adopt. Masaoka and the others deliberately chose to cooperate with their oppressors in the obvious hope that by cooperating they would both mitigate the present circumstances and perhaps have a lien on better treatment later . . .

For the vast majority of Nisei, at least, loyalty was demonstrated by submissiveness to authority. The government said go, and they went, cooperating, organizing, submitting. This submission, this lack of resistance to oppression, had several consequences. In the long run, perhaps, it proved a viable tactic. In the short run, however, it produced, as we shall see, bitterness and fratricide within the Japanese American community.

Sociologist Harry Kitano has suggested that Japanese Americans culturally were so deeply steeped in the tradition of obedience to authority that they would have marched uncomplaining into gas ovens, if Uncle Sam had provided them. This view, understandably, drew vigorous rebuttal.

The JACL decision to cooperate with the government was reached at an emergency meeting of its national leadership in San Francisco early in 1942. A year later, while memory of the event was still fresh, Masaoka wrote a detailed report, which is quoted in part: [10]

In the beginning, three alternatives were discussed. One was out and out opposition in every way possible to the government's evacuation program; another was to seek some compromise, using the threat of opposition as a bargaining weapon; and still another was "constructive cooperation" with the government, not because Japanese Americans conceded the constitutionality of this unprecedented action or the validity of the arguments for such a recourse, but because it was the only reasonable and realistic course at the time.

Number One was ruled out as impossible. As individuals some might oppose evacuation but, as an organization, mass resistance might result in greater evils than even evacuation.

Number Two was rejected as impractical. The government was neither in a mood nor position to compromise . . .

That left only Number Three: Cooperation. . . . The following considerations prompted the unanimous decision to "constructively cooperate" with the government:

1—As Americans, we could do no less . . . If, in the considered judgment of the military commander, "military necessity" dictated the evacuation of all persons of Japanese ancestry, we as patriotic citizens and reasonable people should not be disposed to question that judgment . . . Actually, JACL agreed to cooperate "under protest," believing that this was not only a grave violation of the Constitution but also of human decency . . .

2—To many, a Japanese invasion in force of the Pacific Coast was imminent. If we Japanese Americans had refused to cooperate with the government and the Army was forced to divert large numbers of its troops from preparing defenses to forcibly ejecting us from what were named as prohibited zones, the American people would never have forgiven us for such action. In America's darkest hour, we could not force her to weaken her defenses and invite invasion. And if Japan had launched a landing, timed with the Army's preoccupation with the Japanese American resistance to evacuation, the future would not be worth considering for Japanese Americans in the United States.

3—If resistance proved to be stubborn or forceful, troops might have had to resort to bayonet and rifle fire. If this proved to be the case, the blood of all the Japanese Americans killed, as well as federal soldiers, would have been on our hands.

4—If resistance became widespread, the very groups and interests which might have proved the "military necessity" behind our evacuation might have introduced another reign of terror to drive out Japanese Americans. Some of the older delegates, remembering the race riots and night riders of another day in California when powerful interests desired to force passage of the Japanese Exclusion Law, advised against any move which might incite these groups into action again.

5—If Japanese American opposition to evacuation because of race gained the attention and active sympathy of other "colored" or California-despised minorities, these other nationalities might have joined the demonstrations. Race riots and even civil war might have been the result.

6—In any case, if violence occurred in any form to Japanese Americans or other non-Caucasian races because of the evacuation program, Japan's propagandists would have had a real holiday exploiting the doctrine of race war as against that of ideas and ideals. As it was, they did introduce arguments to that effect in their propaganda aimed at the peoples in Asia and Southwest Pacific. Just imagine what they could have done had race riots resulted.

7—The experience at Terminal Island was a shocking reminder of what might happen if resistance or threat of opposition brought about another twenty-four hour evacuation order.

The people suffered tremendously because there wasn't an organized, supervised removal.

8—Persons of Japanese ancestry had considerable property in the prohibited zones. If some safeguards were to be provided by the government, cooperation was essential.

9—The alien Japanese would have to go as a matter of course . . . The Japanese Americans were duty bound to share the adversity and hardships of a cruel adventure with their parents in the twilight of their lives.

10—This cooperation would be our contribution to the war effort and proof of the Americanism of the Japanese Americans . . .

11—In the long run, cooperation would make it easier for our non-Japanese friends to work in and for our behalf . . .

12—Finally, since the government was determined to evacuate us whether we liked it or not, common sense dictated that we try to make the most of a very difficult situation . . . Cooperation on our part would impose a moral obligation, at least, upon the government to reciprocate that cooperation by working with us in the matter of planning and administration. . . . Cooperation, in a sentence, offered the best opportunity for Japanese Americans to regain their dignity, self-respect and civil rights.

While the JACL decision has been criticized as "accommodationist," it is difficult to suggest alternative policy. Certainly, resistance was out of the question. Military leaders were prepared to use whatever force might be necessary to effect the Evacuation. The image which the Japanese Americans projected by their quiet acquiescence in the removal did no damage to their cause and, as Masaoka foresaw, put their critics on the defensive.

XIII ॐ The Exodus

When President Roosevelt signed Executive Order 9066 on February 19, 1942, Japanese Americans already had endured more than two months of deep torment. First, there had been shame and anger over the way Japan had triggered war, followed by fear and uncertainty about their own status in the United States. The federal government had done nothing substantial to assure them that race and ancestry would not be held against them so long as they behaved as good Americans which, almost without exception, they were anxious to do. Gradually, as the shock of the attack on Pearl Harbor wore off, the rabble-rousers and spiritual descendants of the old-time anti-Oriental elements became more active. What Oswald Garrison Villard called "the sewer system of American journalism" shifted into high gear and was joined by radio commentators of like temperament and political demagogues of which there was no shortage.

Most Japanese Americans conceded that the government's action immediately after Pearl Harbor, taking into custody Issei whose pro-Japan stance was a matter of record, was justified. A nation at war could hardly do less. These men were legally aliens and it made no difference that American law had denied them the right to become naturalized citizens. The tragedy is that such men were judged on the basis of their potential to inflict harm based on emotional ties to an enemy country. Whether they would have committed overt acts against the United States, had they remained free, must remain an unanswered question. The fact is they were not left free, and reasonable people could conclude that the really dangerous element in the Japanese American population had been eliminated.

All this to the contrary, synthetic fear of all Japanese Americans was whipped up. What General DeWitt once described as "the best people" joined in the demand that "something" be done about the possibility that Japanese Americans might harm the war effort. There were few reasonable people willing to stand up and say: "Now wait a minute. Let's take another look. Is this problem really what you say it is?"

The mixed signals Washington and the armed forces had been getting prior to the outbreak of war only confused the situation. The State Department in the fall of 1941 had assigned one of its ace investigators, Curtis Burton Munson, to look into the Japanese American communities. About the same time, Commander Kenneth D. Ringle had been assigned by the Navy to a similar mission. Munson filed a twenty-five-page report, the gist of which was that "there is no Japanese problem." Ringle's finding were similar. Just who read and digested these reports is not known. Army language-experts reading West Coast Japanese American newspapers found the Japanese sections carried Tokyo dispatches following the militarist line. The English-language sections read by the Nisei, however, were not nearly so pro-Japanese. In the end, the voices of those who were convinced of Nisei loyalty were drowned out by the cries of the alarmists who demanded all should be incarcerated because it was impossible to weed out the "dangerous."

The day after Executive Order 9066 was signed, Secretary of War Stimson designated General DeWitt to carry out its provisions. DeWitt was given authority "to prescribe military areas for the protection of vital installations against sabotage and espionage," to remove "any or all persons" from such areas using "the troops you can make available from your general command." [1]

However, the first mass movement of Japanese Americans out of their homes was initiated five days before Executive Order 9066 became effective. Even before the establishment of restricted areas, the Navy began a move to oust a group of Japanese from Terminal Island, a fishing community near San Pedro, California, adjacent to naval facilities. Terminal Island was the home port for a number of ocean-going tuna clippers and many of the women worked in the nearby canneries. A large number of Issei men had been taken into custody after Pearl Harbor. The tuna clippers were kept tied up and a second raid on February 1 resulted in most of the remainder of the community's men being seized. It was a foregone conclusion that the Japanese on Terminal Island must go. Thus, notices put up by the Navy on February 14, ordering Terminal Island residents to leave by March 14, came as no shock. Some had already moved from this sensitive area and many more left following the notice.

Suddenly, on February 25 in a capricious and unnecessarily harsh move the Navy ordered all Japanese Americans to be out by midnight of the twenty-seventh. With most of the men in custody, the burden of moving fell on the women of the some 200 Japanese families still remaining. Near panic swept the fragmented community. Instead of the seventeen days which they had counted on, the residents now had less than three days. For many the physical movement of household goods was impossible in the brief time available and they quickly fell prey to used-furniture dealers who descended on the community. Stoves, washing machines, refrigerators, were sold for almost nothing as frightened women sought to salvage a few dollars. An occasional stouthearted mother refused to be victimized and destroyed things of value rather than see others profit from her toil.

Although the Japanese community in Los Angeles and some Caucasian friends tried to help, finding shelter of sorts for them in other areas, the Terminal Islanders lost heavily. They had to abandon business property, fishing equipment, and household goods. Vessels in which they held only equities had to be abandoned and the equities lost. *Removal and Return* by Leonard Bloom and Ruth Reimer estimates the Terminal Islanders "probably suffered more heavily in the Evacuation than any other occupation or locality group."

At the time Executive Order 9066 was signed nothing was said about declaring martial law which would have legalized military authority over civilians. Aware of the legal problems this might cause, the military through the White House asked Congress to provide legislation making it a federal offense to violate any order issued by a military commander under E.O. 9066. Congress provided this law almost without question, both houses approving the measure by voice vote. A review of the brief discussion that took place before the vote indicates that lawmakers seemed unaware the legislation they were asked to pass would restrict the rights of citizens. In fact, the Nisei were so little known at the time that it seems unlikely any substantial numbers of members of Congress were cognizant of the serious constitutional issues involved. Whether they would have moved with greater caution if they had known of the gravity of their action is a question that never can be answered.

At this juncture it is pertinent to ask whether members of the Roosevelt cabinet were any more aware than Congress of the assault being mounted by the military against the basic rights of an American minority. Francis Biddle, the attorney general, certainly was deeply concerned and expressed his apprehensions on numerous occasions. But he lacked the forcefulness to press his views and he deferred to senior members of the cabinet such as Stimson in view of the gravity of the war situation. Biddle, deplorably, failed to seize an opportunity that would have won him a place of honor in the annals of human rights.

The legal authority that General DeWitt sought was contained in Public Law 503 which President Roosevelt signed on March 21, a few days after Congress passed it. General DeWitt did not wait for this authority. On March 2 he issued Public Proclamation No. 1 which established the western halves of California, Oregon, and Washington and the southern half of Arizona as Military Area No. 1. The remaining portions of these states, with the exception of a tiny sector of Eastern Oregon, tied economically to Idaho, were designated as Military Area No. 2. The language of the proclamation left no doubt that it was aimed at Japanese, Japanese American citizens, German and Italian aliens. The military was still struggling to set up evacuation procedures so no movement was ordered. However, a press release from DeWitt's headquarters made clear that military authorities anticipated removal of all persons of Japanese ancestry from Area No. 1.

The press release went on to state that the restrictions to be enforced in Area No. 1 would not apply to Area No. 2. This amounted to an encouragement to the Issei and Nisei to relocate voluntarily. Approximately 10,000 of them did, although it was a difficult decision. For most Issei, whose assets were frozen, voluntary resettlement in other parts of the country was virtually out of the question. Since the authorities had done nothing to prepare inland areas for the coming of the Japanese Americans, violence and hostility were not uncommon. A federal report had this to say: [2]

> As soon as the San Francisco office was opened, calls began to come in great numbers from sheriffs and other public officials of inland communities protesting the number of Japanese passing through or settling in their jurisdictions. Calls also came from Japanese informing the War Relocation Authority that they were stranded in neighboring states because no one would sell them gasoline or necessary services. There were also frequent calls from the press in areas through which voluntary evacuees were moving. At Klamath Falls, Oregon, several Japanese were arrested to avoid violence. At Yarrington, Nevada, eight were met by hostile citizens and had to return to California. At Swink, Colorado, local residents demanded the recall of evacuees.

By late March it had become apparent that the resentment of the interior states toward continuing evacuation was based upon a complete misunderstanding of the status of the evacuees as well as upon war bred fears and prejudices. Sheriffs from these states frequently reported that "California Japanese were escaping" from the military areas. Officials and residents of the interior regions were not aware that the military authorities were urging the evacuees to leave the West Coast states and establish themselves in inland areas. There was also widespread opinion that California, Washington and Oregon were "dumping undesirables."

Once the restrictive processes were begun, DeWitt, through Bendetsen, newly promoted to colonel, moved quickly. On March 11 the Wartime Civil Control Administration (WCCA) was established with Bendetsen as its director to supervise the Evacuation. Public Proclamation No. 2 followed on March 16, extending certain regulations contained in Proclamation No. 1 to enemy aliens and Japanese Americans in the balance of the Western Defense Command—all of Arizona, California, Oregon, Washington, Idaho, Montana, Nevada, and Utah.

Eight days later, on March 24, DeWitt issued Public Proclamation No. 3. It should have discouraged any Japanese American who managed to remain optimistic to this point. The proclamation established a curfew between 8 P.M. and 6 A.M. for all enemy aliens and Japanese Americans to begin on March 27 in Military Area No. 1. Travel was limited to no more than five miles from place of residence. Voluntary relocation into the interior was still permitted, but travel must take place only during the day.

Meanwhile, it had become apparent in Washington that evacuation of West Coast Japanese Americans, if it was to be done humanely, was a far more complex operation than the Army was prepared to take on. Provost Marshal General Gullion had projected a massive program which would require more troops than was acceptable to the Army chiefs. The decision was to turn over the job of resettling the evacuees, once the Army had moved them out of coastal areas, to civilians. On March 18 President Roosevelt signed still another executive order, No. 9102, creating the War Relocation Authority (WRA) "to assist persons evacuated by the military under Executive Order 9066." Milton S. Eisenhower, a senior bureaucrat in the Department of Agriculture and brother of a rising young military officer named Dwight D. Eisenhower, was named director. Milton Eisenhower held the post only three months; he was happy to leave the confusing, heartbreaking, unprecedented problems WRA faced for a top job in the Office of War Information. Within a week after WRA was formed, Eisenhower was in San Francisco to measure the size and scope of the job Roosevelt had tossed at him. It became obvious to him almost immediately the voluntary evacuation could not continue without widespread disorders and risk of violence. Eisenhower urged Bendetsen to halt uncontrolled evacuation.

That was taken care of when the Army issued Public Proclamation No. 4 on March 27. Effective March 29, all voluntary evacuation out of Military Area No. 1 was prohibited. The entire West Coast Japanese American community was now frozen in position; it was illegal to leave and soon it would be illegal to stay.

It was at this point that two young Nisei, each without knowledge of what the other was doing, stepped forth to challenge the right of the Army to single out Japanese American citizens for discriminatory treatment. These were the "individuals" whom Mike Masaoka, although he had no part in their action, had suggested might do what JACL as an organization could not. One was Gordon K. Hirabayashi, a Quaker and student at the University of Washington. The other was Minoru Yasui, an attorney holding a reserve commission as an infantry lieutenant in the U. S. Army. Hirabayashi violated both the curfew and Evacuation orders which were to come later. Yasui notified the Federal Bureau of Investigation of his intention to violate the curfew order and asked to be jailed. Both were seized and convicted in precedent-setting cases which will be discussed at length in a later chapter. Such was the mood and fear of the times that most Nisei looked askance at the actions of Yasui and Hirabayashi. Later, they were to be hailed as courageous, far-sighted civil rights advocates.

During this period the Army was working furiously to develop a plan to get the Japanese Americans out of Military Area No. 1, and WCCA and WRA were struggling with the problem of what to do with them once the Army rounded them up.

The ultimate decision was to divide the western half of the three West Coast states into 108 "Exclusion Areas," each containing approximately 1,000 Japanese. Exclusion orders were tacked up on utility poles about a week before the date set for evacuating a particular area. These notices instructed the head of each family to register at a WCCA station—set up in schools, churches, and public buildings. Various federal agencies were on hand—U.S. Employment Service, Social Security Board, Public Health, Federal Reserve Bank—to help the Japanese with various problems. How much good they did is a matter of debate. The Japanese usually had six or seven days in which to wind up their affairs, store or sell their possessions, close up their businesses and homes, and show up at an assembly point for transportation to an Assembly Center. The instructions were specific: Bring bedding, extra clothing, and other personal items, but only what you can carry.

The evacuees were sent by bus and train to Assembly Centers hurriedly established at nearby fairgrounds, race tracks, and former Civilian Conservation Corps camps. Twelve of the sites were in California, one in Oregon, one in Washington. The facilities were crude and inadequate. Some families found themselves assigned to quarters only recently vacated by horses, with traces of the former tenants pungently evident. The transition from free citizens to concentration camp inmates was swift and shocking. Many wept themselves to sleep the first night on a straw-filled mattress.

The first areas evacuated were those considered of greatest military importance. The dubious honor of being first went to Bainbridge Island in Puget Sound on the approach to the Bremerton Navy Yard. There were fifty-four Japanese families on the island, almost all of them berry and vegetable farmers. They were notified on March 24 —three and one half months after the outbreak of war—and evacuated March 31. The nearest camp, at the fairgrounds in Puyallup, wasn't ready yet. The Bainbridge Islanders were sent to Manzanar in the Owens Valley of Eastern California not far from Death Valley. Ultimately, they would supply evidence of the provincialism of Japanese Americans and the absence of anything resembling a nationwide consensus. The Bainbridge Islanders were not happy among the California Japanese. By almost constant agitation they finally persuaded the authorities to permit them to join their fellow Washingtonians, most of whom were sent to Minidoka Relocation Center in Idaho.

The next four exclusion orders covered San Pedro, Long Beach, San Diego, and the San Francisco waterfront.

As we have seen, the Evacuation orders were directed "to all persons of Japanese ancestry, both alien and non-alien." Early on, the Army ran into the problem of defining "Japanese ancestry." It came up with a totally racist solution with disquieting parallels to Nazi Germany's anti-Jewish manifestoes. Included among the evacuees "were persons who were only part Japanese, some with as little as one-sixteenth Japanese blood; others who, prior to evacuation, were unaware of their Japanese ancestry; and many who had married Caucasian, Chinese, Filipinos, Negroes, Hawaiians, or Eskimos. Most of these people were American-born, had been through American schools, had not developed Oriental thought patterns or been subjected to so-called Japanese culture." [3] The late Father Hugh T. Lavery who ran an orphanage at the Maryknoll Center in Los Angeles told Bendetsen some of his children were half or one fourth Japanese and asked whether they would be evacuated. According to the priest, Bendetsen replied: "I am determined that if they have one drop of Japanese blood in them, they must go to camp." [4]

Ultimately, the Army relaxed its criteria somewhat but only succeeded in underscoring the racist thrust of the Evacuation program. Eligible for exemption from evacuation, in the Army's own phraseology, were: [5]

1. Families consisting of a Japanese wife, a non-Japanese husband, citizen of the United States or of a friendly nation, and their mixed-blood unemancipated children.

2. Families consisting of a Caucasian mother, citizen of the United States or a friendly nation, and her mixed-blood children by a Japanese father (either dead or separated from the family).

3. Mixed-blood (one-half Japanese or less) individuals, citizens of the United States or of a friendly nation, whose backgrounds have been Caucasian.

4. Japanese unemancipated children who are being reared by Caucasian foster-parents.

5. Japanese wives of non-Japanese spouses serving in the armed forces of the United States.

With notable racist aplomb, the General DeWitt "Final Report" observes: "The execution of the mixed-marriage program has not adversely affected military security, and it has achieved certain benefits: 1—Mixed-blood children are being reared in an American environment; 2—Families have been reunited; 3—Mixed-blood adults predominantly American in appearance and thought have been restored to their families, to their communities, and to their jobs." [6]

With uncharacteristic efficiency, the Army completed its cleanup of Japanese Americans from Military Area No. 1 by June 5, 1942. Almost six months had elapsed since the attack on Pearl Harbor. The tide of war had turned in the Pacific and if the possibility of a Japanese invasion of the U.S. West Coast had ever been viable, it certainly was no longer. But now the Army proceeded to evacuate Military Area No. 2 in California, the eastern half of the state into which, by indirection at least, DeWitt had encouraged the Japanese Americans to move voluntarily to avoid being forced out by the military. The Army's explanation was that the eastern boundary of California approximates the easterly limit of Military Area No. 1 in Washington and Oregon, and the natural forests and mountain barriers "from which it was determined to exclude all Japanese, lie in Military Area No. 2 in California, although these lie in Military Area No. 1 of Washington and Oregon." [7] Whatever the reason—and one suspects political pressure in California had more than a little to do with the decision—it meant more than 9,000 additional Japanese Americans were uprooted, many for the second time. The Evacuation was finally completed August 7, 1942, exactly eight months after the outbreak of war.

The primitive WCCA camps were never intended to be more than temporary holding pens. More permanent quarters for the evacuees —and what to do with them—was the responsibility of Eisenhower's WRA. There was no precedent for the problems they had to solve. They had to start from the ground up, after locating suitable areas, to build communities that would house some 110,000 men, women, and children who had only Japanese ancestry in common, feed them, keep them occupied gainfully if possible, look after their health, educate the children (40,000 were under fifteen years of age), determine who if any should be released from the camps, suggest a system of internal government, and somehow keep the entire experiment from blowing up.

One of the first ideas was to establish a Work Corps among the evacuees to utilize their manpower. Enlistment was to be voluntary. WRA was still wrestling with the details of where Work Corps members would be allowed to work and the wages they would receive when the Los Angeles *Examiner,* a Hearst newspaper, published a story to the effect that the Japanese were to be paid "much more than American soldiers fighting the country's battles overseas." Army privates were being paid $21 per month at the time. The storm of public protest that followed should have warned WRA of the emotionalism and irrationality that would dog almost every decision affecting the Japanese Americans. Eventually, WRA decided on a pay scale of $19 per month for professionals such as doctors, $16 for skilled workers, and $12 for the unskilled. With this kind of income the evacuees had to dip into savings in order to keep up insurance payments and buy small luxuries to brighten drab camp life, depleting resources that would be needed to make the adjustment back to normal life. The idea of a Work Corps ran afoul of so many problems that it was virtually abandoned.

On April 7, while the movement into the WCCA camps was in full swing, Eisenhower and some of his aides met in Salt Lake City with Western governors. Eisenhower told them WRA's plans were still fluid but he was leaning toward establishing fifty to seventy-five communities in the interior states with limited populations which would be kept busy at some or all of the following:

1—Public works, including such things as development of raw land for agricultural production.

2—Production of food, but for evacuee subsistence and not for sale, on federally owned lands.

3—Manufacture of goods such as camouflage nets and cartridge belts which were needed by the military.

4—Private employment inside and outside the camps.

5—Establishment of self-supporting communities which would be managed by the evacuees themselves rather than by the federal government.

Eisenhower explained that the Evacuation was being carried out as a military necessity, that none of the evacuees had been convicted of or ever charged with disloyalty, and asked the governors not to oppose their acceptance into their states. Only the attorney general of Utah and Governor Ralph Carr of Colorado offered their cooperation. They, and Mayor Harry P. Cain of Tacoma, were among the very few Westerners in public office who at war's end could look back with pride and satisfaction on the posture they had assumed with regard to the Evacuation.

Eisenhower then abandoned the idea of numerous small camps and settled on ten self-contained, semi-permanent communities to be guarded by troops. They were located in seven states and all but the two in Arkansas were on federally owned, sparsely populated desert or semi-desert land. Suddenly, huge crews of workmen descended on the sites to lay water lines, install sewage systems, and build military-style barracks of green lumber sheathed by tarpaper. The ten camps were:

Name	Location	Capacity
Central Utah (Topaz)	West-Central Utah	10,000
Colorado River (Poston)	Western Arizona	
Unit 1		10,000
Unit 2		5,000
Unit 3		5,000
Gila River	Central Arizona	
Butte Camp		10,000
Canal Camp		5,000
Granada (Amache)	Southeastern Colorado	8,000
Heart Mountain	Northwestern Wyoming	12,000
Jerome (Denson)	Southeastern Arkansas	10,000
Manzanar	East-Central California	10,000
Minidoka (Hunt)	South-Central Idaho	10,000
Rohwer	Southeastern Arkansas	10,000
Tule Lake (Newell)	North-Central California	16,000

The Army had begun work on Manzanar and Poston as Assembly Centers and they were transferred to WRA. The initial movement of the evacuees into WRA centers was on March 21. A number of volunteers from Los Angeles arrived at Manzanar to help get the camp ready. Soon they were joined by the Bainbridge Island group. By late May, trainloads of Japanese Americans, approximately 500 per train, were leaving the Assembly Centers almost daily for the WRA camps in the interior. Travel was by decrepit, crowded day coaches, some so ancient that they still had gas chandeliers for illumination. The trip from California to Arkansas took as long as five days with shades drawn during the entire period. Some trains from the Los Angeles area to Heart Mountain were routed by way of El Paso, Texas, a hot, dusty, jolting five-day trip. The last Evacuation train left Santa Anita for Manzanar on October 27, just a few days short of eleven months after the start of the war.

The cold statistics of the transfer of a people hide the private agonies of individuals who were seeing their lives destroyed. The problem of just getting by in the Assembly Centers had constituted a new challenge to which the Japanese Americans had responded with customary fortitude. Now movement into the Relocation Centers presented them with new kinds of problems. The Assembly Centers had been in relatively familiar areas adjacent to their homes. The Relocation Centers were in some of the most godforsaken parts of the nation.

In a typical camp designed to hold 10,000 evacuees, barracks buildings were clustered into thirty-six blocks. There were twelve barracks, each 120 feet long and twenty feet wide, to the block. A mess hall and a combination toilet-bath-laundry building served each block. One barrack, totally bare, was set aside to serve as a "recreation" building. What greeted the evacuee family as it moved into its "apartment" is described in a WRA report, *Impounded People*:

> As families and individuals completed the process of being unloaded with their baggage from the buses, registered and signing the forms of induction, they ultimately found themselves in bare rooms about 20 feet square or in unpartitioned barracks. There was nothing in the rooms but Army cots and blankets, no other furniture, no running water, nothing with which to prepare food or the baby's bottle. Everything remained yet to do to make the places habitable. Makeshift furniture had to be built if one could find the lumber. The ground around one's barracks had to be cleaned up.

Although WRA supervised the settlement and operation of the camps, even the most basic services were left in the hands of the evacuees themselves. Men who had been cooks in civilian life opened the mess halls and prepared the food. Others were recruited as pot-scrubbers and dishwashers. The Army Quartermaster Corps supplied the food, but the allowance was 45 cents per day per individual and the camp administration was compelled to remain within this limit. Even so, wildly unfounded charges were heard that the government was coddling the Japanese. Congressman J. Parnell Thomas of the Dies Committee declared wine was being served with meals in the camps. Members of the Dies Committee staff charged that evacuees were being fed so well that they were sending packages of rationed food items to friends outside. The press published these accusations without bothering to check their validity.

The constant sniping of press and politicians did nothing to help the morale of the Japanese Americans who had cooperated in their evacuation in the belief it was their contribution to the war effort. What hurt them most was the feeling of being rejected by their country for no reason other than race. When they had met the initial problems of settling down to the routine of concentration camp life, time permitted them to pause and take cognizance of what had happened to them. And that initiated a new chapter in this regrettable story.

XIV ❧ Turmoil and Travail

After only three months Milton Eisenhower had had enough of the War Relocation Authority and its heartbreaking problems. He was succeeded on June 17, 1942, by his friend and colleague from the Department of Agriculture, Dillon S. Myer. Myer was an excellent administrator, a man of deep compassion with a stubborn respect for justice and human rights that belied his gentle demeanor. He knew no more about Japanese Americans, their history, and their problems, than Eisenhower did. Myer and his aides had only their sense of fair play to guide them in setting and carrying out WRA policy. They were to make some costly mistakes before their education was completed.

Eisenhower's legacy to Myer was a four-point program which he outlined in a letter to President Roosevelt.[1] The letter said, "I cannot help expressing the hope that the American people will grow toward a broader appreciation of the essential Americanism of a great majority of the evacuees and of the difficult sacrifice they are making." He expressed the opinion "that fully 80 to 85 percent of the Nisei are loyal to the United States, perhaps 50 percent of the Issei are passively loyal; but a large portion of the Kibei (American citizens educated in Japan) feel a strong cultural attachment to Japan." His recommendations were:

1—A program of repatriation for those who wished to go to Japan.

2—A strong statement in support of loyal Japanese Americans.

3—More liberal wages for the evacuees.

4—A special program to help evacuees find their place in American life after the war.

Ironically, only the repatriation program materialized in full. However, it was carried out under circumstances that made it little more than semi-voluntary deportation for many embittered Nisei. The "strong statement" in support of the loyal was made only in conjunction with an invitation to step out through the barbed wire fences and volunteer for military service. The $12-$16-$19 wage scale remained unchanged throughout the war even though military pay was more than doubled. And the help given evacuees after the war paled in comparison with the effort that was expended in rushing them into the camps.

Myer became convinced within days of taking over that it would be dreadfully wrong to keep the evacuees locked up for any length of time. Even before the movement into WRA camps was completed, his aides were working on procedures for getting the Japanese Americans out of the camps. Thus, WRA was wrestling with two problems —operating the camps humanely and economically and making them as livable as possible, while resettling the best qualified in other parts of the country not restricted by General DeWitt's Western Defense Command.

The problems produced by these two policies were commented on by WRA in these terms: [2]

> Finally, there was the paradox—the inherent contradiction— that lay in the very nature of the WRA program as it eventually developed. On the one hand, WRA was constantly striving for the greatest possible economy, efficiency, and community service in the operation of relocation centers; on the other hand, it was after November, 1942 encouraging the most energetic, most skillful, and best adjusted evacuee workers, with every device at its command, to leave the centers and resettle in ordinary American communities.

In reality, the movement out of imprisonment began while the evacuees were still in Assembly Centers, awaiting an unknown future. Some of the very areas which had been hostile toward an influx of Japanese Americans suddenly realized the armed forces and war industries were draining them of farm labor. The manpower represented by Japanese Americans in the camps began to look like a likely source of help. WRA, which in vain had sought the cooperation of inland states in accepting the evacuees, now found itself in position to dictate the terms under which they might be released for voluntary work—guarantees of their safety, payment of the going wage, minimum living and working standards, and transportation from and back to the camps when jobs were completed. The Amalgamated Sugar Company in the Nyssa district of Malheur County in Eastern Oregon was the first to qualify. At first, recruiters seeking beet-field labor had little success among Japanese Americans who had endured the West Coast's hostility. But on May 21 a small party from the Portland Assembly Center went out to look over the Nyssa area and reported back that conditions were acceptable. This was the breakthrough. Additional workers were recruited from Portland—almost anything was preferable to idleness in the livestock exposition hall where they were confined. Numerous other counties then complied with the WRA regulations and secured the desperately needed labor. The WRA reported: [3]

> Altogether approximately 10,000 evacuees left WCCA or WRA Centers during 1942 for seasonal agricultural work, principally in Idaho, Utah, Montana, Colorado, and eastern Oregon. Although many of them had occasional unpleasant experiences because of the widespread public misapprehension regarding their status and a few actually ran into situations which appeared momentarily ominous, none reported suffering any bodily harm or any really serious difficulties. By conservative estimates, they probably saved enough sugar beets to make nearly a quarter of a billion pounds of sugar.

Technically, the farm workers were kept confined to the area of employment by an extension of Executive Order 9066. The county or counties where they were needed were declared to be restricted areas which Japanese were prohibited from leaving. In reality, no such precautions were needed. There is no record of a single farm volunteer "escaping." Thus, we have the strange situation of Japanese Americans considered so dangerous to national security that they must be removed from the West Coast and kept under military guard in concentration camps, and these same people being released for work in beet fields under no military control.

In the summer of 1942, efforts were being made to get another group of Japanese Americans out of the camps. These were college students. The Student Relocation Council, formed March 21, 1942 (eight days before the freeze order went into effect), on the Berkeley campus of the University of California, worked vigorously to place Japanese Americans in inland schools.[4] Although this organization was soon replaced by another, in the remaining months before the

June commencements it was able to help about seventy-five Nisei to move to universities and colleges outside the exclusion zone and resume studies.

In May another nongovernmental agency, called the National Student Relocation Council, was formed to carry on the Student Relocation Council's work. Educators and others realized the tragedy of interrupting the education of the brightest among the Nisei. Perhaps the educators believed the Japanese Americans would return someday to their segregated communities and would need trained leaders. It is hardly likely they could have forseen the way the young Nisei have dispersed throughout the nation as the doors of economic opportunity swung open. In any event, the National Student Relocation Council persuaded many leading institutions to accept Japanese American students, handled the paper work required for admission, took care of the necessary military clearance, and even attempted to prepare communities for their coming. Some schools, such as the University of Chicago and Massachusetts Institute of Technology, turned down evacuee-students on the grounds they, the schools, were deeply involved in war-related work. However, by the end of the program the council had found academic homes for about 4,300 Nisei. This was a much larger Nisei enrollment in colleges and universities than in any single prewar year. Many were permitted to study at small, elite liberal arts schools that they never would have been able to afford under ordinary circumstances. The contacts these students made proved invaluable in later years. Without doubt the student relocation program was one of the more significant and uplifting episodes in an otherwise shameful chapter of American history.

By the beginning of 1943, WRA's drive to resettle evacuees in inland America was well under way. On January 4, the first WRA field office was established in Chicago to supervise resettlement through the Midwest.[5] Supervision consisted of locating employers willing to hire Japanese Americans, lining up housing, educating local agencies to the needs of the evacuees, helping to create a favorable public climate, and counseling individual evacuees as they began to trickle in from the camps.

Additional field offices were established in Cleveland, Kansas City, Salt Lake City, Denver, New York, and Little Rock. On the whole the evacuees were absorbed into communities large and small with a minimum of either fanfare or problems.

The key to resettling the evacuees was finding employment. The wartime manpower shortage made it relatively easy to solve that problem. Employers—machine shops, restaurants, factories, farmers —were searching desperately for help and for most of them it mattered little that a prospective employee was being released from a concentration camp. Most of the evacuees proved to be a pleasant surprise. Not only were they well qualified, but they had excellent work habits, were conscientious and reliable. The first evacuees to be hired by a firm were often the best argument for hiring additional evacuees.

By the end of the resettlement program some 35,000 Japanese Americans had been scattered to various parts of the United States, and substantial numbers elected to stay in their new homes rather than return to the West Coast. This accounts for the fact that today there are chapters of the Japanese American Citizens League in places such as Cleveland and Dayton in Ohio, Chicago, Houston, Milwaukee, St. Louis, Indianapolis, Philadelphia, New York, and Washington, D.C.

All evacuees seeking resettlement had to pass security checks, partly so that the public could be assured that their loyalty was certified. The check consisted primarily of making sure that nothing derogatory about these individuals was in the files of the various intelligence agencies. Later, however, a mass loyalty review was undertaken with deplorable results. This episode will be treated in detail later in this chapter.

The first evacuees to leave the camps were Nisei. Even though these citizens had been uprooted along with the aliens, WRA felt citizenship should have some meaning. WRA also took the position that citizens should dominate what little self-government would be permitted within the camps. When Issei in the Gila Center protested the decision to exclude them from the elected council, WRA responded in this manner: [6]

> . . . we believe that the citizenship status . . . of the evacuees who were born in the United States needs to be given special recognition. The fact that . . . all persons of Japanese ancestry were evacuated from the West Coast . . . has caused some of the citizen evacuees to wonder what value their citizenship has. We regret that fact very much. We understand, also, that a few among the alien evacuees have been taunting the young Nisei with this fact, and have stated that the citizenship of the Nisei was valueless. It is our intention, therefore, to help make up for this fact, as much as possible, by giving special recognition to

the citizenship status of the Nisei . . .

A second consideration had a great deal to do with our decision. In general, the Nisei are much more Americanized than are the Issei . . . We are of the opinion that if the Nisei alone are eligible for membership in the community council, the general character of the action taken by the . . . council will be more in keeping with American institutions and practices.

The goal of community self-government was doomed from the beginning. Behind barbed wire, the elected councilmen (who quickly were labeled blockheads by the camp newspapers) could function only as sounding boards for discontent; they were without authority to do more than bring complaints to the attention of WRA administrators and ask for action. The policy inevitably arrayed the Issei, who had been accustomed to community leadership roles, against the Nisei, resulting in a good deal of rancor in the relationship between the two generations. The Issei argued with some validity that in a relocation camp in which all "Japanese" were being treated in a similar manner, citizenship was irrelevant and they as experienced leaders could have headed off much of the unrest that marked community life. Perhaps to placate Issei feelings and give them a sense of usefulness, they were permitted to become block managers with general responsibility for the physical well-being of their areas. They saw to it that the grounds were picked up, the latrines kept tidy, and the boilers fired so there was enough hot water for washing and showers.

The community council was comprised of one member from each block, each block being made up of twelve residential barracks served by a mess hall. WRA in time learned that the block had a life of its own. Some 250 persons lived in each block and they came to have a fellow-feeling and to comprise almost a political unit.

It can be said safely that there were no happy Relocation Centers. All had their problems. At best, camp life was abnormal—subject to uncertainty, fear, frustration, anger, emotional pressures, great physical discomfort, resentment, and beset by an abundance of rumors that fed on boredom and bitterness. In the field of security within the centers, apart from well-publicized incidents such as the Poston strike, the Manzanar and Tule Lake disturbances, the summation in one WRA report provides a fair picture: [7]

The problems of WRA in the field of internal security at the centers were both more simple and more complex than those of the ordinary police department in a city of 10,000 to 15,000 population. They were more simple because WRA was dealing with a group of people who had achieved a high degree of intra-group discipline and had established a noteworthy record for law-abiding behavior in the prewar period. They were more complex because these same people had been scrutinized, questioned, and picked up for questioning to the point where they had almost developed a mass neurosis on the subject of investigations and "informers" even before they entered WRA centers and because they had been set aside from the general population on the basis of fears and suspicions which most of them regarded as ground-less and irrational. With this kind of background, it was hardly surprising that contempt for recognized authority—both govern-mental and parental—should break out among the adolescent groups at relocation centers to a degree that was absolutely un-precedented in the Japanese American population; that gangs should be formed for the specific purpose of "taking care of" in-formers or even residents who were suspected of being "too close" to the administration; and that the appearance of any FBI officers at a center should produce a serious state of community-wide anxiety and tension. These problems were particularly acute and significant at Tule Lake after it became a segregation center, but they existed in some degree at every one of the WRA communi-ties. The only real solution for them, WRA has always felt, lay in removing the evacuated people from the abnormal, highly charged atmosphere of the centers and restoring them to an environment where their ordinary law-abiding and cooperative impulses could reassert themselves.

On the whole, however, the crime record at relocation centers compared quite favorably with that of the ordinary American community of similar size. In fact, a 1944 survey of comparative crime rates . . . indicated that the law was being broken during that period about three times as frequently in ordinary cities as it was in the relocation centers. The centers had their share of gamblers, thieves, prostitutes, gangsters, and even murderers. But these lawless elements were certainly no more typical of the community at large than they are in the average small city. A great majority of the center residents were a psychologically bruised, badly puzzled, and frequently apathetic group of people. But during their stay at the centers they continued their previous practices of religious worship, tried to achieve some semblance of order and dignity in their broken lives, and frequently showed an almost pathetic eagerness to hold their families together and to work back toward their prewar social and economic status.

Once the struggle to make the barracks habitable ended and life settled down to a routine, it was human to look for scapegoats and whipping boys. Those prominent in JACL were quickly, and unfairly, blamed for "selling us down the river" by encouraging cooperation with the military and government in the evacuation. In their psychic torment the evacuees, who could not confront their real tormentors on the "outside," turned upon the JACL, suggesting the Evacuation would not have occurred if the organization had resisted. This, of course, is nonsense. JACL, in attempting to provide leadership for the Japanese American community, adopted the only rational policy under the circumstances. There is no doubt, given the temper of the times, that had the Japanese resisted the Evacuation, force would have been used and blood would have been shed. But for many in the camps there was an emotional need to blame someone, and JACL leaders were available as targets for emotional release. In truth, the cooperative posture of JACL, and the disciplined behavior of the great majority in the camps aided greatly in disarming many of their critics and thus contributed to the radically changed social climate enjoyed by Japanese Americans after the trauma of the war.

In a different sense, another "problem minority" were the Kibei. They were a diverse group, some with strong cultural and sentimental ties to Japan, others violently repelled by Japanese militarism, but all stigmatized and stereotyped by their common inability to speak English fluently. Unable to distinguish the degree to which Kibei were attracted to the Japanese way of life, WRA as well as other government agencies was inclined to lump them all together somewhere between the citizen American-educated Nisei, and the alien Issei.

WRA statistics show that of 71,534 Nisei in the camps, 46,880 were fifteen years of age or older. Dorothy Swaine Thomas and her associates in the volume titled *The Spoilage* reworked WRA figures and found that one of five Nisei, fifteen years of age or older, was a Kibei, if some education in Japan was the decisive criterion. Accepting her figures, we conclude that about 9,300 of the evacuees were Kibei. Although they were to figure prominently in some of the camp disturbances, it is quite unfair to tar the whole group with the same brush. Kibei were among the first to volunteer for service when the Army reopened its ranks to Nisei. In fact, they were among the men accepted as instructors and in the first class of students enrolled by the Military Intelligence Language School, which will be reported on in greater detail in a later chapter. According to the best estimates available, not more than one in nine Kibei was among the renunciants who elected expatriation at the end of the war.

When WRA on July 20, 1942, adopted a tentative policy governing release from the camps, in either ignorance or confusion it flatly denied leave permits to Kibei. On the eve of WRA's policy conference in San Francisco on August 13, a meeting composed largely of Kibei was held at Manzanar to protest this discrimination.[8] The ensuing discussion brought to the surface a deep split in the community between those who, for want of a better term, might be labeled the accommodationists, and the recalcitrants. It would not be accurate to call the recalcitrants pro-Japanese, but certainly they were bitter about the treatment they had received at the hands of the United States government. It may or may not have occurred to them that even in a prison camp they enjoyed freedom of speech.

Unrest festered below the surface in almost every camp. In some instances the friction was a manifestation of hostilities and rivalries which antedated the war. On the night of November 14 at Poston an unpopular Kibei was beaten unconscious by an unidentified group of assailants. Two popular young Nisei were arrested by internal security police.[9] A committee of residents demanded their release. When the administration refused, a strike was called suspending all but the most essential services. The administration then turned loose one of the suspects against whom there was no real evidence, and released the other to the custody of his attorney. It was a good decision. The administration had maintained its authority by holding firm against community pressure, and the military, which was poised to enter the camp, was not called upon.

It was in the face of growing tensions that JACL late in November of 1942 called a historic meeting of its leaders in Salt Lake City. WRA permitted two representatives of each camp to make the trip. Fourteen sessions were held over a period of six days to discuss a wide variety of matters important to Japanese Americans—the way WRA camps were being operated, the resettlement program, funding of JACL operations and JACL's weekly newspaper, *Pacific Citizen*, etc. But undoubtedly the most critical subject was the Nisei's status under Selective Service.

Prior to the outbreak of war Japanese Americans had been drafted like all other Americans. At the time of Pearl Harbor some 3,500

Japanese Americans were in uniform. What happened to them after that seems to have been left to the judgment or whim of the local commander. Some Nisei were discharged summarily for the "convenience" of the government. Many were taken out of combat units and reassigned as hospital corpsmen or to "permanent KP." A few were unaffected. For a brief period after the eruption of war Nisei continued to be accepted for service. Then, abruptly, draft boards ceased calling them up, and presently Nisei began receiving cards notifying them that their 1-A status had been changed to 4-C or 4-F. The 4-C classification was for aliens not subject to military service; 4-F was for persons unfit for military service.

The question now was whether JACL should petition the War Department for restoration of Selective Service obligations. Mike Masaoka, who from his Washington vantage point could see the broad picture, argued strongly for this course "so that we shall be accorded the same privilege of serving our country in the armed forces as that granted to every other American citizen."

Not all the delegates shared his enthusiasm for military service. They were only too acutely aware of resentment among evacuees who were aggrieved over suspension of constitutional rights, and would look with no great favor on risking their lives for the country that had treated them so shabbily. The delegates were aware that the resentment against the government could easily be turned against them.

Masaoka took a longer view. He saw military service as the wedge that would open the way back to normal life for Japanese Americans. The United States government, he reasoned, could not in good conscience discriminate against a people whose sons, husbands, and fathers had shed blood in defense of their country. In the end, the delegates saw the logic of Masaoka's argument and, even though they realized they might face violence when they returned to the camps, voted unanimously to ask the government that had imprisoned them for the right to defend it.

The anticipated violence was not long in coming although the Selective Service decision was only an incidental reason for the outbreak at Manzanar on December 5.[10] This was only two days short of the first anniversary of the Pearl Harbor attack, a fact which newspapers noted in their accounts. The circumstances under which Manzanar was settled made conflict almost inevitable. The first to arrive was a group of JACL leaders who volunteered to pave the way for those who would come later. Their intentions were good, but as it turned out, they were given the better positions open to evacuees since they were on the ground early. They also formed a patriotic organization, the Manzanar Citizens Federation. As in all the camps, controversy and suspicion characterized life at Manzanar. Those who seemed to be cooperating enthusiastically with the Caucasian authorities were looked upon as informers (the Japanese expression was *inu*, meaning "dog") by those who harbored less tractable attitudes.

On the night of December 5 Fred Tayama, a prominent JACL leader, was attacked and seriously injured by a group of masked assailants. A young suspect was arrested and jailed in the town of Independence outside the camp. An angry crowd inside the camp demanded the youth's release and a "death list" of alleged "informers" was read. When gangs started out in search of Tayama and other aggressively pro-American Nisei leaders, the project director authorized the military police to enter the camp. In the confusion that followed, two of the evacuees, one an innocent bystander, were killed by shots fired by the troops. Soldiers patrolled the camp throughout the night while those on the "death list" and their families, sixty-five persons in all, were hurriedly moved to an abandoned Civilian Conservation Corps camp in Death Valley. This action was to become an issue later; it was charged that the WRA had failed to protect patriotic American citizens and had spirited them away, leaving the camp in the hands of dissidents. However, sixteen men were charged with inciting the riot and were moved to a WRA isolation camp at Moab, Utah, or, in the case of aliens, to a Department of Justice internment camp. With leaders of both strong pro- and anti-administration groups removed, Manzanar gradually returned to normal.

Meanwhile, similar violence against JACL leaders broke out in at least two other camps. Saburo Kido's quarters in Poston were invaded one night and he was beaten so badly he was hospitalized for nearly a month. Eight Kibei were apprehended and confessed taking part in the attack. The hospital at the Rohwer camp was invaded and Dr. Tom Yatabe was attacked.

The Evacuation had been justified by the authorities in part by the argument that it was impossible to separate the loyal from the disloyal, and it was presumed by many that some sort of segregation program would be launched in the WRA camps. The violence, which WRA apparently was unable to control, underscored the need for early action. The lack of an adequate system for checking security also was delaying the resettlement program. WRA reported: [11]

One of WRA's most serious bottlenecks in the relocation program at this time was the slowness of leave clearance on an individual basis. Ordinarily, evacuees at the centers would not apply for leave clearance until they had a job rather definitely lined up and were practically ready to leave the relocation center. Then the process of making out the necessary forms, clearing the cases both at the center and in Washington, and securing the information from the files of the Federal Bureau of Investigation would generally take weeks and even months. By the time clearance was finally obtained, the job had frequently disappeared and the applicants, as well as the employers, were left invariably disgruntled and discouraged.

The opportunity for a solution came when the War Department, under urging from both WRA and JACL, finally agreed "to make the Nisei eligible for Army service and thus give them a chance to demonstrate their loyalty in the most effective manner possible." On January 28, 1943, the War Department announced plans to form an all-Nisei combat team of regimental size. Service in a segregated unit was not what Myer and Masaoka had in mind. However, they regarded the decision as a substantial step in the right direction, particularly when it was argued that a few thousand Nisei scattered among millions of troops would be lost from view, but an all-Nisei fighting outfit would be able to dramatize their loyalty.

To expedite the recruiting process, the War Department undertook to look into the background of all draft-age Nisei males through a mass registration program. WRA was told that "a form questionnaire designed to bring out the background and national leanings of individual Nisei was then being prepared by the War Department with the help of Naval Intelligence experts." The questionnaire was to be distributed by recruitment teams visiting each of the WRA camps.[12]

What followed was one of WRA's most serious blunders. WRA figured that since the Army was going to obtain from Nisei males the very kind of information needed for leave clearance, it would be a good idea to broaden the registration program to take in all adults in the camps and turn it into a mass leave-clearance operation.

Unfortunately, neither the Army nor WRA fully appreciated what had happened to the evacuees. Bitterness had continued to fester. The camps tended to create unrest where none had existed. The authorities were inclined to see attitudes strictly in harshly delineated terms of loyalty or disloyalty whereas anger and disillusionment were manifested in many shades of feelings that had little to do with loyalty to either the United States or Japan. One could be resentful of the treatment meted out by the U.S. without wishing to do it harm or supporting Japan. Yet the Army and WRA tried to determine these attitudes with relatively simple questionnaires that showed a total lack of either sensitivity or understanding.

The Army's questionnaire, titled "Statement of United States Citizens of Japanese Ancestry," was to be used to register all male Nisei of draft age for Selective Service. WRA's questionnaire, called "War Relocation Authority Application for Leave Clearance," was patterned after the Army form and would be answered by all Nisei women and Issei of both sexes.

Most of the questions in both forms were innocuous, but two, numbers 27 and 28, were crucial. In the Army form, they read:

Question 27: Are you willing to serve in the armed forces of the United States on combat duty, wherever ordered?

Question 28: Will you swear unqualified allegiance to the United States of America and faithfully defend the United States from any or all attack by foreign or domestic forces, and forswear any form of allegiance or obedience to the Japanese emperor, or any other foreign government, power or organization?

On the WRA form the two questions read:

Question 27: If the opportunity presents itself and you are found qualified, would you be willing to volunteer for the Army Nurse Corps or the WAAC?

Question 28: Will you swear unqualified allegiance to the United States and forswear any form of allegiance or obedience to the Japanese emperor, or any other foreign government, power or organization?

Serious problems arose when the registration began. Many Nisei objected to the idea of serving in a segregated unit although they would have willingly joined up on the same basis as other Americans. Some expressed fear that, in view of their treatment so far, they were being urged to join an outfit that would be sacrificed as cannon fodder. Others qualified their answers, saying in effect they would join the

armed forces only if their rights as citizens were restored. A few
said no, regarding the answer as a clear means of avoiding military
service. The idea of determining loyalty by questionnaire was ridiculous on the face of it. In reality the response to Question 27 was not
any real measure of loyalty or disloyalty. But the Army, having designed the document for this purpose, had no choice but to accept
its findings.

Question 28 posed even greater problems for many Nisei. As they
read the question, they were being asked to forswear an allegiance
which they had never held. Some even regarded it as a trick question
which would be used against them—they felt they were being in-
veigled into admitting they held a prior loyalty to the Japanese
Emperor.

For the Issei, the WRA form presented real problems. Many were
fearful of conditions on the outside. Since the form specified "Leave
Clearance," they feared they would be ejected from the camps and
exposed to the questionable mercies of the very vocal Jap-haters
lurking everywhere. Elderly Issei of both sexes and Nisei women with
young children wondered whether they might be drafted as nurses.
While common sense would dictate the improbability of such a hap-
pening, the atmosphere in the camps was such that anything was
believable.

Question 28 was particularly distressing to the Issei. American
law classified them as "aliens ineligible to citizenship." An affirmative
answer, renouncing allegiance to the only government which recognized them, would in essence make them stateless persons. Very
quickly, Question 28 was revised to say: "Will you swear to abide by
the laws of the United States and take no action which would in any
way interfere with the war effort of the United States?" This the
Issei could live with, but by then they were filled with doubts and
confusion.

Ultimately, the vast majority of the evacuees answered the two
questions affirmatively, but serious damage had been done. Only
1,200 Nisei volunteered for military service from the centers; under
less confused circumstances several times that number might have
stepped forward. In Hawaii, where they had had no mass evacuation,
more than 10,000 volunteered although only 1,500 were being sought.

In all, 11 percent of those eligible to register—about 7,600—refused to fill out the questionnaire or gave "No" or qualified answers
to the two key questions. In the jargon of the camps these were the

No-Nos. Although WRA could understand that few were actively disloyal, it was now necessary to separate them from the others.

Roger Daniels, in his book *Concentration Camps U.S.A.*, affirms that internal local conditions in the camps had a great deal to do with the results of the registration program: [13]

> At five camps everyone registered; at four others a total of only 36 individuals—10 aliens and 26 citizens—refused to register; but at Tule Lake almost a third of the camp population, 3,218 people (1,360 citizens and 1,856 aliens) refused. Dorothy Swaine Thomas and Richard S. Nishimoto, who studied Tule Lake, concluded that administrative blunders were largely responsible for the high degree of non-registration and disloyalty at Tule Lake, but to this almost surely must be added the factor of effective leadership among the "disloyals."

When the Army refused to build a segregation camp, WRA decided one of the existing centers would be used for the No-Nos. Because Tule Lake had the largest number of "disloyals," it was chosen. That meant the "loyals" in Tule Lake had to be transferred to other camps, and the "disloyals" from those camps exchanged for them.

Even as preparations were getting under way, the Senate Committee on Military Affairs made a perfunctory investigation of the registration program and demanded immediate segregation of the "disloyals." This was the stuff of newspaper headlines—thousands of "Japs" in American camps proclaiming loyalty to Hirohito; it all seemed to justify the Evacuation and the continuing hostility against them after they had been placed behind barbed wire.

What the sensation-seekers chose to overlook was that some 17,000 Japanese Americans were settled in various parts of the country during 1943 despite the turmoil in the camps, and many others were volunteering for military service and leaving aged parents and their own young families in care of the government in the camps.

The major movement into and out of Tule Lake began in mid-September, 1943, and was completed in about a month. The incoming numbered 8,575, and to make room for them 6,250 "loyals" were moved to other centers. When accommodations were filled, the movement was halted until additional barracks could be built. In February, 1944, some 1,876 persons were moved in from Manzanar. Additional segregants were sent to Tule Lake from time to time, the total number finally reaching 12,178. Roger Daniels underscores the point that many factors other than loyalty were involved in the decisions that led to confinement at Tule Lake: [14]

> Family loyalties, the desire to remain where they were, and often sheer resentment and disillusionment were as significant as "loyalty" or "disloyalty." An Issei man, age 41, later said: He didn't register because of the rumor that those who registered would be forced to leave Tule Lake and he had no place to go. . . . Eventually, more than 18,000 Japanese Americans were segregated at Tule Lake; almost a third of these were family members of segregants rather than segregants themselves. Another third were "Old Tuleans," many of whom just simply did not want to move.

WRA's goal of developing greater tranquility through more homogeneous centers was never fully realized. Most of the centers other than Tule Lake remained essentially quiet, but some undoubtedly loyal Nisei continued to voice dissatisfaction with the way their government had treated them. Perhaps the most notable manifestation of this unrest was at Heart Mountain where, after Selective Service responsibilities were restored, a "Fair Play Committee" persuaded a number of Nisei to resist the draft until their rights as citizens were restored. Eventually, eighty-five Heart Mountain Nisei were convicted in federal court of draft resistance. However, more than 700 others from that camp reported for their physical examinations as ordered.

Due in large part to the makeup of Tule Lake's population, any expectation that segregation would produce a genuine community was quickly confounded. The initial wave of segregants was scarcely settled before the situation began to deteriorate. A truck accident caused the death of a worker on the camp farms. Some of the dissident leaders used the incident to bring up another issue. Food grown at Tule Lake was being shipped to the other camps, and now the dissidents said that since they were Japanese they should not be required to work for the benefit of the "loyals." When the workers called a strike, WRA sent crews of volunteers from several of the other camps to save the harvest. Although they were housed outside the camp, their presence only aggravated the situation. Before long, bands of pro-Japan toughs were in virtual control of the camp, intimidating the noncommitted and bringing normal activity to a standstill. Violence broke out on November 4. The military unit guarding the camp was called in, and martial law remained in effect for more than two months.

By then it was too late to carry out a proposal studied just before the outbreak. The idea was to segregate the militantly pro-Japan group from what might be called "crypto-loyals," i.e., those who had accepted disloyal status for reasons other than loyalty to or sympathy with Japan. Only too late was it realized that the segregants at Tule Lake were far from being of one mind; once again the officials had displayed a lack of understanding of the "Japanese problem."

After civil control was resumed, it was clear that the militant "disloyals" were firmly in control of the community. Pro-Japan societies, which reorganized and changed their names frequently, constituted a strong and intimidating force whose influence WRA described in this manner: [15]

> The patriotic societies, seeing an unparalleled opportunity to increase their membership and enhance their prestige in the community, stepped up their early-morning demonstrations to a new pitch, kept the community constantly stirred up with a bewildering series of rumors about impending governmental action, and brought all sorts of pressure to bear on the young Nisei and Kibei to renounce their citizenship. In this campaign they were greatly aided by many of the Issei parents who saw in renunciation a means of holding the family together, avoiding Selective Service for their draft-age sons, and increasing the prospects of an early return to Japan. Although the armies of General Mac-Arthur were by this time well entrenched in the Philippines, many of the more fanatical of the residents of Tule Lake were firmly convinced that a Japanese victory was imminent . . .

The matter of renunciation posed deep trauma for many families. Many Nisei teen-agers had accompanied their parents to Tule Lake out of family loyalty or because they were too young to strike out on their own into an uncertain future. On July 1, 1944, Congress passed what was called the Denationalization Act. It enabled an American to divest himself of his citizenship "by making in the United States a formal written renunciation of nationality . . . whenever the United States shall be in a state of war and the attorney general shall approve such renunciation as not contrary to the interests of the United States."

Late in 1944 the Justice Department scheduled renunciation hearings at Tule Lake beginning on December 6. Then, on Sunday, December 17, one day before the Supreme Court ruled in the Endo and Korematsu cases, the War Department announced without warning that exclusion from the West Coast would be ended January 2, 1945. (The Korematsu case upheld the authority of the military to order the Evacuation. In the Endo case the high court ruled that once the loyalty of a citizen had been established, that person could not be kept confined. These and other court cases are discussed in chapter XVI.)

The end of exclusion was greeted with mixed feelings. There was happiness that the evacuees could go home, uncertainty about what awaited them back on the West Coast, fear of hostility, and even reluctance to give up the prison security of the camps for the struggle necessary to start life anew under freedom. Many in the camps had nothing to go back to except sentiment. There was, inevitably, a hard core of evacuees whose readjustment to normal life was beset by difficulties. But thousands who had resettled in interior America and sunk roots deep into the soil of their adopted communities never did go back.

One day after the Army canceled its exclusion orders, WRA announced that regardless of the course of the war the relocation camps would be closed before the end of 1945, and the entire WRA program would be wrapped up before June 30, 1946.

Exclusion's end did not apply automatically to the segregants at Tule Lake. And since they remained under restraint, many Nisei— confused, resentful, or under unbearable pressure—continued to file renunciation of citizenship forms during the winter and spring of 1944–45. In all, some 5,700 citizens filed these forms, about 95 percent of them being Tule Lake residents.

After Japan surrendered on August 15, 1945, the Justice Department continued its efforts to deport all renunciants and aliens still in its internment camps. But by then many of the renunciants had changed their minds, and they and their families appealed to WRA for rehearings. Myer was sympathetic, and since WRA had been absorbed into the Department of the Interior early in 1944, it was in position to enlist the powerful influence of Secretary Harold L. Ickes. His intercession produced hearings that won reprieves for many.

Nevertheless, 4,724 persons left for Japan as repatriates or expatriates. Aliens repatriated to Japan numbered 1,659. They were accompanied by 1,949 American citizens, virtually all minors. And there were 1,116 citizen-renunciants, 930 of them being above the age of twenty. They were mostly Kibei.

In 1959, the Justice Department announced that a total of 5,766 Japanese Americans had renounced their citizenship during the entire war period, 5,409 had asked that citizenship be restored, and as of that date 4,978 had regained citizenship.

The exodus from the camps, unfortunately, was not as well organized as the Evacuation. There was no military timetable to hasten the process, nor did it have anywhere near the logistical and moral support of the Army that had attended the Evacuation. Only a few officers who had served with Nisei overseas were assigned to public relations duty on the West Coast where in most areas hostility still ran high. WRA officials redirected their resettlement efforts to the West. Churches and other human relations groups provided heartwarming support. But the years had taken their toll. Jobs had disappeared. Businesses had vanished. In many cases property left behind was gone—stolen, vandalized, or ruined by neglect. Some markets refused to accept produce from Japanese farmers. Still, there was nothing to do but make the best of it, and gradually the antagonism began to recede.

As a people, the Japanese Americans had confronted a challenge few are ever compelled to endure, and their response by any standard was magnificent. Few others would have endured as much and kept the faith.

XV ✿ Proving Their Loyalty

In the war in which we are now engaged racial affinities are not severed by migration. The Japanese race is an enemy race and while many second and third generation Japanese born on United States soil, possessed of United States citizenship, have become "Americanized," the racial strains are undiluted . . . It, therefore, follows that along the vital Pacific Coast over 112,000 potential enemies, of Japanese extraction, are at large today. There are indications that these are organized and ready for concerted action at a favorable opportunity. The very fact that no sabotage has taken place to date is a disturbing and confirming indication that such action will be taken.

This quotation is from the memorandum General John L. DeWitt sent to the secretary of war on February 14, 1942, a peculiar Valentine's Day message.[1] DeWitt, chief of the Western Defense Command in San Francisco, was echoing the views which California's attorney general, Earl Warren, expressed a dozen days earlier at a private conference of California sheriffs and district attorneys. On February 20, Walter Lippmann, the eminent commentator, was to give nationwide expression to these same views in his syndicated column.

What is it these men were saying? They were alleging that the enemy being fought by the United States was a race, not a nation. They were charging that only immigrants of certain racial origins could become good Americans. They were alleging that Japanese immigrants and their citizen-children were guilty before the fact, and the fact was only supposition. (DeWitt also completely overlooked the fact that the 120,000 "potential enemies" was the total Japanese American population on the West Coast including infants, schoolgirls, and the aged.)

A politician, a general, and a political pundit, and after them many editors and commentators advanced these same arguments. Here we have adequate warning against accepting unquestioningly the views of the elite and seemingly the most learned of our society.

Less than a year after General DeWitt voiced his unabashedly racist charges, President Franklin D. Roosevelt issued another statement which should be measured against the first. Roosevelt, who had authorized the Evacuation by signing Executive Order 9066, apparently had changed his mind to the extent of addressing a letter on February 1, 1943, to War Secretary Henry L. Stimson in which he declared: [2]

> The proposal of the War Department to organize a combat team consisting of loyal American citizens of Japanese descent has my full approval . . . No loyal citizen of the United States should be denied the democratic right to exercise the responsibilities of citizenship, regardless of his ancestry. The principle on which this country was founded and by which it has always been governed, is that Americanism is a matter of mind and heart; Americanism is not, and never was, a matter of race or ancestry. A good American is one who is loyal to this country and to our creed of liberty and democracy. Every loyal American citizen should be given an opportunity to serve this country wherever his skills will make the greatest contribution—production, agriculture, government service, or other work essential to the war effort.

As we have seen in an earlier chapter, Japanese Americans received the same treatment as other ethnic groups under the Selective Service Act prior to the outbreak of war. Approximately 3,500 Nisei had been drafted before December 7, 1941, but the attack on Pearl Harbor caused the Army to alter its policy. Not only were Nisei reclassified as unwanted by draft boards, but some already in uniform were discharged for no reason other than that of their race. Roosevelt's approval of the Army's decision to organize an all-Nisei combat team would change all that, even though 110,000 human beings had been uprooted, the majority in violation of their civil rights as citizens. Now the Army saw no illogic in inviting Nisei to step out of concentration camps in their own country and volunteer to fight in defense of that nation.

In reality, however, a great many Japanese Americans were already deeply involved in important military duties for which they were uniquely qualified. Even before Pearl Harbor, Nisei had been part of a Japanese-language training program at the Presidio in San Francisco. U.S. intelligence specialists had recognized well before the outbreak of war that American armed forces were severely handicapped by the absence of Japanese-language specialists who could serve in intelligence and other capacities. A small military-intelligence language school was set up at the Presidio with a class of fifty-eight Nisei and two Caucasians, and three Nisei instructors. When war erupted, this program was greatly expanded. During the evacuation the Army shifted the school to Camp Savage, Minnesota, and then later to nearby Fort Snelling.

The greatest difficulty facing the program was the recruitment of qualified students. Nisei, for the most part, were not proficient in the Japanese language, particularly in reading and writing. Kibei were best qualified, but if they had received a major part of their education in Japan they were regarded as the least likely to be loyal and their English was often inadequate. Nevertheless, Kibei responded enthusiastically to the language program and served with distinction as teachers and students.

(The U.S. Navy also established a language school but, unlike the Army, refused to accept Nisei as students. However, the Navy recruited a faculty made up largely of Issei and Kibei civilians. It was established at the University of California in Berkeley before Pearl Harbor, then shifted to the University of Colorado.)

The efforts of WRA and JACL to get Selective Service regulations changed were outlined in an earlier chapter. After a good deal of backstage discussions, with Assistant Secretary of War John J. McCloy (who had endorsed the Evacuation) supporting the Nisei, Stimson approved plans for the 442nd Regimental Combat Team. Mike Masaoka and George Inagaki, JACL representatives in Washington, were summond to the Pentagon a few days before the announcement on January 28, 1943, and given advance word. Masaoka volunteered on the spot, and Inagaki also asked to be inducted. Masaoka eventually joined the 442nd while Inagaki was sent to the language school.

The 442nd was activated February 1, 1943, and soon cadres of Nisei non-coms from various inland military camps began to arrive at Camp Shelby, Mississippi, to begin preparations for training the men soon to arrive.[3] While the response from the WRA camps was disappointing, a totally different reaction was encountered in Hawaii. The reason for the difference is worthy of study.

In Hawaii, the target of the first Japanese attack, the authorities were well aware of the disciplined behavior of the Japanese American community, and the instant patriotic response of the citizens. Rumors which circulated on the mainland about sabotage during the Pearl Harbor attack were known to be false. However, security officials had kept dossiers on a number of Issei and Kibei who were considered potentially dangerous and they were quickly taken into custody in a screening process reminiscent of the procedures followed in Great Britain concerning European nationals. During the entire course of the Pacific war, 1,440 Japanese aliens and American citizens were taken into custody in Hawaii. Of that number, 981 were sent to the mainland to relocation or alien detention centers.

More than 1,500 men of Japanese ancestry from Hawaii had been inducted into the Army prior to December 7.[4] They continued to serve in their respective units until the spring of 1942 when they were assembled into a special organization called the Hawaii Provisional Battalion. In June the name was changed to 100th Infantry Battalion, Separate, and the outfit dispatched to Camp McCoy, Wisconsin, for combat training. The 100th was at Camp Shelby for its final tuneup when their brothers and friends from Hawaii began to arrive for service with the 442nd. In all, nearly 2,700 Hawaii Nisci, selected from among more than 10,000 volunteers, joined about 1,500 mainlanders. The Hawaiian response without doubt reflected the confidence, for whatever reason, the military command showed in the Japanese Americans. There had been much discussion about moving Hawaii's 160,000 Japanese Americans to the West Coast, or confining them on one of the islands. In the end, it was decided that the Japanese Americans, who comprised one third of the Islands' labor force, were virtually indispensable to the economy and war effort, and General Delos C. Emmons, the theater commander, ruled they would not be disturbed. Pragmatism won out over hysteria, but the Japanese Americans responded with an unsullied record of loyalty and a significant civilian contribution to the war effort in addition to a magnificent combat record.

On August 21, 1943, the 100th Battalion set out across the Atlantic, landing at Oran in North Africa where it was assigned to the 34th Division. The 100th landed at Salerno, Italy, on September 22, just thirteen days after the first Yanks had stormed ashore. It went into action a few days later, and in rapid succession took part in battles at Volturno, the Rapido River, and Cassino. In each encounter the 100th performed with great distinction but at enormous cost. Casualties soon numbered more than the strength of the battalion. The wounded went back into the line as quickly as they were able to fight. In the battle for the Abbey of Monte Cassino the 100th's losses were so heavy the battalion was almost eliminated as an effective unit.

Reinforcements came from the 442nd training back in Mississippi. Virtually all its 1st Battalion was sent to join the 100th. Restored to effective strength, the 100th was shifted to the Anzio Beachhead near Rome on March 26, 1944. U.S. forces had landed at Anzio in January but were unable to expand their narrow perimeter and suffered heavy casualties. The 100th played a key role in the breakout from the beachhead in late May and early June and drove northward along the coast, taking Lanuvio and La Toretto in an intense thirty-six-hour battle and finally driving on to the key town of Civitavecchia. There they were joined on June 11, 1944, by the 2nd and 3rd battalions of the 442nd. The 100th formed the 1st Battalion, although it was allowed to keep its identity as the 100th in deference to its proud combat record. The three battalions, which made up the 442nd Regimental Combat Team, now became part of the 34th Infantry Division. The 442nd's senior officers were Caucasians, all its enlisted personnel and many of its junior officers Nisei.

Through the summer of 1944, following Italy's surrender, the 442nd took part in the Rome-Arno campaign driving German troops northward along Italy's west coast. On reaching the Arno River, which runs through Florence and to the sea near Pisa, the 442nd was pulled out of the line and sent back to Naples on September 6 for a much-needed rest. The 442nd's anti-tank company had been detached in mid-July and assigned to the First Airborne Task Force which was to spearhead the invasion of Southern France. However, at Naples the combat team was reinforced by 672 replacements from Camp Shelby. They were quickly welcomed and integrated. On September 27 the 442nd sailed for Marseilles to join the Seventh Army which was already in action in the Rhone Valley of France.

The fighting ahead was some of the heaviest the 442nd was to encounter. The Seventh Army's momentum was spent by the time the Nisei arrived. Nazi forces in the Vosges Mountains were dug in with their backs to the nearby German frontier. The 442nd reached the front lines early in October and during the next six weeks performed with exceptional gallantry. In this relatively brief campaign the Nisei achieved every objective they were assigned, including the rescue of the "Lost Battalion," the 1st Battalion of the 141st Infantry Regiment made up largely of Texans. The Nisei not only broke through and rescued 211 men—all that remained of the battalion—they also drove on to seize the high ground that had been the original objective.

Before the 442nd was relieved, it had experienced nearly a month of continuous fighting and suffered more than 800 casualties including 140 dead. The high cost of the operation did not go unnoticed. The Texans gave the 442nd a plaque which read:

> To the 442nd Infantry Regiment
> With Deep Sincerity and Utmost Appreciation
> For the Gallant Fight to Effect Our Rescue
> After We Had Been Isolated for Seven Days
> 1st Battalion, 141st Infantry Regiment
> Biffontaine, France
> From 24th to 30th October
> 1944

The action just described, called the Battle of Bruyeres, resulted in the award of three of the seven Presidential Distinguished Unit Citations won by the 442nd. When the 442nd was reassigned on November 17, the commander of the 36th Division in which it had been serving, Major General John E. Dahlquist, wrote:

> 1. The 36th Division regrets that the 442nd Combat Team must be detached and sent on to other duties. The period during which you served, October 14 to November 18, 1944, was one of hard, intense fighting through terrain as difficult as any army has encountered.
> 2. The courage, steadfastness, and willingness of your officers and men were equal to any ever displayed by United States troops.
> 3. Every officer and man of the Division joins me in sending our best personal regards and good wishes to every member of your command, and we hope that we may be honored again by having you as a member of our Division.

The 442nd's next assignment, the only easy one the outfit was to enjoy, was well deserved. Nearly 2,000 of its men were in hospitals and the regiment was at half strength even with the arrival of 382 replacements. The 442nd was based near Nice on the French Riviera and its responsibility was to guard against a German thrust from Northern Italy against Marseilles which would disrupt supply lines and isolate American forces in the Rhone Valley. Most of the action was light as patrols sought to intercept spies and infiltrators, and artillery duels broke out only sporadically.

Late in March, 1945, the "champagne campaign" ended. The 552nd Field Artillery had been ordered north to cover the crossing of the Rhine. The 442nd Infantry and its engineering company, the 232nd, left for Italy. Their new assignment was destruction of the western anchor of the Gothic Line, a defense system built across Northern Italy by the Germans. The Gothic Line had been breached by Allied forces near the center, but the western anchor in extremely rugged country near the coast appeared impregnable. From April 5 until the end of the war in Italy on May 2, the three infantry battalions of the 442nd and the engineers slugged ahead at great cost, finally capturing strongpoints that had withstood other American assaults for five months. A few days later Nazi Germany surrendered.

The 442nd and 100th had served with distinction in seven major campaigns and suffered 9,486 casualties including 600 dead. Its men had been awarded more than 18,000 individual decorations, among them one Congressional Medal of Honor, fifty-two Distinguished Service Crosses, one Distinguished Service Medal, nearly 600 Silver Stars, more than 5,000 Bronze Stars. As a unit the 442nd had won forty-three Division Commendations, thirteen Army Commendations, and seven Presidential Distinguished Unit Citations.

The casual reader may respond to this impressive list of decorations with two questions:

—Had the men of the 442nd been of a different color, would there have been more Medal of Honor winners?

—Would they have fought as valiantly against Japan?

The questions deserve answers.

It is strange indeed that only one Nisei received the Medal of Honor —Pfc. Sadao S. Munemori, who sacrificed his life to save two of his comrades by covering a German grenade with his body—while fifty-two Nisei won the next highest award, the Distinguished Service Cross. The record shows that a substantial number of Nisei were recommended for the Medal of Honor. But in each case the Distinguished Service Cross was awarded. Obviously the Medal of Honor recommendations were being downgraded. At war's end, this situation was brought to the attention of Senator Elbert Thomas, chairman of the Military Affairs Committee. Senator Thomas ordered an investigation. Recommendations for decorations then pending were reviewed, and Munemori became the first Nisei to win the Medal of Honor. Since then, Nisei have won the highest award in the Korean and Indochina wars.

The role of Japanese Americans in the Pacific war was a high-priority military secret for a long time, partly to protect the Nisei themselves, partly to prevent the enemy from learning that skilled linguists were translating intercepted messages and documents and interrogating prisoners.[5] Even before December 7, 1941, Japanese American soldiers were among GIs stationed in the Philippines. Some among these men were captured after the surrender of Corregidor. Others were considered so important to the war effort that they were evacuated to Australia on General Douglas MacArthur's orders. Most Nisei who served in the Pacific were linguists although a number of them, particularly those in the China-Burma-India theater, also doubled as combat infantrymen.

The largest number of Nisei was dispatched to the Allied Translator and Interpreter Section (ATIS) immediately after completing the Military Intelligence Language School course. ATIS was an inter-Allied activity established just outside Brisbane, Australia, in 1942. It numbered about twenty linguists, including eight Nisei, when taken over by Colonel Sidney F. Mashbir in early October, 1942. By the end of the war nearly 4,000 Nisei were attached to ATIS, serving with scores of units all over the far-flung Pacific theater. Mostly they worked in teams pairing Nisei with a lesser knowledge of Japanese together with a Kibei whose English was somewhat deficient. For the most part ATIS was a rear-echelon organization and manpower pool from which specialists were drawn for combat duty. Colonel Mashbir has written in his autobiography, *I Was an American Spy*: [6]

> Men were ordered in and out of action, detachments were flown to combat units and back to the rear when the unit was relieved, the only requirement being that the request for orders be sent through G-2 to the Adjutant General so that Gen. Charles Willoughby would be cognizant of what was taking place.

From the Solomon Islands to Okinawa and beyond into the Occupation the Nisei served with great distinction. Some died. Many were decorated. In addition to the normal hazards of combat, the Nisei faced an unavoidable risk. Mashbir writes: [7]

> The Nisei were up against another hazard. Right from the start of the war, all Nisei serving with the combat troops were under suspicion from their Caucasian comrades, and furthermore, when they got into a battle zone they were often fired at by both sides. I was recently discussing with a major of infantry who served through the Aleutian campaign the frightful peril in which these lads were constantly placed because of their Oriental features. The danger was often intensified by the fact that Japanese soldiers very frequently donned American uniforms, taken from our dead,

in order to try to penetrate our lines. The major told me that one
night the Japanese launched an attack on our forces at midnight. It was early in the campaign and the troops were not yet
battle-trained. Many of the men, therefore, including the Nisei,
had undressed. In the resulting scramble in the dark with men
running around partly dressed, several of the Nisei very narrowly
escaped death at the hands of their comrades.

The Nisei linguists served in all theaters of the Pacific war. Some
were assigned to Australian combat units and they emerged with
letters of commendation even though their service had been accepted
initially with reluctance. When serving with combat units, translation
and interrogation were only part of their duties. They fought with
weapons alongside their comrades of whatever color. Frequently, they
were able to persuade Japanese to surrender, thus eliminating the
dangerous necessity of digging them out of caves and entrenchments.
Often, they crept close to enemy lines in the jungles, overheard officers
giving commands, and relayed information about Japanese plans to
their own officers. How many lives their skills saved will never be
known, but beyond question many men are alive today as a consequence of the dedication of the Nisei linguists. Colonel Mashbir pays
tribute to them in these words: [8]

> I want to make an unequivocal statement in regard to the Ameri-
> cans of Japanese ancestry who, being American citizens, fought
> by our side in the war. Had it not been for the American Nisei,
> that part of the war in the Pacific which was dependent upon
> Intelligence gleaned from captured documents and prisoners of
> war would have been a far more hazardous, long-drawn-out
> affair.
>
> The United States of America owes a debt to these men and
> to their families which it can never fully repay. At a highly con-
> servative estimate, thousands of American lives were preserved
> and millions of dollars in materiel were saved as a result of their
> contribution to the war effort.

In addition to the linguists and the men of the 442nd, the vagaries
of war found a small number of Nisei in more conventional military
roles. They were to be seen from India to Alaska and throughout
Europe, but not in the Navy. Even though the Navy did not hesitate
to borrow Nisei linguists from the Army, its color line kept Japanese
Americans out of naval uniform. The Army Air Corps, however, accepted a few Nisei, the best known being Ben Kuroki, a Nebraska farm

boy. Soon after Pearl Harbor when he volunteered, Kuroki had to virtually fight his way into uniform. As a gunner in a bomber, he flew thirty missions against targets in Europe and North Africa, then volunteered for a tour of duty in the Pacific, flying twenty-eight additional missions in B-29 bombers. Other Nisei and even a few Issei served in Office of War Information propaganda units, in the hush-hush Office of Strategic Services as psychological warfare specialists, the Army map service, as monitors of Japanese broadcasts, and in other agencies where their knowledge of Japanese was invaluable.

The Selective Service System has reported that 33,300 Japanese Americans, about half from the mainland and half from Hawaii, served in World War II. These included nurses, doctors and other medical personnel, and members of the Women's Army Corps, as well as merchant mariners. The Military-Intelligence Language School graduated some 6,000 Nisei, more than half of whom reached the Pacific theater before VJ-Day. Most of the others joined the Allied Occupation Army in Japan where, in more peaceful duty, they proved as valuable as those who had been in combat. Many of these men were among the first to be sent to Korea when war broke out there in the summer of 1950. Since all adult Koreans spoke Japanese but few understood English, the Nisei linguists were once more in demand.

In the hindsight of history, there can be no doubt that Mike Masaoka was right when he told JACL leaders in their wartime Salt Lake conference that military service for Nisei was imperative if they were to claim their rightful place in postwar America. Newspaper stories from the war fronts about Nisei courage and sacrifice dramatized their loyalty as nothing else could, and underscored the injustice of their incarceration. In the postwar fight to repeal discriminatory laws, the Japanese Americans could cite their war record to silence their foes and win popular support. In Hawaii, the Nisei war record helped them win unprecedented political power. And tens of thousands of war veterans, who had served alongside the Nisei or had come to know them by reputation, demanded that justice be done. It is probably correct to say that the wartime sacrifices of Japanese Americans in uniform was the largest single factor in changing the status of their people from a despised, discriminated-against minority to near-total acceptance as full-fledged Americans.

Yet there are dissenting voices. Professor Roger Daniels, for one, sees high significance in the fact that numbers of Nisei chose to refuse military service. In his book, *Concentration Camps U.S.A.*, published in 1972 and written during the glory period of campus revolts against the Vietnam War and establishmentarian ideas, Daniels says the record of draft-resistance [9] "calls into question the stereotype of the Japanese American victim of oppression during World War II who met his fate with stoic resignation and responded only with super-patriotism." He continues: "This stereotype, like most, has some basis in reality. Many Japanese Americans, conforming to the JACL line, honestly felt that the only way they could ever win a place for themselves in America was by being better Americans than most. Whether or not this kind of passive submission is the proper way for free men to respond to injustice and racism, is, of course, a matter of opinion. But it is important to note that not all 'loyal' Japanese Americans submitted . . . There are those, however, who will find more heroism in resistance than in patient resignation."

It can be argued, of course, that Daniels is engaging in a bit of historical revisionism, passing judgment on actions during the 1942–45 war years from the popular wisdom of a quarter century later when social forces unleashed by World War II had created a drastically different mood and standards of values in the United States. Nor is it accurate to describe that act of volunteering for military service as "passive submission" and "patient resignation."

It may take a longer perspective than is available at this time to evaluate the impact of the Japanese American military record on the course of their history as Americans. Be that as it may, there are many who will agree with a California representative, Charles H. Wilson, who during a special congressional tribute to the Nisei nearly two decades after the end of World War II, declared: "I think we can say with truth that it was the Japanese American fighting men that proved to our government of that day the loyalty and patriotism of the Nisei."

XVI ❧ The Struggle for Justice

The Japanese Americans are not necessarily a litigious people who seek relief from oppression by frequent appeals to the courts. Or to public opinion, for that matter. But they learned early in their struggle for equality and justice that the United States was a nation of laws, most of which were designed to protect people's rights. But laws also could be utilized to perpetuate injustices. Inevitably, in their search for justice and equal opportunity, they became involved in a number of landmark lawsuits in the general field of human and civil rights. They sought relief through favorable interpretation of oppressive laws, or by the passage or repeal of specific laws, particularly after the Japanese American Citizens League appeared on the scene.

One of the first things the Issei immigrants learned about life in America was that a vast gulf separated citizens from aliens. At first the majority of Issei had no desire to exchange their Japanese status for American citizenship. But as their tenure in the New World lengthened, the Issei realized they were handicapped by permanent alien status and were compelled to fight for equality from a position of weakness. They were, of course, unable to hold public office and were denied careers in the one profession which would have enabled them to confront their tormentors effectively—the law. In addition, many states reserved for citizens, or those who had declared intent to become naturalized citizens,[1] licenses to practice various other professions.

It was logical, then, that early in their American experience some Issei should seek citizenship. And because the process of naturalization was left to local officials, interpretation of the laws was uneven and the petitions of a number of Issei—such as Joseph Heco—were indeed accepted.

Congress had provided for naturalization of aliens through the Act of March 26, 1790, three years after the Constitution was ratified. The act provided that "any alien, being a free white person who shall

245

have resided within the limits and under the jurisdiction of the United States for a term of two years, may be admitted to become a citizen thereof." After the Civil War, in 1873, the act was amended to include "persons of African nativity or descent" among the eligible. No reference was made to persons other than white or black. Most of the Chinese and Japanese who petitioned for naturalization under the 1873 law were turned down. The litigation that followed their denial thus centered around the meaning of "free white persons" and whether races not specifically named in the statute were or were not eligible to citizenship.

The first known naturalization suit brought by an Issei was filed in 1894 by one Saito in Massachusetts. Saito, admittedly of the "Mongolian" race, asked a federal district court whether under naturalization statutes he should be classified as "a free white person." The court ruled that the Founding Fathers clearly intended to limit citizenship to the Caucasian race, and since Saito was of the yellow race, he was not eligible. It is important to note that denial was based not on the shade of Saito's skin, but on race.

In *The Bamboo People*,[2] a study of the law and Japanese Americans, Frank Chuman reports he found at least six other challenges of the naturalization statutes by Issei. Each is interesting enough to merit mention.

In 1908 Buntaro Kumagai, a Japanese alien who had enlisted in the U.S. Army, sought citizenship under an 1862 law providing naturalization for "any alien" who had served honorably in the armed forces. The federal district court in the state of Washington denied Kumagai's application on the ground that "any alien" meant any alien who was white, even though the law did not so specify. Two years later Namiyo Bessho, who had served five years in the U.S. Navy, sought naturalization in Norfolk, Virginia, contending the words "any alien" in the statute should be employed without restriction. He also was turned down.

In 1918 Congress, apparently unaware of the problems posed by the Civil War statute, extended the right of naturalization to "all aliens" who had served in the U.S. armed forces in World War I. Three years later Hidemitsu Toyota petitioned for naturalization under that law in a Massachusetts court. Toyota had enlisted in the Coast Guard in 1913 and was still a member of that service at the time of the suit. The Massachusetts court granted Toyota's petition, but a federal court canceled the certificate. Ultimately, the U.S. Supreme Court ruled in 1925 that "it has long been the national policy to maintain the distinction of color and race" in naturalization statutes and Congress hadn't meant to change that policy in recognizing veterans of military service.

Another war veteran, Ichizo Sato, was naturalized by a federal court in Hawaii in 1923 on the basis of Army service. But when he sought registration as a voter in Sacramento, California, Sato was refused. The California Supreme Court held that citizenship matters were in the hands of Congress, that federal courts had no authority to extend provisions of naturalization laws, and a Japanese alien certainly wasn't eligible for naturalization.

Another Issei, Takuji Yamashita, who thought he had been naturalized in a Washington state court in 1906, was tripped up when he sought to exercise his rights in 1922 by organizing a corporation. The Washington secretary of state ruled that only citizens could organize a corporation and that Yamashita, being an alien, was not eligible. Yamashita filed suit. The state supreme court ruled against Yamashita, and the decision was upheld in the U.S. Supreme Court which decided that his naturalization sixteen years earlier was null and void.

Land ownership was among the rights denied Japanese immigrants by many states taking advantage of their peculiar status as "aliens ineligible to citizenship." Without the legal right to own land, Issei farmers were doomed to remain migrant workers, hired hands, and tenant farmers or sharecroppers who, under California law, could lease any piece of property for no more than three years. It was primarily to challenge this situation that suit was filed in 1922 on behalf of Takao Ozawa, born in Japan but brought to the United States at an early age. Ozawa was graduated from high school in Berkeley and attended the University of California. He took a tack somewhat different from the earlier lawsuits. The thrust of his logic was that since Orientals were not specifically denied naturalization by Congress, he should be as eligible as a free white person. It was an argument that gave the court a graceful out if it had wanted to extend citizenship to Orientals. But the Supreme Court was not in such a mood. It ruled that even though the lawmakers had failed to *exclude* the yellow races of Asia, it would be necessary to name them in addition to "free white persons" if they were to be *included* among the favored.

This decision was followed in 1924 by congressional revision of immigration laws that effectively sealed off entry of Japanese, and no further efforts were made to gain citizenship for Issei as a group until after the end of World War II.

However, the matter of citizenship for the parent generation was high among the concerns of the infant Japanese American Citizens League, whose members were Americans by birth. After its first national convention in 1930, JACL pressed vigorously for citizenship for Issei who had enlisted in the U.S. armed forces in World War I, and for the repeal of the Cable Act. Both issues involved simple justice. Inexperienced as JACL was, its members lobbied for a change in the two laws and eventually succeeded. The victories affected relatively few individuals, but the principle involved—a breakthrough in the wall of racially discriminatory laws—was a critical one. Only about 700 Issei veterans benefited. There is no record of the number of Nisei women who were able to regain the citizenship lost automatically as the result of the marriage to aliens, but they were a relative handful.

JACL in 1930 was hardly more than an embryo organization. After several false starts, a small group of Nisei from California, Oregon, and Washington met in Seattle to form a "national" organization concerned primarily with civic matters. It was, in fact, the only Nisei body to extend over as much as three states. Those attracted to it were earnest Japanese Americans in their late teens and early twenties, deeply concerned about their political, economic, and social future as Americans but not quite sure what they could, or should, do about it. Some Issei leaders recognized JACL's potential— since it was made up of citizens it was in position to wield an influence denied the alien parent generation—and supported its activities. JACL members were encouraged by both their leaders and the Issei to register and vote to maximize their power as citizens. But their numbers were infinitesimal and their strength as a political force virtually negligible. Adding to these drawbacks was the nationwide economic Depression which had hit the Japanese American communities as hard as or harder than the rest of the country.

JACL grew slowly during its first decade, adding gradually to its numbers as Nisei reached maturity. By 1940, it had some fifty chapters divided into Southern California, Northern California, and Northwest district councils. A fourth district encompassing Utah and Idaho was brought into the organization in 1940. By the time of the Evacuation in 1942 there were sixty-six chapters, all but ten of them in the coastal zones from which the members were barred. Oddly enough, JACL never gained a foothold in Hawaii. A major reason was that the political and social climate encountered by Japanese Americans there was somewhat less harsh than that on the mainland.

JACL membership soared after the attack on Pearl Harbor. Many new members recognized JACL as the only patriotic organization able to speak for Japanese Americans; they may have ignored it in the past but now they found it prudent to support it and hoped to be supported by it in turn. Others obviously felt that membership, somehow, would signal their Americanism when questions of loyalty to the United States were being raised on the flimsiest of grounds. Unfortunately, the organization's dedicated and vigorous efforts to serve and defend the Japanese American community proved unavailing in the hysterical and hate-filled months after Pearl Harbor.

The temper of those times is described accurately by John K. Emmerson, a Japan specialist during a long and distinguished career in the U.S. foreign service, in his book *The Japanese Thread*: [3]

> Americans, stunned and bewildered, found it easy to hate the Japanese enemy. An Oriental face was immediately suspect; Chinese labeled themselves as such in self-protection . . . Galvanized into action, government agencies—all too late—tried to cover their chagrin over the disastrous failure of intelligence before Pearl Harbor by turning in every direction to unearth sources of disloyalty, sabotage, subversion and espionage. The so-called day of infamy had cast suspicion on every person and everything identifiable as Japanese. There followed the indefensible forced evacuation of 100,000 Japanese from California, including thousands of American citizens, and their incarceration for the duration of the war in concentration camps euphemistically named relocation centers.

JACL's policy of demonstrating loyalty (and hoping for sympathetic treatment after the emergency) by complete cooperation with the government despite the injustice of the Evacuation was reached reluctantly at the extraordinary meeting of its leaders in San Francisco in March of 1942. In various localities JACL members served as buffers between government and military officials on one side, and the Japanese American population on the other. They helped cut red tape, gathered and distributed food, assisted confused and bewildered individuals—in other words, providing the services federal and local authorities were unable or unwilling to make available. Under the circumstances there was no time to think of challenging the government's right to incarcerate Japanese Americans.

However, there were individuals who, on their own, decided to stand up for their rights. One was Gordon Hirabayashi, a student at the University of Washington, who as a matter of principle refused to obey the Army's curfew order requiring all Japanese Americans to be in their homes between 8 P.M. and 6 A.M. When the Evacuation order became effective, Hirabayashi declined to report. Another was Minoru Yasui, a Portland, Oregon, attorney. An Army Reserve officer, Yasui had been called into service, then sent home after one day. He challenged the curfew order on the ground that the military had no right to impose its will on civilians without declaring martial law. Both Hirabayashi and Yasui chose to become prisoners of conscience, violating military orders not out of disloyalty, but because they believed their government's actions were illegal. Both surrendered peacefully and their presence behind bars posed something of an embarrassment for authorities. Still another Nisei who resisted the Evacuation was Fred Korematsu, a young Californian who apparently was moved less by ideological considerations than by a simple unwillingness to be forced out of his home and community for no understandable reason.

Although JACL's Mike Masaoka had suggested the desirability of a court test of the Evacuation and curfew orders, the organization had no direct involvement in any of these cases. Later, when the Supreme Court heard appeals, JACL filed *amicus curiae* briefs.

By the time the movement into Assembly Centers began, most JACL chapters had disbanded "for the duration." While JACL members took leadership roles in the camps, chapters as such were ineffective or nonexistent. Late-joiners who had sought shelter under the JACL umbrella were not really committed to it. When hostility toward JACL mounted, many rejected the organization. Nonetheless, dedicated JACLers carried on from the transplanted national headquarters in Salt Lake City. Masaoka and George Inagaki operated out of Washington, meeting with government officials, members of Congress, and influential individuals, until they were inducted into the Army. In 1943, JACL offices were opened in Denver, Chicago, and New York, manned by people willing to forgo excellent employment opportunities in favor of serving their people on salaries which barely met minimum needs. They contended against hostility ranging from denial of hospital service to cemetery accommodations, literally from cradle to grave. Most of their financial support came from chapters which had remained intact in the intermountain area.

It was during this dark period that the Supreme Court began to rule on appeals in the litigation set in motion by the Evacuation. The early decisions had not been encouraging.

The Hirabayashi and Yasui cases were the first to be heard. Hirabayashi had been imprisoned in Seattle for five months before a federal district court heard his case. He had admitted readily that he had violated the curfew order and had not registered for evacuation. Hirabayashi's defense was based on the contention that these orders were illegal and he would be waiving his rights as an American citizen by submitting to them.[4]

Despite the seriousness of the case, there were comic overtones.[5] Hirabayashi's Issei father had been called as a witness, and when he became confused, Gordon, the defendant, was pressed into service as an interpreter. The jury took only a few minutes to determine that Gordon was, first, of Japanese ancestry, and second, had violated the curfew and Evacuation orders. The judge sentenced Hirabayashi thirty days on each count, to be served consecutively, a total of sixty days. Hirabayashi had heard that prisoners facing ninety-day sentences could be sent out to a road camp, and since he was anxious to get out of jail, asked the court to extend his term. The judge laughed and changed the sentence to ninety days on each count, to run concurrently. That change was to have a profound effect on the course of litigation involving Japanese Americans, and will be discussed later in this chapter. After Hirabayashi's routine appeal, he was permitted to live with friends in Spokane for several months before being ordered to report to a federal prison camp near Tucson, Arizona. Because federal authorities did not have funds to escort him to Tucson, Hirabayashi hitchhiked, stopping en route to visit his family in Weiser, Idaho, and friends in Salt Lake City.

Yasui had been employed by the Japanese consulate in Chicago after graduation from law school.[6] At war's outbreak he resigned and returned to Portland. He notified authorities of his intention to violate the curfew order as a test of its legality and was arrested. Hirabayashi had been given many privileges during his imprisonment and eventually was put in charge of his section as unofficial "mayor." Yasui, in contrast, was kept in solitary confinement and denied access to barber, typewriter, razor, and manicure scissors. After nine months Yasui was tried in federal district court where Judge Alger Fee returned a strange ruling: The curfew order was unconstitutional as it applied to American citizens, but Yasui had lost his citizenship by having worked for the Japanese consular office; being an alien, therefore, Yasui was guilty.

Because of the constitutional issues involved, both the Yasui and Hirabayashi verdicts went directly to the Supreme Court, which ruled on the two cases together on June 21, 1943.

In the Hirabayashi case the high court found unanimously that the Army's curfew order was a lawful exercise of its power.[7] It also ruled that the rights of Japanese Americans under the Fifth Amendment (". . . nor shall any person . . . be deprived of life, liberty, or property, without due process of law") were not being violated because in a wartime situation citizens of one ethnic ancestry may be placed in a different category from other citizens in view of the danger of espionage and sabotage.

The Supreme Court chose not to rule on the legality of the Evacuation, seizing on the fact that Hirabayashi had been sentenced to two concurrent terms. The line of reasoning was that if he were guilty of one count, there was no point in hearing the second charge since he would be serving time on the two simultaneously. In effect, the high court chose the out of saying that since Hirabayashi had been found guilty unanimously of violating the curfew, there was no need to rule on the second charge. Thus, the matter of the Evacuation's legality was not addressed until nearly a year and a half later when the Supreme Court ruled on the Korematsu case.

Two curious points, aside from the court's refusal to consider the legality of the Evacuation, were raised by the Hirabayashi decisions. First was the court's contention that the military, under special circumstances, has the legal right to discriminate against certain groups of citizens based on their ethnic background. How this could be justified under the Fourteenth Amendment, guaranteeing citizens equal protection of the laws, was never explained. In this case the Army's Western Defense Command had ruled that because of their ancestry, Japanese Americans had "attachments" to the enemy and could be of greater danger to the nation than Americans of other ancestry. This decision, sanctified by the Supreme Court, establishes troubling precedents for a nation whose citizens are derived from numerous ethnic backgrounds.

The second point is that the military had made, and the high court had not questioned, allegations about the potential disloyalty of Japanese Americans. Military authorities had accepted the racist contentions developed over a half century of anti-Orientalism and the Supreme Court had made no effort to test their validity. Only long afterward was it determined that the potential for disloyalty among Japanese Americans had been grossly exaggerated and distorted by hysteria, selfish economic interests, and political opportunism. To these factors must be added the failure of the press to exercise its traditional responsibility of questioning allegations and digging for the truth. As a matter of fact, much of the West Coast press not only accepted and published as gospel the most hysterical of charges, but also used them to carry on what amounted to an editorial vendetta against Japanese Americans and what few supporters they had. The facts are that despite widely aired fears of espionage and sabotage, not a single charge was filed against Japanese Americans on these counts.

In Yasui's appeal, the same constitutional issues found in the Hirabayashi case were ruled applicable. However, the Supreme Court overruled the contention that Yasui had lost his American citizenship. The legality of the Evacuation was not an issue in the Yasui case. That matter was to be tested later in the Korematsu and Endo cases.

No strong legal or ideological considerations had motivated Fred Toyosaburo Korematsu, a Nisei nurseryman in Oakland, California. He simply didn't want to be evacuated for personal reasons. Korematsu had been arrested for failing to obey evacuation orders, convicted of the charge, placed on probation for five years, and sent off to the camp he had sought to avoid. A flaming California civil libertarian, Wayne M. Collins, took Korematsu's appeal to the Supreme Court.

Mitsuye Endo's case was somewhat different. American-born, as were all the others who took their grievances to the Supreme Court, she had been employed by the state of California prior to the war. She was chosen by a San Francisco attorney, James Purcell, as a guinea pig to test the federal government's authority to imprison Japanese Americans without charge or trial. With her permission a *habeas corpus* petition was filed on her behalf in July, 1942, shortly before she was moved from an Assembly Center to the Tule Lake WRA camp. It took a whole year for a federal judge to rule that the government had acted legally in depriving Mitsuye Endo of her freedom. Purcell promptly appealed.

The Korematsu case was heard by the Supreme Court October 11 and 12, 1944, and oral arguments in the Endo case also were heard on the twelfth. Just a little more than two months later the high court announced its judgment. The court acknowledged, six to three, that the Army had the authority to order citizens of Japanese ancestry from specific military areas. Korematsu was ruled guilty of remaining in a prohibited area. Mr. Justice Hugo Black, speaking for the majority, wrote that Korematsu "was excluded because we are at war with the Japanese Empire, because the properly constituted military authorities feared an invasion of our West Coast and felt constrained to take proper security measures, because they decided that the military urgency of the situation demanded that all citizens of Japanese ancestry be segregated from the West Coast temporarily, and finally, because Congress, reposing its confidence in this time of war in our military leaders—as inevitably it must—determined that they should have the power to do just this."

However, it is significant that the court's united front on issues pertaining to the Nisei as demonstrated in the Yasui and Hirabayashi cases was broken. Justices Owen J. Roberts, Frank Murphy, and Robert H. Jackson found Korematsu's constitutional rights had been violated. Murphy described the mass incarceration of Japanese Americans, as contrasted to the individual hearings provided persons of German and Italian ancestry, a clear case of legalized racism. "Racial discrimination in any form and in any degree," he contended, "has no justifiable part whatsoever in our democratic way of life." Jackson raised an issue which has continued to disturb civil libertarians. He charged that the court's majority validated the principle of racial discrimination in an emergency, and he warned that this principle is a "loaded weapon ready for the hand of any authority that can bring forward a plausible claim of an urgent need."

If a small crack had been chiseled into the legalized restrictions against Nisei by the Korematsu decision, they were brought tumbling down in the Mitsuye Endo case.[8] The Supreme Court found unanimously that since the Evacuation was a security measure, once her loyalty had been established she could not be kept in custody; as an American citizen she was free to come and go as she pleased anywhere in the United States, and that of course included the West Coast.

Thus the Endo decision had the effect of bringing the inglorious Evacuation episode to an end, spurring the various government agencies to speed up a program actually begun earlier that fall. WRA officials had been growing progressively more disturbed by the continued incarceration of Japanese Americans while the military need for keeping them off the West Coast had vanished. Under WRA pressure the Army quietly had been allowing a few selected evacuees to return to their homes. Some 2,000 of them were back in the restricted area by the time the Supreme Court announced its judgment. WRA quickly announced the movement out of the camps would be speeded up and all the centers closed before the end of 1945 regardless of what happened in the war. Eventually, of course, the Army would have had to make some sort of decision about the fate of the people it had herded into concentration camps. However, there is no doubt that the litigation pressed by Hirabayashi and Yasui served to make the courts aware of the constitutional dilemmas posed by the Evacuation, and later the Korematsu and Endo cases hurried the tortuous course of justice by forcing the Army to revoke its exclusion orders before it was willing to face the issue.

The trek back to the West Coast was about to get under way in earnest, but back to what? Jobs, savings, and property had vanished. Much of the hostility hadn't; in fact, the racists had taken advantage of the exile of Japanese Americans to demand their permanent exclusion. For the evacuees, in addition to the demands of re-establishing themselves and making up for three years of lost time, the fight to seek legal redress for the many kinds of legalized injustice that still remained was just getting started.

Initially, however, it was necessary to rebuild an economic base. The War Relocation Authority assumed responsibility for basic needs such as transportation from the camps back to the West Coast and help with temporary housing, but the government's pitifully inadequate performance was in contrast to the dispatch with which the Japanese Americans had been moved out of their homes. As well intentioned as WRA was, the task of restoring individual and community life was beyond its resources. That could be accomplished only by time and the energies and determination of the Japanese Americans themselves with a helping hand from such organizations as the Pacific Coast Committee on American Principles and Fair Play. JACL offices were established in San Francisco, Los Angeles, and Seattle to assist returning evacuees, but a more far-reaching program was even then taking shape.

It was unveiled at what was designated as JACL's Ninth Biennial Convention, held in Denver in late February of 1946.[9] (The emergency conference held in Salt Lake City in 1942, and another sparsely attended conference in 1944 were designated as the Seventh and Eighth conventions.) Twenty chapters were represented in Denver, but only two—San Francisco and San Jose—were reactivated West Coast chapters. They represented 1,547 active members and 1,177

associates (meaning they were not affiliated with any particular chapters), up substantially from the wartime low of 865 and 940 associates.

The Denver convention had opened on an euphoric note. The war
was over, the Nisei had come through their ordeal with their loyalty
firmly established, and now the time was ripe for a frontal assault
on legalized discrimination. But the delegates were hardly prepared
for the sweeping program that the league's wartime president, Saburo
Kido, proposed. He demanded a mandate from JACL to seek naturalization rights for the Issei, indemnity from the federal government
for monetary losses suffered in the Evacuation, and ultimately, elimination of racial discrimination in immigration laws.

The fact Japanese aliens were by law ineligible for citizenship had
been at the root of their problems. A law that would make citizenship
attainable without regard to race would be the cornerstone of the
fight to see that the sacrifices paid in the Evacuation would not have
been in vain. Mike Masaoka, freshly returned from service with the
442nd in Europe, was dispatched by JACL to Washington to lobby
for legal justice.

But first there were a good many other matters that required urgent
attention.

XVII ☙ Tumbling Barriers

Even before any substantial numbers of Japanese Americans began to return to California the state legislature threw up a roadblock, in the form of a mandate to press escheat cases, in an effort to discourage their coming home. Escheat cases referred to allegedly illegal purchases of land by Japanese aliens. Ever since 1920, when aliens ineligible to citizenship (meaning Japanese) were prohibited from owning land in California, a sort of cat and mouse game had been under way. Issei farmers bought land in the names of their minor citizen-children, duly deeding it to them as gifts, and operating the farms as trustees. This was a perfectly legal maneuver and probably would not have been questioned if aliens other than Japanese had been involved. Sporadically, however, these transfers of property had been challenged in escheat suits with the state confiscating the land when it won. Early in 1945, when it became evident the Japanese Americans would be coming back to California, the legislature appropriated $200,000 to be used by the attorney general to press escheat actions.[1] To encourage filing of such cases, county governments were offered half of whatever the escheated property was sold for.

Between 1944 and 1948 some 200 escheat suits were filed. The defendants had a choice of fighting the suits in court or "compromising" the action by paying the state half of the land's appraised value to quiet title. Such payments amounted to nothing more than extortion. Yet, to avoid almost certain confiscation of their property, a dozen cases were "compromised" by payment of more than $230,000.

A few landowners, unwilling to submit to such officially inspired outrage, went to court. The most notable of these cases involved Fred Oyama,[2] born in California in 1928. He was sixteen years old at the time the state brought escheat action. The facts of the case were that Oyama's parents, Kajiro and Kohide Oyama, Japanese aliens, had bought six acres of farmland near San Diego in 1934, and two additional acres in 1937. Both were in Fred's name. In 1935 the elder

Oyama went to court and was named legal guardian of his minor son's estate. From time to time Oyama went back to court to seek, and be granted, approval for various business transactions on behalf of his son's property. Every action had been legal and above board. The Oyama family was evacuated in 1942. Then, unexpectedly, the escheat suit was filed in 1944, at a time the Oyamas could not return to California to defend themselves against a charge that the two parcels had been purchased with intent to violate the alien land law.

While the Oyama case was making its way through the California court system, hostile old-line California elements introduced a proposal to make existing alien land laws a part of the state constitution.[3] It was called Proposition 15 and titled "Validation of Legislative Amendments to Alien Land Law." Proposition 15 was pushed by powerful, well-financed interests. The opposition was led by a still financially shaky JACL. With a war chest of only slightly more than $100,000, JACL sought to convince California voters of the injustice of Proposition 15 through the newspapers, an informational pamphlet, and frequent public appearances.

Just five days before the election on November 5, 1946, the California Supreme Court upheld the state's seizure of Oyama's land. The outlook for defeating Proposition 15 appeared dark, but fortunately the California of 1946 was not the California of 1920. New generations had reached voting age. Veterans of World War II brought to the election their own point of view. The influx of tens of thousands of war workers unindoctrinated in California's anti-Orientalism introduced a strong new element to the electorate. To all of these elements the JACL argument was persuasive and together with reasonable members of the old California population, they defeated Proposition 15 by a margin of 1,143,780 to 797,067.

The Oyama decision was appealed to the U.S. Supreme Court with JACL and other organizations filing *amicus curiae* briefs. Finally, on January 19, 1948, another long step toward equal treatment under the laws was achieved when the California verdict was reversed. Unfortunately, instead of attacking the alien land law head on, the high tribunal focused on Fred Oyama's rights as an American citizen. It found that California's alien land law clearly discriminated against Fred in that obstacles, which would not apply to minors of other ethnic origins, were placed in the way of Fred's right to receive property from his parents. The decision had the effect of making the alien land law unenforceable as it related to ownership by citizen-minors of Japanese ancestry, and eventually the pending escheat cases were dropped. A frontal attack on the alien land law itself was to come later.

Meanwhile, JACL was moving to carry out the mandate of its Denver convention on the national scene. Working out of his apartment in Washington, Mike Masaoka registered as a lobbyist and began a determined campaign to acquaint Congress with JACL's goals. One observer has noted that Masaoka skillfully exploited the sense of guilt that Americans were coming to feel concerning the Evacuation and a new social climate among legislators partially compounded of the revelations concerning the behavior of Nazi Germany toward another minority. Masaoka's strategy was relatively simple. He would find the source of power in the various pertinent committees, then devise ways of meeting them so that he could present his case. Masaoka's natural eloquence was reinforced by his obvious sincerity. Robert M. Cullum, a former WRA employee who worked with Masaoka during this period, has suggested that the angels were on JACL's side—all it sought was equity and justice—and Masaoka orchestrated it all in a campaign based on tireless work.

Perhaps the first significant victory was in the Soldier Brides Act, designed to enable American servicemen to marry Japanese women and bring them home to the United States.[4] Without such an act, the brides would have been barred by the provisions of the 1924 immigration law. President Truman signed the measure on July 22, 1947. It provided that "the alien spouse of an American veteran or serviceman, irrespective of race, may enter the United States for permanent residence, provided that the marriage took place within 30 days after the enactment of the Act."

The key words were "irrespective of race." They signaled significant progress in Congress and the nation at large on racial attitudes. The changing attitudes were further underscored by the report of Truman's Presidential Committee on Civil Rights, released October 20, 1947. One part of the report dealt with Japanese Americans and recommended passage of "evacuation claims and naturalization legislation" and urged the various states "to repeal discriminatory laws." Masaoka, a consultant to the committee, obviously had some input.[5] The report became the basis of President Truman's civil rights program recommended to Congress in 1948.

The significant words appeared again in a bill, signed June 1, 1948, offering citizenship "irrespective of race" to aliens who had served in the American armed forces during World War I or World War II, without the necessity of taking the usual examinations. The inclusion of World War I gave Issei, who had not availed themselves of their right to naturalization in 1935, a new opportunity.

In terms of numbers affected, another JACL-backed bill—to block the arbitrary deportation of certain classes of Japanese aliens—was more important. These included treaty merchants—persons who had entered the United States before the war as merchants and business-men and who had acquired citizen- or resident-alien spouses and citizen-children—students, and temporary visitors who had spent the war years here. President Truman signed the measure on July 1, 1948. The bill made the Japanese, as other aliens, eligible to seek suspension of deportation on a plea of economic hardship to their citizen families, or on grounds of seven years continuous residence in the United States.

Even before President Truman's civil rights message, Congress in response to Masaoka's efforts had begun consideration of a bill to compensate evacuees for material losses. The Evacuation Claims Act was passed without dissent and President Truman signed it on July 2, 1948. By the deadline of January 3, 1950, 23,689 claims totaling $131,949,176 were filed. (The Federal Reserve Bank in 1942 had estimated the loss at $400,000,000.) Sixty percent of the claims were for less than $2,500, representing loss of household items; 73 percent were under $5,000.

Typically, the Department of Justice, which administered the claims program, misunderstood the intent of Congress, which was to offer the evacuees some sort of compensation for their losses. The bureaucrats took the position that their responsibility was to challenge every claim. In all of 1950 they approved only 137 of 211 claims; the successful claimants had asked an average of $1,030 each and the government agreed to pay an average of $450. It had cost the govern-ment an average of $1,400 per case to find that a payment of $450 was justified.[6] At this rate it would have taken ten years to settle all the claims with far more being spent to administer the program than to pay the claimants. Congress then ordered a simplified procedure whereby the claimants could be paid three fourths of the amount of a claim, or $2,500, whichever was less, without question. Even so, the final claim wasn't settled until 1965. A total of about $38,000,000 was paid, approximately ten cents for each dollar of loss. Inflation had eroded the purchasing power of the award even further. Many persons, unable to come up with the documentation needed to prove loss, had failed to file claims or were turned down when they did. The program had not taken into account loss of time or earning

The bitter road "home." At war's end, aliens who felt they had no future in the United States asked to be sent to Japan. Here, some of them board an American military transport. NATIONAL ARCHIVES

Nisei soldiers stationed in Japan were among the first to be rushed to Korea when war broke out in 1950. Cpl. Susumu Shinagawa of Hawaii was captured, returned home to a tearful greeting after prisoner exchange. U.S. ARMY PHOTO

But others weren't so fortunate. Bronze Star medal awarded posthumously to Pfc. Yoshinobu Gusukuma of Hawaii was presented to his father, Gazo Shiroma, by Lieutenant General John W. O'Daniel. U.S. ARMY PHOTO

Exemplary conduct of Japanese American civilians and soldiers opened way to citizenship for Asians. Mass swearing-in ceremony was held in Honolulu. HAWAII TIMES PHOTO

Raisuke Fujii of Seattle, newly naturalized as an American citizen, shows his wife how to operate a voting machine. Fujii came to the United States in 1906, his wife in 1915. ELMER OGAWA

Where Japanese immigrants had cultivated truck gardens, their offspring became scientific farmers on a large scale. Bob Sakata of Brighton, Colorado, farms several thousand acres. TAK MURAKAMI COLLECTION

Dr. Newton Wesley (Uyesugi) of Chicago, pioneer developer of contact lenses, displays models he uses in lectures. TAK MURAKAMI COLLECTION

First Nisei jurist on the mainland was John Aiso of Los Angeles, appointed by Governor Earl Warren. PACIFIC CITIZEN

Japanese Americans are about evenly divided between Christians and Buddhists. Bishop Kenryu Tsuji, born and educated in Canada, heads Buddhist Churches of America. TAK MURAKAMI COLLECTION

Pioneer labor contractor Naoichi Hokazono is commemorated in stained glass in Colorado State Capitol window designed by Issei artist Yuri Noda. TOM MASAMORI COLLECTION

War Relocation Camps were quickly abandoned but the dead were re-membered in pilgrimages. The Rev. Unryu Sugiyama of Denver conducts services at Granada campsite in southeastern Colorado. TOM MASAMORI COLLECTION

Many Sansei were swept up by social-protest movements. These Los Angeles Sansei march in an anti-war protest. PACIFIC CITIZEN

Nisei quickly took advantage of economic and professional opportunity after World War II. Minoru Yamasaki, who heads his own architectural firm in Troy, Michigan, has designed scores of outstanding buildings including World Trade Center in New York City.

First Nisei to win stardom on Broadway was Pat Suzuki, singer and actress. TAK MURAKAMI COLLECTION

Actor George Takei can handle Japanese roles as well as Shakespeare or fly a Star Trek spaceship. VISUAL COMMUNICATIONS

George Ariyoshi, a Democrat of Hawaii, became first Nisei to be elected governor. PACIFIC CITIZEN

District Judge Robert M. Takasugi of Los Angeles, first mainland Nisei to be named to the federal bench. ERNIE AYALA

U.S. Senator Daniel K. Inouye (far right), first Nisei in Congress, was a member of the committee that conducted the Watergate hearings. Inouye, a Democrat, was elected Hawaii's first representative in Congress in 1959, elected to the Senate in 1962. PACIFIC CITIZEN

Hawaii's other senator is Spark M. Matsunaga, also a Democrat. Like Inouye, Matsunaga served in the House of Representatives and is a decorated veteran of World War II. FUMI KUWAYAMA

Senator S. I. Hayakawa, California Republican, was elected in his first political race after winning fame as the no-nonsense president of strife-ridden San Francisco State.

Democrat Norman Y. Mineta (left) was elected to Congress in 1974 after serving as mayor of San Jose. ASSOCIATED PRESS

MR. MATSUI

Newest Japanese American member of Congress is Robert T. Matsui, former Sacramento city councilman, elected in 1978. Matsui is a Democrat.

power. Masaoka observed that "the psychological aspect of the legislation may far outweigh the financial benefits." [7]

Of greater and more lasting significance was JACL's successful drive to win naturalization for the parent generation, a victory somewhat marred by accusations of compromise with principle. As it turned out, the noble proposal to extend citizenship to the Issei became tangled in the vicious political in-fighting of Senator Joseph McCarthy's anti-Communist crusade. From JACL's viewpoint, the winning of naturalization rights for the Issei was the keystone of its postwar program. Masaoka would have preferred to see a simple measure eliminating race as a consideration in the naturalization of aliens, but the obvious way often is not the route taken in Washington. In the end, Masaoka's strategy became of necessity one of getting whatever help he could from whatever source without alienating either liberals or conservatives.

Soon after the end of World War II, Congressman Walter H. Judd, a Minnesota Republican and former medical missionary in China, became interested in legislation to remove racial discrimination from immigration and naturalization laws. He filed such a measure in 1947, and it quickly moved through the House but became stranded in the Senate. In 1949, with Masaoka's encouragement, he introduced a similar bill. It passed the House unanimously, but the Senate turned down broad changes in the law. The bill the Senate passed limited naturalization to Japanese already in the United States. A conference committee restored the House provision but added rigid security measures in keeping with the current political climate. The overwhelming fear in Congress at the time was Communist infiltration of the government and the nation; basic human rights were seriously jeopardized by some of the acts to control communism. Because of these provisions, President Truman vetoed the immigration and naturalization measure even though it carried out a part of his civil rights program.

Masaoka, representing the JACL's Anti-Discrimination Committee, supported the effort to override the veto, which failed. His rationale for pushing a measure that compromised civil rights was that since a bill containing even harsher internal security provisions was already in the legislative mill, the President should have signed the bill providing naturalization for the Issei.[8]

The measure that Masaoka referred to was the Internal Security Act of 1950, also known as the McCarran concentration camp measure. Its Title II authorized the President to order detention without trial of persons suspected as potential spies or saboteurs in case of invasion, insurrection, or declaration of war. In effect, Title II codified the incarceration of Japanese Americans during World War II and made the same kind of treatment a possibility for all citizens in a future emergency. President Truman vetoed the Internal Security Act, declaring: ". . . the bill opens a Pandora's Box of opportunities for official condemnation of organizations and individuals for perfectly honest opinions. The basic error of these sections is that they move in the direction of suppressing opinion and belief—a long step toward totalitarianism." But such was the fear of communism stirred up by McCarthy that Congress passed the detention measure over the veto. Masaoka explains that JACL not only opposed Title II, but also Title I which was directed at controlling allegedly subversive activities. It is to JACL's credit that some years later, after the dust had a chance to settle, its National Committee to Repeal the Emergency Detention Act mounted a frontal attack on the concentration camp law. Ultimately, Congress repealed the law and President Nixon signed the measure in September of 1971.

In the 1952 congressional session, Masaoka plotted a new and direct assault on discriminatory provisions of the immigration and naturalization laws. Judd was anxious to lead the fight once more. However, the Republican congressman ran into Democratic Speaker Sam Rayburn's partisanship. As Judd recalled recently for JACL researcher Harry Takagi, Rayburn realized the Judd bill would pass but he wanted the Democrats to get credit for it. So Rayburn persuaded Judd to let Francis Walter, a Democrat from Pennsylvania and also a friend of JACL, introduce the bill. Pat McCarran, the Nevada Democrat whose name oddly enough was attached to the concentration camp bill, was persuaded to sponsor a bill in the Senate similar to Walter's and the measure came to be known as the Walter-McCarran Act. It was substantially more comprehensive than the original Judd bill had been. The Walter-McCarran measure provided in effect for repeal of the Oriental Exclusion Act of 1924, extending to all Asian nations a token immigration quota, and eliminating race as a barrier to naturalization. These were provisions that President Truman approved. But he opposed other provisions of the act which he felt implanted more firmly into law the internal security measures which were part of the concentration camp law. Once more the desirable immigration and naturalization reforms fell victim to a veto directed against unrelated measures.

Congress passed the Walter-McCarran Act just as JACL was about to meet in convention in San Francisco. The veto came while the Nisei were in session. In a late-night strategy meeting, Masaoka urged all JACL members to telegraph their senators and congressmen, and write to editors of hometown newspapers to ask that the veto be overridden. Congress acted quickly, the House voting 278 to 113, and the Senate 57 to 26, to defeat the President. Harry Takagi, who was at the convention, recalls:

"I can never forget the emotional scene that resulted when the delegates were told that the bill had been passed. It was the culmination of our dreams, an extremely emotional moment. I can't think of any other legislative action that so united the JACL. The bill established our parents as the legal equal of other Americans; it gave the Japanese equality with all other immigrants, and that was a principle we had been struggling for from the very beginning."

Some observers downplay the importance of JACL's effort to override the veto, asserting that rebellious Democrats had joined Republicans to ride roughshod over Truman's wishes in the past and probably were ripe for another revolt. These same observers suggest JACL took an extremely parochial position in judging the immigration and naturalization provisions affecting the Japanese to be more important than the repressive internal security portions of the measure.

To this, Congressman Judd has a reply: "In politics you cannot draw up a bill that pleases everybody. You ought to go ahead and get the best you can. JACL, I think, wisely agreed to support the Walter-McCarran Bill. I've never had a qualm about this. There has never been one incident to indicate the un-wisdom of the decision. Most progress in government comes from minorities who have a cause, who are dedicated to it and are convinced it is right, and will work at it— which was JACL's role." [9]

It did not take long for the Issei to avail themselves of the privilege of joining their children in American citizenship. By 1965, about 46,000 of them had become citizens of a country in which they had labored hard and to which they had contributed much. Overall, JACL, through the skill of its representative, Masaoka, probably gained much more influence in Washington than it enjoyed with the Japanese American community at large. Its record is an interesting example of the way in which a relatively small but well-organized group can achieve results when it focuses upon clear but limited objectives, particularly when those objectives right basic wrongs.

However, not even Masaoka's skills and JACL's earnest concerns could have brought about the important legislative measures discussed in this chapter if the behavior of the Japanese Americans themselves had not been exemplary. In later years when revolt became a popular credo, activists among the younger generation of Japanese Americans condemned the Issei and Nisei for having accepted the government's Evacuation order. They criticized Nisei men for stepping out of the concentration camps to offer their lives in the service of the nation that had betrayed them. JACL and Masaoka had urged Japanese Americans to cooperate with their government, unjust though its demands seemed at the time, as a patriotic duty in the clearly expressed hope that their sacrifice in the name of loyalty would lead to the righting of wrongs when the emergency was ended. That hope bore fruit as Masaoka seized every opportunity to tell the story of the loyalty of Japanese Americans, dramatically demonstrated by their record on both the military and home fronts. That record proved to be a telling argument for righting historic wrongs.

While all this was going on, Japanese Americans under JACL leadership continued to chip away at other discriminatory laws. In 1944 the Colorado state legislature had voted narrowly to submit an anti-alien land law to the people as a constitutional amendment. The proposal was defeated by a substantial margin. In Utah, however, the legislature did pass an alien land law during the war years. In February, 1947, the Utah legislature repealed the law under heavy pressure from veterans' groups whose support had been rallied by JACL. Two years later another victory was scored in Oregon. There the State Supreme Court reversed a lower court decision in a suit brought by Kenji Namba, a Nisei. Namba and his father, an alien, had sought to lease farmland in 1947. The state ruled that since no treaty existed between Japan and the United States, the lease was invalid. The high court found that the ruling was an infringement upon the equal protection provision of the Fourteenth Amendment and declared the entire alien land law illegal.

In each instance, however, there were minor points left unsettled which made continued litigation necessary. Two landmark cases finally provided definite judgments. The first was brought by Sei Fujii, a veteran Issei newspaper publisher in Los Angeles.[10] In the Oyama case the courts supported the plaintiff but had avoided ruling on the legality of California's alien land law. Fujii purchased an unimproved city lot to provoke a direct test of the land law. The state responded by moving to escheat the property. However, a new element was introduced into the legal picture. A district court ruled that the United Nations Charter, to which the United States subscribed, now enjoyed constitutional force within the country. The charter guaranteed rights and freedoms "without distinction of any kind such as race, color, sex, language, religious, political or other opinion, national or social origin, property, birth or other status." Therefore, the court ruled, California's alien land law was "untenable and unenforceable." The majority of the California Supreme Court in the spring of 1952 also found the alien land law was a violation of the equal protection clauses of both state and federal constitutions. Chief Justice Phil S. Gibson had this to say in the majority opinion:

> The California Alien Land Law is obviously designed and administered as an instrument effectuating racial discrimination, and the most searching examination discloses no circumstances justifying classification on that basis. There is nothing to indicate that those alien residents who are racially ineligible for citizenship possess characteristics which are dangerous to the legitimate interests of the state, or that they, as a class, might use the land for purposes injurious to public morals, safety, or welfare. Accordingly, we hold that the Alien Land Law is invalid as in violation of the 14th Amendment.

The Fujii case thus established the rights of aliens under the Constitution. The second major case, brought by the five sons of Mrs. Haruye Masaoka on her behalf, addressed the California alien land law from the viewpoint of citizen rights.[11] The sons were Ike, Henry, Tad, Mike, of JACL fame, and Joe Grant, all American-born. They transferred title to a lot in Pasadena to their mother, an alien, and proposed to build a home on the property for her use during her lifetime. After her death, the property would revert to the sons. Under the law, however, such a transfer of property was illegal, the state could enforce escheat proceedings, and the citizen-sons would lose their investment. In other words, the Masaoka sons' concern for the comfort and welfare of their mother, which would be considered laudatory under other circumstances, would result in the state penalizing the sons for their charity. The brief filed for the sons did not overlook the fact that three of them had been wounded in action with the 442nd Regimental Combat Team and a fourth had died in combat.

A superior court judge who heard the Masaoka case held the alien land law was unconstitutional because it violated the Fourteenth Amendment. Judge Thurmond Clarke declared the alien land law was directed against persons of Japanese ancestry solely because of their race, that in seeking to prevent them from owning property it violated the equal protection clause, and was unconstitutional "both as to the alien mother and the citizen-son." When the state appealed, the California Supreme Court in the summer of 1952 cited its decision in the Fujii case, returned just three months earlier, as the reason for upholding the lower court decision.

California's forty-year campaign to deny Japanese immigrants in perpetuity the right to till the land except as laborers or tenant farmers had been thoroughly discredited. But there remained one detail of legal housekeeping. The alien land law had been ruled unenforceable and illegal, but it remained in the statute books. In 1956 JACL launched a campaign to repeal the law by the most impressive route possible—a direct vote of the people in a general election. The repeal measure was titled Proposition 13. Thanks to the almost total reversal in public opinion, victory was relatively easy. The newspapers, city and county governing bodies, political leaders, community organizations, labor unions, veterans groups—all of them had endorsed the alien land law when it was first proposed in 1913 and again in 1920— now joined in what amounted to a virtual crusade to wipe the slate clean. JACL leaders campaigned with characteristic zeal but the changing tide of public opinion made their work easy. More than 2.5 million Californians voted for repeal, winning by a two to one margin.[12] Now there remained no legal barriers in the Golden State to prevent Orientals from buying farmland, homes, business buildings, or other real property on the same basis as anyone else.

California had been the bellwether of legalized discrimination by state governments. The changes taking place in California soon were reflected elsewhere; one by one other states took the steps necessary to rid themselves of the taint. But the last of the alien land laws was not eliminated until 1966 when voters of the state of Washington, on the third effort spearheaded by JACL, finally removed this racist legislation from the law books.

However, it should be noted that the campaign for human and civil rights was moving forward on a broad front during the postwar decades. For example, in 1948 the U.S. Supreme Court in the case of *Takahashi* v. *Fish and Game Commission* ruled that California's denial of commercial fishing licenses to Japanese was unconstitutional. The decision had little practical effect since the Issei role in commercial fishing had been wiped out by the Evacuation and they were too old to start over. It was a victory of principle, with such diverse groups as the Congress of Industrial Organizations, the American Veterans Committee, and the National Association for the Advancement of Colored

People joining JACL in the suit. By the same token JACL filed *amicus curiae* briefs in suits successfully challenging the legality of whites-only restrictive covenants on real estate, the segregation of Mexican American children in California schools, and a wide variety of civil rights test cases in which the rights of all Americans, not just the Japanese American minority, were involved. JACL was approaching a level of maturity from where it could look out and express concern on issues beyond its own ethnic interests. Most of the major battles affecting rights of Japanese Americans directly had been won, but two larger matters remained to be addressed.

The first was statehood for the territory of Hawaii. Statehood, with all the benefits and responsibilities of such status, had been a goal of many residents of the Islands since the 1920's. But the large Oriental population—nearly 40 percent of the total was of Japanese descent at one time—had led to fears among some that Hawaii would be dominated economically and politically by people of doubtful allegiance. The performance of Japanese Americans in World War II largely dispelled those fears. Now statehood became a challenge to be met by all Japanese Americans. In the national arena statehood was snagged —as the naturalization measure had been—by extraneous issues. Both Hawaii and Alaska were candidates for statehood. It was obvious Hawaii would go Democratic, Alaska Republican. Hawaii, from the viewpoint of population and development, was better prepared for statehood, but it continued to be delayed as politicians jockeyed for whatever political advantage might accrue from bringing in one or the other first. Finally, it was agreed Alaska could come in first. A presidential proclamation designated Alaska as the forty-ninth state on January 3, 1959. Hawaii by presidential proclamation became the fiftieth state on August 21 that same year.

The honor of becoming Hawaii's first senators went to two oldtime Caucasian pols. But the new state's solo seat in the House of Representatives went to Daniel K. Inouye, the first Nisei in Congress. For Japanese Americans the appearance of a Nisei on the national political scene was as significant as statehood for the Islands. Today Inouye is a senior member of the Senate, a respected member of the inner circle of the Democratic Party's moderate wing.

The other matter was the elimination of the traditional bias in favor of immigration from Northern Europe continued in the Walter-McCarran Act. The so-called National Origins system discriminated against peoples of what was known as the Asia-Pacific Triangle. Under the 1952 law Japan had been allowed an annual immigration quota of 185 but, in contrast to non-Asian countries, ancestry was decisive; anyone of Japanese ancestry entering the United States was charged against that quota. JACL filed a 110-page document arguing for termination of the National Origins system. "The Immigration and Nationality Act," it pointed out, "while removing race as a complete barrier to immigration, limits that liberalization by applying to only the nations of the Asia-Pacific Triangle, or attributable by race to that Triangle, the special discrimination that ancestry, and not place of birth, determines the quota area to which one is chargeable for immigration purposes."

President Truman had denounced the radically discriminatory aspects of the 1952 immigration law, as did Presidents Eisenhower and Kennedy. Finally, the law was changed by Congress during Lyndon Johnson's presidency. In October, 1965, in a ceremony held at Ellis Island, site of the former immigration station in New York harbor, Johnson signed an amendment to the 1952 law eliminating its discriminatory features. It would have been more appropriate had he chosen Angel Island in San Francisco Bay where tens of thousands of Chinese and Japanese immigrants had been held and frequently harassed by insensitive immigration officials. Under the amendment the law would admit up to 350,000 immigrants annually chosen not on the basis of race, nationality, or religious creed, but on the basis of skills needed by the United States and relationship to persons already here. Among the guests invited to witness the signing was Masaoka who had played such an important role in the long, difficult, and finally successful assault on racially discriminatory laws.

Twenty years had passed since the end of World War II, and in that period Japanese Americans had seen improvements in their lot which few could have envisioned. Most of the credit must be given to the Japanese American Citizens League which identified the issues, planned the strategy for addressing them, then carried out the campaign against prejudice and for justice. JACL fought from a position of political weakness but moral strength. This moral position was exploited skillfully, nationally and locally. Some changes might have come even without JACL's efforts, it is true, but it is hardly conceivable that so much could have been achieved so soon without the organization's vigorous, dedicated, and well-devised efforts.

Among a substantial proportion of the Japanese American community JACL has won few plaudits. Hostilities born of the Evacuation era have burned deep into the souls of many. It is true that different policies and different tactics might have been employed at various junctures in the recent history of the Japanese Americans. But it is also true that the leaders may look back on an eminently successful struggle in the period since 1945 and, if virtue is its own reward, reflect with satisfaction on what they have achieved. The status of the Japanese American community today would be far different had it not been for the JACL's efforts, and successes, reported in this chapter.

XVIII ✿ Comeback

In view of the long, stubborn history of anti-Orientalism and the bitterness engendered by World War II, only a surprisingly brief period was required to achieve the primary human rights goals of Japanese Americans.

Less than three years after war's end, in July of 1948, President Truman signed the Japanese American Evacuation Claims Act designed to compensate the evacuees in small part for the material losses they had suffered. Although the Department of Justice made grudging payment of only token sums, Mike Masaoka observed that a major triumph had been won in that Congress "recognized the error of the evacuation and the justice of the claims."

Four years later, in the summer of 1952, a far more significant measure became law—the Walter-McCarran Act eliminating race as a consideration in American immigration and naturalization laws. In effect, it repealed the Immigration Act of 1924 that branded Asians as unworthy of acceptance as immigrants, and opened citizenship to aliens regardless of race. Henceforth, since Issei were made eligible for naturalization, they could not be discriminated against as "persons ineligible to citizenship." This measure made anti-alien land laws moot, but they were laid permanently to rest by the Oyama, Fujii, and Masaoka court tests in the early 1950's, and the overwhelming California vote on Proposition 13 in 1956 that repealed formally the unenforceable alien land laws.

Thus, within a decade after World War II, the legal barriers that had blocked total Japanese American participation in the nation's life had been eliminated. It was a remarkable achievement made possible by the exemplary conduct of Japanese Americans during the war and JACL skill in exploiting a new popular understanding of past injustices.

The reversal of popular attitudes toward Japanese Americans is all the more remarkable in that other American racial minorities, although they had not been subject to mass imprisonment, were only beginning their final struggle for equality. It was not until May 17, 1954, in the case of *Brown* v. *Board of Education*, that the U.S. Supreme Court struck down the longstanding "separate but equal" doctrine and ruled that racial segregation in public schools was unconstitutional. This was the first step in the realization of truly significant changes in American attitudes toward equal treatment for black Americans. Three years later, in September of 1957, President Dwight D. Eisenhower ordered U. S. troops into Little Rock, Arkansas, to enforce a federal court order requiring the previously all-white Central High School to enroll black students. In 1960, public facilities were desegregated following a series of lunch counter sit-ins by blacks and whites together. But in 1963, a full decade after former "enemy alien" Japanese had been extended citizenship rights, black Americans were still fighting for equality. On August 28 of that year Dr. Martin Luther King delivered his "I have a dream" speech before some 200,000 persons taking part in a human rights rally in Washington. King declared: "I have a dream that this nation will rise up and live out of the true meaning of its creed, 'We hold these truths to be self-evident, that all men are created equal.'"

Rank and file Japanese Americans on the whole looked with sympathy on the black struggle in common with most Americans of good will, but with a few notable exceptions gave them little active support. Mostly, they were thoroughly preoccupied with the routines of the work-a-day world, making up for years of repression and the disruption of the Evacuation—rearing families, building businesses and job seniority, seeking their share of the good life. Despite the more tolerant environment, this was not easy. The median age of Issei males at the time of the evacuation was fifty-five, the women forty-seven. Nisei had a median age of only seventeen years. Having lost virtually all that they had saved and built prior to the war, many Issei found an economic comeback virtually impossible. For them, and for the younger Nisei, there was no GI bill to help ease the transition back to normal life. And yet, the Issei's traditional diligence, fortitude, and ability to persevere enabled most of them to come back, often in jobs for which they had little experience. Men who had farmed for years moved into the cities and became gardeners. Shopkeepers worked as waiters and dishwashers until they could set aside enough capital to go into business. Step by step they made their way back.

During 1964–66, roughly two decades after the end of the Evacuation period, the Japanese American Research Project at the University of California at Los Angeles interviewed a random sample of 1,002 Issei. Assistant Professor Darrel Montero, now of the University of Maryland, reported on some of these findings in 1978. He writes: [1]

> In order to determine the extent to which the Issei felt they had achieved their goals in life, we asked our respondents: "Have you achieved the place in life that you wanted for yourself and your family?" Three in four Issei reported that they had in fact achieved their goals. When asked what factors had contributed to their success, three-quarters of the Issei reported that diligence, hard work, honesty and thrift were responsible. Other reasons which contributed to the Issei's success (in order of frequency) included health, good luck, and shrewdness.
>
> In order to determine how the Issei are faring economically, we asked if they were financially dependent upon their children for support. Six in ten of our respondents reported that they are completely financially independent of their offspring. In contrast, however, almost one in five reported that they received over one-half of their financial support from their children.

While Issei were inclined to think of success (*seiko*, in Japanese) in economic terms, many undoubtedly would agree with the suggestion that their greatest achievement was in producing and rearing the Nisei generation despite the wide generational and cultural gap that separated them. Burdened by the pressures of keeping their families fed, clothed, and sheltered, few Issei had the time to be companions to their children. Many were old enough to be grandparents of their own offspring. The product of strict upbringings in Japan, Issei found it difficult to accept the free and easy customs the Nisei learned at school and from their white classmates. Language was a barrier that blocked family discussions that might have brought about an understanding of cultural differences. American dating habits, which Nisei quickly adopted, scandalized the Issei. In the late 1930's, Japan's military aggression in China became another source of conflict in Japanese American families with the Issei defending Japan's actions and Nisei criticizing them. It was common for Issei to regard their children as disrespectful, lazy, thoughtless, ill-mannered, and for the Nisei to consider their parents hopelessly rigid and old-fashioned.

The evacuation experience did much to modify these perceptions. Each generation came to respect the fortitude with which the other bore up under injustice and hardship. While some Issei resented the way Nisei moved into the vacuum left by the arrest of community leaders, most were willing to concede that the English-speaking younger generation must now take over. Many Issei urged their children to relocate to Midwestern and Eastern cities rather than stagnate in the camps, and when the Nisei had established themselves the parents joined them to start a new life. On the other hand, there were stormy family sessions in the camps with the Issei parents unable to overcome their affection for the homeland and unwilling to permit their children to cut familial ties by leaving the camps to head out on their own.

At the end of the war, readjustment was another wrenching experience which the Nisei could cope with much more easily than their parents. In their sunset years, the Issei watched with satisfaction as the Nisei began their climb up the economic, social, and political ladder, reaching goals that the Issei had dreamed about but knew they would never realize. In the Nisei, they saw the extension of their own hopes and Nisei accomplishments gave them much to be proud of.

Where Issei farmers had eked out a living on a few acres of truck crops tended as carefully as gardens, their sons extended their operations over hundreds and sometimes thousands of acres. The Issei truck gardener farmed with the help of his family. His sons were quick to utilize machinery and the latest scientific techniques developed at the agricultural schools. The Issei took his produce to market in a rickety truck piled high with crates; his son sent huge trailer-loads to the cannery or heavily laden refrigerated semi-trucks to markets on the other side of the continent.

Other Issei were delighted that the educations their sons and daughters had acquired, often at great family sacrifice, were beginning to pay off. Back in the 1930's, when the doors of job opportunity seldom opened for Japanese Americans, Nisei educated as engineers were pumping gas in service stations, business majors helped run the family grocery store, trained teachers went home to the farm or transplanted seedlings in the nursery. It was not at all uncommon for young men who had a Phi Beta Kappa key hidden away in a drawer at home to be working fifteen hours a day in a fruit stand because there was no other employment to be had.

The education and the diligent work-habits developed during the hard times proved to be priceless assets when at last, under the pressures of wartime manpower shortages and WRA's determined efforts to find employment for the relocatees, job opportunities opened up. At war's end, thousands of Nisei who had relocated to places such as Chicago, Cleveland, St. Louis, New York, Washington, D.C., Denver, and Salt Lake City decided to remain. They had sunk their roots deep into friendly soil. They had little to draw them back to the West Coast other than memories. But thousands of others went "home" and quickly made the best of a changed environment. Largely liberated from the millstone of anti-Orientalism, they found their skills were salable. They obtained employment as engineers and architects, city planners and technicians, teachers and administrators, chemists and laboratory aides. Nisei doctors, dentists, and attorneys found they were developing multiracial practices. This is not to say that racial discrimination had been eliminated. Stubborn pockets of bigotry remained, but they became the exception rather than the rule and could be attacked effectively.

The story of Earl Warren is illustrative of the West's, and the nation's, changing regard for Japanese Americans. A product of traditional California politics, Warren as attorney general in 1942 had been one of the most vigorous advocates of Evacuation. He was among the "best people" whose opinions of the "Japanese problem" helped persuade General DeWitt that the Evacuation was necessary. Then, as governor of California, Warren strongly opposed the return of the evacuees to the West Coast.

But once the U.S. Supreme Court in the Endo case ruled they could return, and the federal government made it official policy, Warren urged their acceptance and moved to protect them from hoodlum elements. In one of his last acts as governor before going to Washington as Chief Justice of the Supreme Court in 1953, Warren named John Aiso as a municipal court judge in Los Angeles. He was the first mainland Nisei to attain a judicial position. Aiso said that he felt Warren's recognition that a Nisei was worthy of serving in the judicial system of his beloved California was his signal that he had been wrong about the Evacuation. Some observers believe that Warren's realization of the injustice inflicted on Japanese Americans had much to do with the strong liberal stance in defense of human rights that characterized the Warren court. In that sense, one journalist has suggested, the Nisei may have paid the ransom that finally liberated the blacks. In life Warren could never bring himself to admit he had erred in 1942. But in his memoirs, published posthumously, Warren wrote: [2]

. . . I have since deeply regretted the removal order and my own testimony advocating it, because it was not in keeping with our American concept of freedom and the rights of citizens. Whenever I thought of the innocent little children who were torn from home, school friends, and congenial surroundings, I was conscience-stricken. It was wrong to react so impulsively, without positive evidence of disloyalty, even though we felt we had a good motive in the security of our state. It demonstrates the cruelty of war when fear, get-tough military psychology, propaganda and racial antagonism combine with one's responsibility for public security to produce such acts.

After Aiso's appointment, other Nisei were named to the bench in various parts of the West, as well as in Philadelphia. Senior in rank among them is Federal District Judge Robert Takasugi in Los Angeles. Nisei ran for and were elected to a variety of posts—city councils, school boards, municipal clerkships—until such achievements became almost commonplace. Two Nisei are members of the California State Assembly, Paul Bannai, a Republican, and Floyd Mori, Democrat. A roster of Asian Americans elected to public posts, compiled in 1979 by Don T. Nakanishi of UCLA, lists nearly 100 from mainland states. Other Japanese Americans were elected presidents of civic clubs and library boards, attesting to their acceptance in an integrated society. And they have made a substantial splash on the national political scene.

Hawaii's Daniel K. Inouye led the way when he was elected the state's first congressman in 1959. He was re-elected in 1960, then elected to the Senate in 1962. When Inouye moved up to the Senate, Spark M. Matsunaga won his House seat. And when Hawaii was given a second House seat, Patsy Takemoto Mink won it. At one time Hawaii's entire congressional delegation was of Asian descent—Inouye and Hiram Fong in the Senate, and Matsunaga and Mink in the House. When Fong retired in 1976, Matsunaga defeated Mink in the Democratic primary and went on to win the seat handily. Meanwhile, they have been joined by three Nisei from the mainland. The first to enter Congress was Norman Y. Mineta, the former mayor of San Jose, who was elected to represent California's 13th District in 1974. He was re-elected in 1976 and 1978. A second Japanese American, Robert T. Matsui, former Sacramento city councilman, was elected from California's 3rd District in 1978. All these Nisei are Democrats and labored long in the political vineyards to gain party support. Samuel Ichiye Hayakawa took a different road. Born in Canada, he was a well-known semanticist when a sensational campus revolt propelled him into the national spotlight. Student radicals had all but paralyzed San Francisco State College in 1968 when Hayakawa, a professor of English approaching retirement age, accepted its presidency. Parlaying firmness and flamboyance—prime time TV showed him, tam-o'-shanter perched on his graying head, leaping aboard a rebel sound-truck and jerking loudspeaker wires loose—he put down the revolt and restored order. Conservative Californians cheered and radicals (including some Japanese American students) jeered.

At age seventy-two Hayakawa rode the crest of that fame to run for the U.S. Senate on the Republican ticket in 1976. He won by nearly a quarter million votes. That 3,748,973 Californians would cast their ballots for a naturalized Japanese American to represent them in the Senate of the United States was a remarkable phenomenon. This was persuasive evidence that for all practical purposes the "Yellow Peril" had been laid to rest.

But Hayakawa's victory drew scant applause from some young Japanese Americans who regarded him as a hopeless reactionary. There is no way to determine how many Japanese American Democrats crossed party lines to vote for Hayakawa, but in many cases political ideology proved dominant over ethnic affinity.

The Japanese American community did not escape the polarization that divided the nation during the Vietnam War period. As the Nisei as a group grew older and more established economically, they tended to become more conservative. They viewed with increasing uneasiness what they perceived to be the radicalization of an important Sansei segment. The concern turned to alarm as Sansei activists, adopting the long hair and rhetoric that had become the hallmark of the radical movement, sided with Cesar Chavez and his agricultural workers in their struggle against farmers of the Central Valley, some of whom were Nisei.

The new activism surfaced in ways unique to the Japanese Americans. One of its earlier manifestations was the controversy over the title of a history of the Japanese in the United States commissioned by JACL's Japanese American Research Project. The title the author selected was "Nisei," with a sub-title, "The Quiet Americans. The Story of a People."

Without having seen the manuscript, an authorized committee of the JACL, the National JACL Ethnic Concern Committee, objected strenuously to the word "quiet," charging it perpetuated "a negative racial stereotype" of Japanese Americans. Presumably, quietness was an undesirable trait since outspokenness had become the popular stance. The committee asserted in a widely circulated resolution that it found the term "The Quiet American" (sic) "noxious to us and to practically every Nisei to whom we have spoken," and went on to say "the 'New Nisei,' the Sansei, along with future generations, find and will find the description even more offensive." [3] The resolution declared that "quiet" may be interpreted by some as being opposed to "violent" and "this may have racist undertones similar to the commonly used phrase, 'the Japanese made it on their own, why can't they?' " (This point was amplified later by a statement that it was feared "the title will add fuel to the explosive tensions that exist between Blacks and the Japanese," with the possibility it might contribute "to possible violence against Japanese." There is no evidence black-Japanese tensions at the time were any greater than black-white tensions.) When the committee brought up the possibility of a boycott—"We feel so strongly about the title that we may be compelled to initiate, or join with others in a general effort to boycott the purchase of the book"—the controversy became far from quiet. The committee said it would prefer to have the sub-title "The Quiet Americans" deleted, but inexplicably went on to say that if a descriptive phrase were necessary, "Better Americans" from the JACL motto "Better Americans in a Greater America," or "Determined Americans" would be "more appropriate and acceptable."

Another group, calling itself the San Francisco Center for Japanese American Studies, sent a telegram to the publisher urging the book be held up "until adequate community discussion be held to resolve the issue of the book title." One of the three signing the telegram was Dr. Clifford Uyeda, a physician, who a decade later was to become national president of JACL.

The author, standing firm on his title, contended that in an overview of the 100-year history of the Japanese in the United States, the adjective was accurate and appropriate, and any other interpretation of the facts would be revisionist history, which he found unacceptable. The committee that had commissioned the book stood by the author's prerogative of choosing his title, just as it supported his right to report the facts as he found them. Howard Cady, representing the publisher, said never in his career as an editor had he experienced such a furor over one inoffensive word in the title of a book.

The effort to force a change in the title was indisputably arrogant, but in keeping with the temper of the times. Raymond Uno, later to become a JACL president and a Salt Lake City judge, saw the controversy as a manifestation of the conflict then raging between those in power and those who felt the establishment was irresponsive and insensitive: [4]

> To a large degree, the stand that JACL has taken [in the title controversy] is similar to the stand that many university administrations have taken regarding many vital issues . . . When all recourse to correct what in the eyes of those who feel deeply injured are closed, the only answer is to reject the establishment and in some instances openly defy, demonstrate, protest and in a number of instances to react violently.
>
> The people that are concerned with what is happening to our country and the way it is happening and who have observed the gross injustices and the cavalier and downright callous handling of many of our most crucial and critical problems feel that the only way to set things right is to destroy everything that is now in existence that represents the establishment. When rejection is so complete and the prospects for the future so bleak and the frustrations so intolerable for those who must suffer them, there is no sacrifice too great, no price too high to pay to bring about change . . .
>
> For those who have not been involved on a grass roots level in working to alleviate the problems of the poor, the deprived, the disadvantaged and the forgotten, the hurt is not as keen; their frustration not as severe, the disappointment not as intense, but for the others it is a devastatingly humiliating and inexcusable breech of human understanding and good will. Therefore, if there is anything possible, if there is any way possible that this title can be changed I urge upon all those people who may have any influence whatsoever to change the title, to do so.

In the end both the author and the JACL leadership decided to retain "Quiet" as neither offensive nor inaccurate, but the controversy had proved that whatever the demeanor of Japanese Americans historically, segments of the contemporary generation were quiet no longer. By the time the matter was settled, the issue had become a matter of principle, with both sides adamant and both sides ignoring the fact that they were arguing about one word in a 160,000-word manuscript. Thanks in part to the publicity generated by the con troversy, the book enjoyed a substantial sale and criticism quickly dwindled once the public read it.

This experience proved, as Uno had observed, that some Nisei and Sansei could identify with the oppressed, even in so oblique a man ner as protesting the title of a book, and would depart far enough from the traditional behavioral norms to cry out and demonstrate. But others, who only so recently had been among the repressed, could turn their backs so completely on that experience that they were repelled by the rhetoric and anger of the activists.

Hayakawa has made some perceptive comments on this matter: [5]

> I am proud that Mary Furuyama was my aunt. She, like other Japanese immigrants of her generation, exhibited in her life the best qualities of her background culture—patience, industry, the ability to suffer misfortune without complaint, and the total absence of paranoia.
>
> If the Japanese had been paranoiac about the injustices in flicted upon them, as fashionable radicalism today urges all minorities to be, they would merely have reinforced the preju dices against them. But because they accepted with quiet dig nity the insanities of a wartime climate of opinion, prejudice against them has all but disappeared, even in California, the original home of all the propaganda against the "Yellow Peril." The radical left, like the radical right, is unwilling or unable to understand that paranoia is a mental illness, not a program of social action. . . .
>
> The image of the Japanese as quiet, conforming and eager to adapt to the majority culture was vehemently rejected by some Japanese Americans, especially the student radicals among the Sansei in the late 1960s. The Sansei, or third generation, the grandchildren of the Issei, as a rule do not speak, read, or write Japanese. The radicals among them declared proudly that they were not quiet, like the generation of their parents. They be lieved in loud protest against American imperialism and capital ism. As they tooled around in their Jaguars and Corvettes, they cried, "Down with the white power structure!" Believing them selves to be racially oppressed, they called each other "brother" and "sister" and shouted "Right on!" in fashionable imitation of radical blacks.
>
> . . . the Sansei who tried to seek their ethnic identity by

emulating the radical posture of their white and black college peers were caught in a dilemma. The more they rejected quietness, conformity, discipline, and the "stereotype" of the well-behaved Japanese in the mistaken belief that such traits are "the result of submission to white racist oppression," the farther they got from their cultural roots. . . . I am not unsympathetic to the young person trying to find out, as the grandchild of immigrants, "who he is." Nor do I deny that discrimination can make a person feel less than a whole human being. However, I deplore the present fashion of magnifying discrimination against Japanese Americans as a way of getting into the act. The Japanese in America are not being discriminated against in any economic, or even social, way today.

The foregoing section on the young activists should not be construed as denigrating in any way their idealism and activities. They had been swept up by the tide of dissent and revolt that characterized America in the 1960's and the early 1970's and their fervor jolted many of the older Nisei out of their complacency. If the activists had manufactured a cause and had been jousting with an empty symbol in the "Quiet" title, they also were responsible for at least three significant accomplishments.

The first was repeal of Title II of the Internal Security Act, mentioned in the previous chapter. Elimination of this law, providing for imprisonment without trial of persons considered to be security risks in time of war, insurrection or invasion, had appeared to be a "mission impossible" in view of popular concern with activist dissent. Nonetheless, on the initiative and persistence of Nisei and Sansei activists, the national JACL authorized the Committee to Repeal the Emergency Detention Act. The committee then launched a vigorous educational campaign to inform Americans of the existence of the "concentration camp law." Senator Dan Inouye and Congressman Spark Matsunaga introduced bills in their respective chambers and President Nixon signed the repeal in the fall of 1971.

Hitherto, Japanese Americans had concentrated on measures and reports affecting them directly—for example, Evacuation claims, anti-alien laws, citizenship for the Issei, and restructuring of immigration regulations. Title II was a law that authorized violation of the civil rights of all Americans, and it was particularly satisfying that a group whose rights had been abridged was responsible for its elimination.

Activists were also behind the move to get a formal recision of Executive Order 9066, signed by President Roosevelt on February 19, 1942, as the first step in authorizing the military to clear the West Coast of Japanese Americans. The federal government took the attitude that E.O. 9066 was a wartime measure and expired automatically at the termination of hostilities. JACL sought some more-specific action. Finally, on February 19, 1976, as a Bicentennial Year gesture recognizing "our national mistake as well as our national achievements," President Gerald Ford signed a proclamation burying E.O. 9066. "We now know what we should have known then," the proclamation read, "not only was that evacuation wrong, but Japanese Americans were and are loyal Americans." The proclamation acknowledged that because there was no formal statement of the termination of E.O. 9066, "there is concern among many Japanese Americans that there may yet be some life in that obsolete document. I think it is appropriate, in this our Bicentennial Year, to remove all doubt on that matter, and to make clear our commitment in the future . . . I call upon the American people to affirm with me this American Promise—that we have learned from the tragedy of that long-ago experience forever to treasure liberty and justice for each individual American, and resolve that this kind of action shall never again be repeated."

While the campaign against E.O. 9066 had widespread JACL support, a small group of determined activists carried virtually the entire burden in the effort to win a pardon for Iva Toguri d'Aquino. Born in California, she was visiting relatives in Japan when war flared in 1941. She stubbornly refused to give up her American citizenship. To support herself, she took a job as typist at Radio Tokyo. At the urging of an Australian army officer captured in Singapore and assigned to work at Radio Tokyo, she agreed to host a program of music, humor, nostalgia and news, beamed to American servicemen. Her script was written for her by the Australian and other prisoners of war. Iva Toguri was one of thirteen English-speaking women announcers on Radio Tokyo. When war ended, American occupation authorities arrested her as "Tokyo Rose," a name American servicemen gave to all female announcers heard on Radio Tokyo. Returned to San Francisco, she was indicted on eight counts of treasonable offenses by a federal grand jury and charged. After a fifty-six-day trial in 1949, she was found guilty on one count: "That on a day during October 1944, the exact date being to the grand jurors unknown, defendant in the offices of the Broadcasting Corporation of Japan did speak into a microphone concerning the loss of ships." What she allegedly had said was: "Orphans of the Pacific. You really are orphans now. How will you get home, now that all your ships are sunk?" [6] Iva Toguri was sentenced to ten years in federal prison. She was released after serving six years and two months and joined her family in Chicago.

Independent investigation showed many irregularities in the trial. Japanese witnesses who had testified against her admitted they had perjured themselves in fear of reprisal by American occupation officials. The Nisei at the time of her trial were busily trying to reestablish themselves. Suspicions against their loyalty were still fresh, and they felt hardly in a position to speak out on behalf of one of their number accused of treason. Gradually, support for her built up, and JACL established a committee to work with her attorney, Wayne Collins, Jr., to seek justice for her. In one of his last acts before yielding the presidency to Jimmy Carter in January of 1977, Gerald Ford signed an unconditional pardon.

Meanwhile, some significant socio-economic changes were overtaking the rank and file of Japanese Americans. Perhaps the most thorough study of these phenomena was undertaken by Professor Montero with the support of the Japanese American Research Project while he was at UCLA. Montero surveyed 2,304 Nisei and 802 Sansei from all parts of the country and found: [7]

—Japanese Americans have the highest median education level among both whites and nonwhites.

—They have a median income which nearly matches that of white Americans.

—They are twice as likely to be employed as professionals than are members of society as a whole.

—Four in ten of older Nisei say one or more of their best friends is non-Japanese. Among younger Nisei, six in ten say their best friends are non-Japanese. Among Sansei who have married non-Japanese, nine of ten say one or both of their two closest friends are non-Japanese.

—The higher the occupational and educational achievement, the more likely that Nisei and Sansei will move out of the ethnic orbit.

—Only one third of Nisei professionals choose a Japanese American organization as their favorite, compared to eight in ten of service workers.

—Among younger Sansei, seven in ten are marrying non-Japanese.

Montero's study also showed vast changes in residential patterns from prewar days when social and economic pressures kept Japanese Americans in Oriental ghettos. He found only 4 percent in predominantly Japanese neighborhoods, 38 percent in mixed neighborhoods, and 58 percent in predominantly non-Japanese neighborhoods.

The Japanese American dedication to the work ethic, thrift, commitment to progress through education, and respect for socio-economic "success"—in a now-nonhostile environment—undoubtedly was responsible for the rapid upward movement. What does the drift away from Japanese American communities portend? Montero answered:

> Our findings suggest that on every indicator of assimilation it is the socio-economically successful Nisei who are the most cut off from the ethnic community. Since the majority of our Nisei respondents are making considerable economic strides, this suggests an accelerating rate of assimilation for the Japanese American population as a whole. Ironically, that very assimilation may suggest the demise of some of the Japanese American community's traditional values which were so instrumental in catapulting its members to these heights. The demise of these values in turn may serve to bring about the leveling off of the Nisei and Sansei's socio-economic achievement. As their values become congruent with the larger American society, Japanese Americans most likely will begin to mirror the achievement patterns of American society in general.

While Montero's findings were published in 1978, his surveys were made more than a decade earlier. However, the trends that his research uncovered, particularly the number of mixed-racial marriages and the drift away from the Japanese American communities, have been accelerated. While no firm figures are available, substantially more than half the Sansei marriages are with non-Japanese.

Still another study supports Montero's findings generally, but provides some different details. Thomas Sowell,[8] an economics professor at UCLA who also is black, in a *Commentary* magazine article has quoted 1978 Urban Institute data showing that if the American national average income were set at 100 percent, the income of Jews would be 170 percent followed by Japanese with 132 percent. Other ethnic groups above the national average are Poles with 115 percent, Italians and Chinese 112 percent, Germans and Anglo-Saxons 107 percent, Irish 103 percent. Below the national average were Filipinos with 99 percent, West Indians 94 percent, Mexicans 76 percent, Puerto Ricans 63 percent, blacks 62 percent, and Indians 60 percent.

A thorough analysis of these findings is outside the scope of this volume. Suffice it to say that Sowell himself has recognized that experience is an important factor in income differences; the four lowest income groups were at least two decades younger than the Jews (forty-six), and therefore it is understandable they were making less money. On the other hand the Japanese (thirty-two), second in income, are shown by U. S. census figures to be fourteen years younger than the Jews on average and only slightly older than the U.S. national average (twenty-eight). This indicates their average income will continue to rise. However, comparisons such as Sowell makes are tricky at best and should be accepted only as interesting indicators.

Nobu Miyoshi, assistant clinical professor of social work in psychiatry at the University of Pennsylvania School of Medicine, found that the degree of assimilation found by Montero has not been without cost. In a paper completed in 1978, she reported: [9]

> The Sansei are in a quandary over their identification with their dual cultural heritages—the American and Japanese—thus creating a sense of estrangement, on some levels, in relation to both. The Sansei receive strong overt messages from their parents to become "white," i.e., to subscribe to the legacies of American society, almost exclusively. On the other hand the Sansei themselves are not white but they themselves have yearnings for validation of their attitudes and values that are unlike those encountered in their outside society. It is also suggested that the Sansei are subconsciously stirred by covert messages to identify with their ethnic culture by their Nisei parents who feel some ambivalence in not promoting a closer connection with the past of their Issei parents.

Miyoshi also reports on the phenomenon of the Sansei—most of whom were born too late to experience the Evacuation, or were too young to remember much about it—showing a great deal of interest in what had happened to their parents and grandparents. On the other hand, many Nisei find difficulty talking about the Evacuation. Some feel a sense of shame at having been rejected by their own country, if only temporarily, and having been imprisoned by their own government, and are reluctant to discuss the matter. Miyoshi writes: [10]

> It is difficult to know the Nisei's actual reaction to their children's plea to tell them about their personal attitudes and experiences in the concentration camps. Parents, who in many other respects willingly devote themselves to the needs of their children

appear not to hear what the Sansei are asking of them. Remarks that are frequently heard among the Nisei parents are: "We don't tell because they [Sansei] don't ask." "Past is past, why dig up forgotten memories? The future is important." "Why burden our children? Why instill doubts in our children?" etc. Among the possible contributing factors related to the defensive posture of the Nisei, two will be mentioned here.

The pervasive protective attitude of the Nisei parents toward their children applies, somewhat, to their desire to shield the Sansei from knowledge of their camp experiences. They want to see their children integrate into the major society with less prejudicial impact than they had. I have perceived that the Nisei parents generally regard their children's social adjustment with satisfaction.

The second contributing factor is the Nisei's possible concern that they will break down in the presence of their children. Nisei are aware of the deep emotions displayed by some of their colleagues when they forthrightly confronted their own attitudes about camp. Perhaps a tolerable way to cope with the whole episode of incarceration at the present time is to dwell on the lighter and even nostalgic remembrances associated with the sustaining and warm communal life shared among the internees while they faced a common ordeal.

There is reason to doubt that any substantial number of Nisei fear "they will break down" over recollections of the Evacuation. After all, more than a third of a century has passed since the uprooting, and while that was a traumatic and unforgettable experience, Nisei have gone through many memorable times since then. The inclination of many Nisei to "dwell on the lighter and even nostalgic remembrances" may be compared to men who talk about the amusing episodes of military life rather than dwelling on the horror of battle, or to women who remember the pleasure of motherhood rather than the pain of childbirth.

In any event, in the early 1970's, some three decades after the Evacuation, a movement began among younger Japanese Americans to seek some form of recompense from their government for the material loss of their basic human rights. At first they called it a "reparations" movement but some were troubled that the word implied the fact of one nation seeking payment for damages from another. At a JACL meeting in Southern California, John Dean, who had only recently acquired a measure of notoriety for confessing his part in the Watergate scandal, suggested the word "redress" and offered to help the Japanese Americans to obtain it. The term was quickly adopted. Spirited discussion about the merits of redress and the form it should take followed in the Japanese American press. At JACL's national convention in Salt Lake City during July, 1978, the National Committee for Redress unveiled a proposal to seek $25,000, tax-free, for each evacuee. Since approximately 120,000 Japanese Americans spent time in the camps, the total to be sought was about $3 billion, an impressive sum even in these inflationary times. After the proposal was amended to include among beneficiaries the heirs of deceased evacuees and persons of Japanese ancestry from Central and South America interned in the United States, official convention delegates approved it unanimously. Dr. Clifford Uyeda was chairman of the Redress Committee and he was elected National JACL president for the next biennium.

In the months that followed, JACL toned down monetary indemnity and focused on the principle of compensation for a wrong. JACL also opted for the "commission" approach despite some internal opposition. The Nisei senators, Inouye, Matsunaga, and Hayakawa, were joined by California Democrat Alan Cranston, Idaho Democrat Frank Church, and Idaho Republican James A. McClure in sponsoring a bill to set up a commission to investigate the redress proposal and determine what action should be recommended to Congress. A similar bill was introduced in the House co-sponsored by 128 members.

Many factors unconnected with the Evacuation—inflation and an economic recession, the 1980 presidential campaign, trade with Japan and the imbalance of payments, the energy crisis—may have a part in determining the fate of the redress proposal. It is a measure that deserves to be considered strictly on the principal issues, namely whether an injustice was done to an American minority on a racial basis, and if so, whether the aggrieved should be recompensed and in what way. However, such are the times and the reality of American politics and prejudices that extraneous issues are likely to cloud congressional judgment.

Despite the unanimous JACL convention mandate, the Japanese American community is far from being of one voice on the merits of the redress proposal. Many members, particularly those who have put the past behind them in establishing a niche for themselves in America, would just as soon forget the whole thing. On the other hand, proponents of redress emphasize the importance of not permitting

America to forget what wrong the nation inflicted on a helpless minority, and cite as the "American way" the principle of seeking monetary damages for injury.

Whatever form and substance Congress gives to the redress proposal, the decisions of JACL to confront their government head on on an issue of importance to both marks an important milestone in the eventful history of Japanese Americans. Only time will tell whether it was a wise move based on confidence and maturity, or an ill-advised action of a group spurred by emotion and high idealism without an understanding of prejudices, diehard misconceptions, and the realities of a less-than-perfect political system.

But even without a satisfactory settlement of the matter—and no settlement would satisfy all elements of a Japanese American community as splinterized as the greater American community of which it is a part—the status the Japanese Americans have achieved in the United States despite monumental obstacles speaks eloquently of their qualities as a people. When their ancestors came east to America, they brought to this nation worthy ingredients to enrich the mosaic of the U.S.A.

ꙮ Appendix A

JAPANESE IN THE UNITED STATES
(U.S. Census by Race and Sex)

	Total	Male	Female
1870	55	47	8
1880	148	134	14
1890	2,039	1,780	259
1900	24,326	23,341	985
1910	72,157	63,070	9,087
1920	111,010	72,707	38,303
1930	138,834	81,771	57,063
1940	126,947	71,967	54,980
1950	141,768	76,649	65,119
1960	260,059	124,323	135,736
1970	591,290		

Note: Figures through the 1960 census are for the coterminous mainland U.S. New Nisei families and immigration from Japan which in the years 1951 to 1960 amounted to 46,250 account for the increase in the 1960 census. Figures for 1970 include the new states of Hawaii and Alaska for the first time, with Hawaii providing 217,307 of the total and Alaska 916. The changed sex imbalance of 1960 continued in the 1970 census. Based on a 20 percent sample, a technique usually employed by the census bureau which produced a population total of 588,324, slightly smaller than the actual count reported above, the census found 271,453 males and 316,871 females in the Japanese population.

✵ Appendix B

UNITED STATES DEPARTMENT OF JUSTICE
IMMIGRATION AND NATURALIZATION SERVICE
WASHINGTON, D.C.—MARCH 17, 1969

IMMIGRATION FROM JAPAN
FISCAL YEARS 1861–1968 [1]

Period	Number
Total	356,558
1861–1870	186
1871–1880	149
1881–1890	2,270
1891–1900	25,942
1901–1910	129,797
1911–1920	83,837
1921–1930	33,462
1931–1940	1,948
1941–1950	1,555
1951–1960	46,250
1961	4,490
1962	4,054
1963	4,147
1964	3,774
1965	3,294
1966	3,468
1967	4,125
1968	3,810

[1] No record of immigration from Japan until 1861.

✿ Appendix C

California Alien Land Law
Approved May 19, 1913

THE PEOPLE OF THE STATE OF CALIFORNIA DO ENACT AS FOLLOWS:

Section 1. All aliens eligible to citizenship under the laws of the United States may acquire, possess, enjoy, transmit and inherit real property, or any interest therein, in this State, in the same manner and to the same extent as citizens of the United States, except as otherwise provided by the laws of this State.

Section 2. All aliens other than those mentioned in section one of this act may acquire, possess, enjoy and transfer real property, or any interest therein, in this State, in the manner and to the extent and for the purposes prescribed by any treaty now existing between the government of the United States and the nation or country of which such alien is a citizen or subject and not otherwise, and may in addition thereto lease lands in this State for agricultural purposes for a term not exceeding three years.

Section 3. Any company, association or corporation organized under the laws of this or any other State or nation, of which a majority of the members are aliens other than those specified in section one of this act, or in which a majority of the issued capital stock is owned by such aliens, may acquire, possess, enjoy and convey real property, or any interest therein, in this State, in the manner and to the extent and for the purposes prescribed by any treaty now existing between the government of the United States and the nation or country of which such members or stockholders are citizens or subjects, and not otherwise, and may in addition thereto lease lands in this State for agricultural purposes for a term not exceeding three years.

Section 4. Whenever it appears to the court in any probate proceeding that by reason of the provisions of this act any heir or devisee can not take real property in this State which, but for said provisions, said heir or devisee would take as such, the court, instead of ordering a distribution of such real property to such heir or devisee, shall order a sale of said real property to

307

be made in the manner provided by law for probate sales of real property, and the proceeds of such sale shall be distributed to such heir or devisee in lieu of such real property.

Section 5.   Any real property hereafter acquired in fee in violation of the provisions of this act by any alien mentioned in section two of this act, or by any company, association, or corporation mentioned in section three of this act, shall escheat to, and become and remain the property of the State of California. The attorney general shall institute proceedings to have the escheat of such real property adjudged and enforced in the manner provided by section 474 of the Political Code and title eight, part three of the Code of Civil Procedure. Upon the entry of final judgment in such proceedings, the title to such real property shall pass to the State of California. The provisions of this section and of sections two and three of this act shall not apply to any real property hereafter acquired in the enforcement or in satisfaction of any lien now existing upon, or interest in such property, so long as such real property so acquired shall remain the property of the alien, company, association or corporation acquiring the same in such manner.

Section 6.   Any leasehold or other interest in real property less than the fee, hereafter acquired in violation of the provisions of this act by any alien mentioned in section two of this act, or by any company, association or corporation mentioned in section three of this act, shall escheat to the State of California. The attorney general shall institute proceedings to have such escheat adjudged and enforced as provided in section five of this act. In such proceedings the court shall determine and adjudge the value of such leasehold, or other interest in such real property, and enter judgment for the State for the amount thereof together with costs. Thereupon the court shall order a sale of the real property covered by such leasehold, or other interest, in the manner provided by section 1271 of the Code of Civil Procedure. Out of the proceeds arising from such sale, the amount of the judgment rendered for the State shall be paid into the State treasury and the balance shall be deposited with and distributed by the court in accordance with the interest of the parties therein.

Section 7.   Nothing in this act shall be construed as a limitation upon the power of the State to enact laws with respect to the acquisition, holding or disposal by aliens of real property in this State.

Section 8.   All acts and parts of acts inconsistent or in conflict with the provisions of this act, are hereby repealed.

✹ Appendix D

MEMORIAL PRESENTED TO THE PRESIDENT WHILE AT SAN FRANCISCO ON SEPTEMBER 18, 1919.

The Japanese Association of America
No. 444 Bush Street, San Francisco, California

Honorable Woodrow Wilson,
President of the United States of America,
San Francisco, California.

Mr. President: The Japanese Association of America, on behalf of resident Japanese in the State of California, extends greetings to you and begs to add its voice of welcome to that of the great state which you now honor by your presence. It sincerely hopes that the noble task in which you are now engaged may be fully realized, and that world peace and happiness may be ultimate rewards of the labors for humanity to which your great efforts are devoted.

The Japanese people of this state, trusting implicitly in the lofty spirit of justice and fair dealing which have characterized your every public act and expression, take advantage of your presence in California to lay before you a few facts and figures bearing upon their relations to the community in which they reside, and they venture to ask for them your respectful and disinterested consideration.

The cry against our people may be historically traced as far back as 1887, when there were no more than 400 Japanese in the entire state. The so-called Japanese question did not, however, assume an acute character until 1906, when the school question arose. Unfortunately that question was settled by the politicians and not determined upon its true merits. At any rate, ever since that date, the Japanese "question" has become an issue of a most complicated nature—political, economic, racial, diplomatic— always resulting in the suffering of the Japanese residents. A few of the more familiar cases might be mentioned. The "Gentlemen's Agreement," under the workings of which America prohibits Japanese immigration, has been so strictly administered by the Japanese government that there has

309

been no immigration from Japan. The alien land law of this state, enacted in 1913, prohibits Japanese ownership of land and limits the terms of lease to three years.

The limitation strikes at the very foundation of farming so far as the Japanese are concerned, and the limitation is substantially interfering with all Japanese agricultural enterprises. Not satisfied with these annoying measures, innumerable anti-Japanese bills were introduced at the last session of the State Legislature. One of these proposed to deprive the Japanese of the right to lease land while another proposed to segregate Japanese children in the public schools.

These facts, not to mention others, have tended to strain the historic friendly relations between the United States and Japan. We regret the situation. However, the Japanese residents, on the whole, have so far entertained the faith that the American government would eventually protect them and render them justice and peace. A great deal of anxiety has, in the meantime, been experienced by them. This is but natural, and this unrest has been reflected across the ocean. Some of us who feel that we are better acquainted with the situation have taken the position that our best course must come from education and we have been doing our utmost in what we characterize as an "Americanization campaign." We point out to our fellow-countrymen the better elements in American civilization, urging them to strive for their own improvement and better fit themselves for American life, hoping thereby to be relieved of the anxiety created and reinforced by the constant agitation against them. Our Americanization campaign will prove fruitless unless backed by true sympathy on the part of Americans. We regret to say that even to these efforts on our part there has been given but little response or sympathy.

May we not then appeal to you, Mr. President, and ask your powerful aid in so adjusting our condition on this coast that we may engage in legitimate pursuits and live in peace?

A census of the Japanese in California, taken in September, 1918, shows the following facts: The total Japanese population is 68,983, composed of 41,842 male adults, 12,232 female adults, 7,877 male children and 7,031 female children. Of these the farmers and their families number 19,044, while farm laborers and their families count 18,968. In other words, more than 50 percent of the Japanese in the state are engaged in agriculture and horticulture. The remainder are engaged in commerce, in domestic service, transportation, factories, canneries, etc.

The Japanese in agriculture constitute the most important element in number as well as in other respects. And thus it happens that whatever hostility now exists is generally directed against this particular element. The status of this element may be briefly stated. The most recent investigations show the number and acreage of farms cultivated by Japanese under various methods as follows:

CALIFORNIA FARMS UNDER JAPANESE MANAGEMENT

	Ownership		Tenant		Contract		Total	
	Number	Area	Number	Area	Number	Area	Number	Area
Northern coast ...	39	2,155	223	8,839	13	1,400	275	12,414
Sacramento Valley ..	146	6,811	1,220	117,057	14	4,040	1,380	127,906
San Joaquin Valley ..	10	6,315	367	57,779	28	3,703	405	67,797
Livingston	34	1,751	5	125	...	.....	39	1,876
Central California ..	182	9,723	549	40,758	...	.....	828	50,481
Southern coast ...	31	600	308	30,493	65	14,465	855	45,558
Totals .	442	27,355	2,672	255,051	120	23,608	3,780	306,037
Southern California ..	84	2,950	2,266	81,650	...	.....	2,350	84,600
Grand totals ..	526	30,305	4,938	336,701	120	23,608	6,130	390,637

Again, the following table shows the crops raised by the Japanese farmers, as well as their values:

Product	Acreage	Yield per Acre	Total Yield
Grapes	47,439	$150	$ 7,115,850
Berries	5,968	700	3,580,800
Fruits	29,210	150	7,381,500
Greens	17,852	300	5,355,600
Potatoes	18,830	135	2,542,050
Onions	9,251	250	2,312,750
Asparagus	9,927	150	1,489,050
Tomatoes	10,616	160	1,698,560
Celery	3,568	300	1,070,400

Product	Acreage	Yield per Acre	Total Yield
Cantaloupes	9,581	250	2,395,250
Beans	77,107	70	5,397,490
Rice	16,640	160	2,662,400
Seeds	15,847	160	2,535,520
Sugar beets	51,604	70	3,612,280
Hay and cereals	15,753	50	787,650
Corn	7,845	60	470,700
Hops	1,260	180	226,800
Ornamental flowers and plants	298	. . .	450,000
Cotton	18,000	100	1,800,000
Miscellaneous	5,084	. . .	491,070
Totals	371,680	. . .	$53,375,720

To illustrate more concretely how the Japanese farmers have achieved their present position the following illustration may be given. In 1918 Japanese farmers in the Sacramento Valley contributed more than 1,000,000 sacks of rice to the food supply of the United States and its allies. They planted 25,000 acres to rice in the five counties of Sutter, Yuba, Colusa, Glenn and Butte. This year the total acreage devoted to the same industry has increased to 140,000, of which 33,000 acres are cultivated by Japanese. They expect to harvest 9,400,000 bushels. Of these the Japanese share is expected to reach 2,400,000 bushels.

This immensely prosperous industry, which in eight years has assumed a commanding position in the Sacramento Valley, was first put on a safe commercial basis and proved a success by Japanese. Japanese were not the first to try rice in California, but they were the first to make it a commercial proposition. They were the first to apply with practical success the experimental results of the government rice station at Biggs. And they were the ones who stuck to rice through all the years before the industry emerged from its uncertainties and became firmly established.

The Japanese demonstrated success and the American farmers who have since been getting rich out of the industry and who now greatly outnumber the Japanese rice planters must admit that their prosperity is founded on the structure built by the daring and persistence of the Japanese.

There is something more. This pioneering developed a huge food production on land that in most cases will not grow anything else. It is admitted that the rice industry has been created out of nothing.

Certainly the lands on which it has been built up were next to nothing before the persistent industry of the pioneers demonstrated that rice would grow on them. It is a curious fact that rice can not be grown successfully in California except on the poorest lands. The very conditions that spoil the land for other crops are the ones necessary to the success of rice. On good soils rice grows so rankly that the heads do not mature until too late, bringing the harvest past the beginning of the rainy season. Hardpan close to the surface, the bane of land where it occurs, is essential to rice growing. Rice fields must be kept flooded through the growing season. Consequently hardpan must be presented to hold the water. Most of the lands now devoted to rice are so impregnated with alkali that only salt grass grew on them before.

The growers had everything to learn. Americans were at a loss because the varieties they were familiar with in the South were not successful. And though a Japanese rice, the Wataribune variety, finally became the commonest one grown, even Japanese farmers familiar with rice growing in their own country were no better off. In Japan rice is cultivated intensively. The young plants are germinated in seed beds to be transplanted in small paddies, where they are cultivated by hand. Such methods are impossible in rice growing on a large scale as it is practiced in California.

Consequently the early rice growers, Japanese and American, lost money. Most of them quit. But one Japanese stuck to it and thereby earned the title of pioneer in California rice growing. That was K. Ikuta, who never quit, but is still growing and successfully. And ten years ago the land now devoted to rice growing was worth no more than $10 an acre. No one will now sell the same land for less than $100. The rental on these lands varies from $35 to $45. Is not this a substantial creation of wealth for the state?

Again, vast acres along the lower Sacramento and the San Joaquin reclaimed from an original condition of swamp and tule beds, long reaches of orchard and vineyard on the east side of the San Joaquin and Sacramento Valleys developed from a semidesert, where at the best only crops of hay or grain were produced before, great areas of garden and orchard in the Santa Clara Valley which, in like fashion, have sprung up on former hay fields, and many other improvements in various parts of the state testify to the pioneering of the Japanese.

An American writer says:

> The most striking feature of Japanese farming in California has been this development of successful orchards, vineyards or gardens on land that was either completely out of use or else employed for far less profitable purposes. Ignorant of the facts of the case, we have been inclined to believe in California that Japanese farmers have merely taken over lands and farms of American farmers and continued the business as they found it. The slightest study, however, shows this conclusion to be a complete error.
>
> The Japanese farmer in California has always been a great developer and improver. Where he has taken over lands that were in use before his time he has almost always, if not always, put them to a far higher use and made them far more valuable than they were before.

But with a great proportion of the lands he now farms he has developed them out of nothing, or next to nothing.

He is the skillful agriculturist who has done so much to bring out the riches of the vast delta of the San Joaquin and the Sacramento. He is the vine planter who has transformed the poor clay lands of Florin, Acampo and Lodi into rich vineyards. He is the horticulturist who dared to settle on the shifting sands of Livingston, in Merced County, and Bowles, in Fresno County, and turned those wastes into valuable orchard and vineyard. He is the adventurer who had the nerve to level the formidable "hog wallow" lands along the thermal belt in Tulare County and plant on them the oranges and vines, the proved success of which has changed these spring sheep pastures into another prosperous extension of the citrus region of California. He is the persistent experimenter who hung on in rice growing until it became a success.

In all this and in much more the Japanese farmer was the pioneer. It must not be thought that he struck out these successes for himself alone. He does not enjoy alone the wealth he created and the prosperity he produced. In all these places his daring and industry immensely increased the value not only of the lands he had bought or leased, but as well of those of the American landholders in the vicinity. His success as a pioneer was the example that brought many times his number of American farmers to these localities to engage with profit in the industries which he had demonstrated for their benefit.

Prosperous as the Japanese farmers in California are, it is just to say that they have produced for American farmers many times the wealth they have gained for themselves. In the enhancement of land values alone Japanese farmers have added millions to the total wealth of the state. This means not only the enlarged value of the lands they have farmed and improved, but also the increased value of the neighboring lands. In all the once hopeless districts in which Japanese farmers have made a success the American farmers who came after have them to thank.

Of course, these achievements are not without sacrifices. In many other places in California besides the river regions the Japanese farmers have met, fought with and overcome unhealthful conditions. They have not overcome them without fearful losses. In Fresno County alone, in the earlier days of development, when water and sanitary conditions were bad, the Japanese lost 3,000 lives. It is not too much to say that the lives of these Japanese boys were expended in the service of the state and the United States.

Furthermore, the Japanese farmer has never been content to do merely as well as the American farmer under whom he learned farming in California. When he has not been pioneering new land he has always found a way to make the soil produce a better and more profitable crop than it did before.

Perhaps the most brilliant example of Japanese agricultural pioneering in California is the colony at Livingston. That unique colony in Merced County, where Japanese and American live and work in friendly cooperation, animated by common purposes of good citizenship, still remains the highest example of Japanese settlement in California.

The Japanese of Livingston, where 85 percent of their numbers are Christians, have in the past year organized a church and called a pastor. The new church, which is nondenominational, was organized, the Livingston Japanese explain, because the older people of the colony cannot understand services in English. The idea is that eventually all, Japanese and Americans, shall go to the same church, but at present the elders who do not speak much English, and the little children, go to the Japanese church and Sunday school while the older children attend the American church.

The Colony Association owns ten acres which has been set aside for the church buildings and a public park. The Association meeting hall, in the park, has been enlarged and now serves for church services as well as for public meetings. American citizens of the community have presented the Japanese meeting hall with a large American flag and a portrait of President Wilson.

Let one of the colonists speak.

> The following points are, in my opinion, the most conspicuous reasons, among others, why the Japanese colonists in this place are able to keep their social order comparatively systematically:
>
> In the first place, the pioneer Japanese settlers here bought their lands and cultivated them with their own hands.
>
> In the second place, I must not forget to point out the kindness of our American neighbors to us.
>
> The third point is the fact that most of the Japanese residents in this place are followers of Christianity.
>
> Lastly, there is one thing that I want to call to the attention of thoughtful Americans and Japanese in California. It is the question of the Japanese farmers in California. I do not mean to discuss the immigration problem, which has been discussed by many able persons. But we must admit the fact that, because of the Alien Land Law, prohibiting the ownership of land by Japanese and prohibiting land leases for more than three years, most of the Japanese in the state, with their families, are forced to wander about from one place to another without any definite aim of settling down.
>
> Under such circumstances must they not only earn their living, but support their families and give their children education. Most of their children, being native born citizens of this country, naturally look on this country as their own fatherland, and consequently it is needless to

say that it is the duty of their parents as well as of society to give them a sound education and to make them good and able citizens of the United States. Education does not always give a man personality. Building up of manhood and noble personality depends largely on the conditions of the home and outside influences in childhood and boyhood. I believe, therefore, that with a strong conviction of our responsibility for the future life of our second generation, we must take it as our solemn duty to give our younger generation better conditions at home and more favorable surroundings. It is undoubtedly a hard and complicated problem to fill these conditions, how to improve our home life and how and what to do to change the social conditions. If I am allowed to speak frankly, I say that we must get down to the bottom of the problem and make a complete change in the system of our life. This is the fundamental and essential point of the problem presented to us. By changing the system I mean that some of those who are in the cities or in the country already improved, should go into the untouched lands, where they can build up their homes and create new society. The Japanese pioneers of Livingston followed this system when they established a colony in this place.

A brief statement may here be made concerning the anti-Japanese agitation in California. Before taking up the alleged reasons upon which the agitation is based we may be allowed to quote one of the best general statements on the subject, which was prepared by Prof. P. J. Treat of Stanford University, an acknowledged authority on Oriental history. He says:

It was in 1905 that the first suspicion of friction appeared. And in the next nine years a series of incidents occasioned some ill feeling, but it must be remembered that the friction was always between popular groups: the official relations were always cordial.

The occasions for controversy were found in both the United States and in the Far East. In the United States it arose from the agitation for the exclusion of the Japanese immigrants. This movement began in California about 1905. It had small basis in fact, for there were relatively few Japanese in this country, but if their number continued to increase as rapidly as it had since 1900 a real social and economic problem would be soon presented. Instead of meeting this problem through diplomatic channels, the agitators, remembering the Chinese exclusion movement of an earlier generation, commenced direct action. This took the form of the so-called "schoolboy incident" in San Francisco. Using the excuse that school facilities were lacking after the great fire in 1906, the school board ordered all Oriental students to attend a designated school. The Japanese, recognizing the motive which prompted this action, justly resented it. And it was the more ungracious because at the time of the earthquake and fire the Japanese

Red Cross had contributed to the relief of San Francisco more money than all other foreign countries combined. They had eagerly seized this opportunity of showing their appreciation of all that the United States had done for Japan in the past. The action of a local school board soon became a national and an international question. With the legal aspects we are not concerned here. The matter was settled, between the federal government and San Francisco, by a compromise. The Japanese students were admitted to all the schools as of old, and President Roosevelt promised to take up the question of immigration with Japan.

When the matter was presented in proper form, the Japanese at once met our requests. Practically all thoughtful Japanese realized the dangers involved in a mass immigration of people from a land with low standards of living to one where they were high. The understanding took the form of the "Gentlemen's Agreement," under which Japan promised not to give passports to laborers desiring to emigrate to the United States, and our Government in turn agreed not to subject the Japanese to the humiliation of an exclusion act. Since this agreement went into effect in 1907, it has met every need. No one has found ground for questioning the scrupulous good faith of the Japanese foreign office in the issue of passports. In fact the admission of Japanese, under the passport system, has worked out with fewer abuses than the admission of Chinese under the exclusion laws which we administer ourselves.

Unfortunately this good understanding did not quiet the agitation on the Pacific Coast. In the California Legislature in 1909, 1911 and 1913 a number of measures were proposed which would have caused discrimination against the Japanese residents of the state. These were reported to the Japanese press, and even though not passed they kept alive the resentment. Japanese who accepted our views regarding immigration did not hesitate to assert that such Japanese as were admitted to our country should enjoy rights and privileges equal to those of any alien. A crisis was reached when, in 1913, a bill was proposed at Sacramento which would deny to Japanese the right to acquire land or to lease it for more than three years. The purpose of this bill was to prevent the accumulation of agricultural land by the industrious and thrifty Japanese farmers. But the danger was largely imaginary because, due to the "Gentlemen's Agreement," very few Japanese could enter the country, and in 1913 less than 13,000 acres were actually owned by them. In spite of the efforts of the national administration, the bill was passed in a modified form, which made it apply only to "aliens ineligible to citizenship." This class included, specifically, the Chinese, and, by interpretation, all aliens who were not "free white persons" or persons of African nativity or descent. The act,

moreover, especially asserted that it respected all treaty obligations.
Thus the responsibility was thrown back upon the federal government, whose naturalization laws apparently debarred Japanese from
citizenship. At the time Professor H. A. Millis, a well known econo-
mist who had made the most careful study of the Japanese in the
Western States, did not hesitate to assert that the law was "unjust,
impolite and unnecessary legislation." Against this land law the
Japanese government protested, and our administration defended the
legality of the act. But as an effort was made on both sides to avoid
trouble, the issue was never joined, and the exchange of notes never
completed. But the so-called "Alien Land Law" did more to disturb friendly relations than the immigration controversy seven years
before. Happily, there has been no renewal of the anti-Japanese
agitation in California. In 1915 Japan made a notable exhibit at the
Panama-Pacific Exposition, which was properly appreciated, and
since that time a better understanding has been established between
the labor organizations of California and Japan.

The immigration from Japan by years since 1908 has been as
follows:

1908	15,803	1914	8,929
1909	3,111	1915	8,613
1910	2,720	1916	8,680
1911	4,520	1917	8,991
1912	6,136	1918	10,213
1913	8,281		

Among the most commonly used arguments against the Japanese are
the charges that they are non-assimilable, that they underbid prices, that
their standard of living is lower and that their power to work is greater,
and that their birth rate is higher. They say "the Caucasians and Asiatic
races are unassimilable." "The leopard cannot change its spots." "The
Creator made the two races different and different they will remain." If
this is true, it can not be answered. Is it a misfortune that the Creator did
not keep them apart? But America came to Japan first. At any rate, they
assert in the same breath that "The Japanese are intensely distinct and
self-conscious as a race and nation. Those who come here come as
Japanese. They have no thought of becoming Americans." But this is not
true. The facts previously given prove it. The racial difference, even if it
tends to discourage amalgamation, by no means prevents assimilation. The
history of modern Japan is a clear proof that the Japanese are assimilable.
The Japanese in California are assimilated to a degree unrecognized by
anti-Japanese Americans. The native born Japanese are 100 percent American, while foreign born Japanese are at least 50 percent American in spite
of the many obstacles put in their way. Their spiritual attitude toward, and

material contributions to, the various enterprises of the late war eloquently testify to this effect.

In the early days of Japanese immigration it is true that the Japanese did underbid to a certain degree. But that is true of all immigrants until they have become familiar with American industrial life and have mastered the art of bargaining advantageously. Since 1907 the Japanese have been enjoying a scarcity value. Today, they are earning more than other races similarly engaged. On farms the common Japanese laborer is getting $4.50 a day, while others are paid $4. This argument, if true in the past, is no longer a fact.

The above argument is, of course, based on another, namely that the Japanese are satisfied with a lower standard of living. They say, speaking of the Japanese: "Accustomed to live on a little rice and dried fish, to sleep on a board, and to do with very few of the comforts of life, no white man can hope to hold the field against them." This picture of the Japanese is not quite true. But it is true that the prevailing standard of living among the Japanese immigrants was low in the past. They could then earn on the farm no more than $1 or $1.50 a day. On such wages they could not indulge in the standard of living enjoyed by American workingmen. This fault is nothing innate with the Japanese. They were compelled to live cheaply because of their limited earning capacity. With their increased earning power their standards rose. Their present standards of living are not inferior; as a matter of fact, they are superior to those which prevail among other immigrant races. At this point it should be noted that as yet many Japanese men are single, as the sex distribution above given shows, and these are mostly without their own homes. Thus they spend relatively a small portion of their earnings on actual living. The rest is spent on things largely for display, good clothes, gold watches, diamond rings, etc. This is not a commendable habit, but display seems to be an inevitable accompaniment of their nomadic life. When their mode of life becomes normalized by marriage and settlement, these things of display will be changed to things of living. Then their expenses of living will constitute no problem.

The Japanese nation is characterized by industry and perseverance, so naturally the Japanese who are here possess the power of endurance and the habit of industry. But it appears rather strange that Americans should complain of these facts, for they themselves take pride in these very characteristics. Those Japanese who are even slightly acquainted with American history can not but be impressed by the degree of these qualities with which Americans have converted the once wild west into a fertile land. The Japanese, as they have been conditioned upon arrival in this country, have found that the best asset they possessed consisted in those characteristics that helped them to get on an independent footing. So they worked and worked hard and as is charged, perhaps overworked as some of them still do. American farmers who complain that their Japanese neighbors work longer hours must realize that the latter are handicapped in many other respects to make them successful. The most noteworthy of these is their ignorance of the American methods of disposing of their produce. The Japanese farmers greatly lack the commercial ability possessed by the Americans. Consequently they think that they must produce more than their American neighbors. Even if this position is a mistake, they have at least thought so. But why do they struggle so hard? The majority of these Japanese farmers lacked educational opportunities at home. Recognizing this, it impels them to work very hard so that they can give their children a chance to get education. It is a well known fact that the Japanese will do anything to get an education or to enable their children to obtain it. So far as we know, the Japanese farmers work hard not so much for their own enjoyment of life, but because they think of the future welfare of their children first. Of course, this is not altogether wise, and we are trying to point out to them that they, too, must develop. We are advising them as best we know how, not to work so hard as to cause their neighbors to criticise them, and to create some leisure for self-development. At the same time, it appears even to us rather strange that the Americans should complain of Japanese industry. But if Americans insist that Japanese should work no more than so many hours, that can be easily accomplished. Admit them into the unions and make them obey the union rules. This simple method will do away with the problem except perhaps for those engaged in agriculture. Farmers, too, in time, might be habituated to shorter hours of labor.

Of late, much eloquence has been spent in condemning the Japanese birth rate. It is alleged that the Japanese power of fecundity is notoriously high, furnishing ground for the fear that the Japanese will become the dominating race in California. The white races will be driven from the land. Hence the terrible "yellow peril." But in reality, we are not even certain that the birth rate among the Japanese is very high. We have no statistics to prove it. No one, so far as we know, has studied this subject scientifically. No one has given us statistics showing even elementary facts such as sex distribution, marital condition, age composition, etc., of the Japanese population. Yet without these facts we can not make a comparative study of the birth rate between any two races. But let it be granted, for the sake of expediency, that the Japanese birth rate in California is higher than, say, the American birth rate. Even if this is true, it can not be established as a racial trait of the Japanese. It is probably due to their inferior social, economic and intellectual status. The ignorant always suffer from high birth rate, which are always accompanied by high death rates. But as they advance, their power of fecundity falls. This is an established fact. The birth rate among "old" immigrant races is fast falling. As the Japanese emerge from their present status, their birth rate, too, will surely fall. Thus the allegation that the Japanese will dominate California and will drive the white races from the land is a reality that exists only in the mind of agitators.

Finally we beg to state a few facts concerning the more important of our positive efforts to uplift the Japanese residents. These may be classified under four headings: An organized movement for Americanization, the protection of Japanese immigrants, religious work, and schools for immigrants and their children.

The origin of our more or less organized movement for Americanization can be traced back to 1900. We first directed our effort to what we called social education and economic development. We tried to impart to our fellow countrymen elementary facts of American civilization so that they could better fit themselves for American life. We tried to teach them that assimilation was the first step for their success. Then we tried to convince them that by contributing to the national interests of America they could attain their own economic development.

In 1918, when the American government laid down the general plan of the "Americanization campaign," we made it the foundation of our work. In fact, we joined the movement. The Japanese associations of San Francisco, Los Angeles, Portland, and Seattle assumed the responsibility of directing the campaign in the coast states, Nevada, Utah and Colorado.

The San Francisco Association employs a man educated in America to canvass the northern half of the state. His function was to organize, in conjunction with the local associations, work for the campaign. Meetings were held at which men and women familiar with America addressed the Japanese. These addresses are for the purpose of acquainting the local Japanese with America. The topics discussed are such as American history, spirit, politics, economics, industry, religion, education, society, customs and manners, hygiene, care of children, cooking, housekeeping, etc. Besides lectures, pamphlets on these subjects have been prepared, and these are freely distributed. We have asked the Japanese schools, churches, YMCA, YWCA, clubs and other associations, newspapers and magazines to help us in our campaign, and they are enthusiastically responding. The Japanese Agricultural Association is also doing most effective work. We are also making a special effort to facilitate learning of the English language. We are helping to organize classes for women and children newly arrived and securing proper teachers for them. We are also helping them to select textbooks so they can learn the language, and, at the same time, become familiar with America. Such is the nature and scope of our Americanization campaign.

To protect new arrivals, mostly women and children, we are cooperating with every institution connected with immigration at the time of their arrival and after their landing in America. We distribute at ports of departure pamphlets on what they should know on the voyage and in America. We send one of our secretaries to the immigration station every time a ship arrives to facilitate the needs of newcomers. We do what we can for the unfortunate immigrants, acting as go-between for such and the Federal Bureau of Immigration. We make special efforts to protect wives whose husbands for various reasons fail to meet them at the station. We do our best to see that Japanese immigrants are accorded proper treatment from immigration officials. Our relations with these officials have been very cordial, and we are grateful.

The earlier Japanese immigrants were mostly students and for many years students formed the bulk of Japanese immigrants. They began to come to America about forty years ago. The Christian missionaries saw a chance to do proselyting work among the young Japanese. First they taught them English and helped them to secure jobs. As the number of Japanese increased missions were established. These conducted religious meetings and schools and provided rooming facilities. The various denominations together now maintain fifty-nine missions in America and Canada. These are doubtless helping the Japanese in many ways. But Professor Millis says: "These missions are for Japanese alone, and a recognition of a difference between them and other races and a condition which lessens their value as an assimilative force." This indictment is, we are inclined to think, worthy of serious consideration by all who are interested in religious instruction as well as in the real Christianization of the Japanese. A stigma is attached to "mission" Christianity in the mind of many Japanese Christians, and they prefer to attend American churches and they do. The mission work, if properly instituted, will no doubt have a far-reaching influence in Americanizing Japanese immigrants.

Aside from the school for instructing Japanese in English, there are seventy-five so-called "supplementary" schools for teaching children the Japanese language. These are attended by the Japanese pupils after the public schools close for the day. They are primarily for the study of the Japanese language and are not intended to perpetuate the traditions and moral concepts of Japan. Of course, these are criticized by hostile Americans. But says Professor Millis, "They are supplementary schools, and at the worst, there is much less in them to be adversely criticized than in the parochial schools attended by so many children of the South and European immigrants. No real problem is yet evident connected with Japanese children on American soil." These are some of the more obvious facts concerning the status of Japanese residents in California.

In conclusion, Mr. President, the undersigned, in their official capacity as representatives of their countrymen, have thought this a fitting opportunity for directing your attention to the status of our people on this coast. We approach you in no spirit of complaint. If we have grievances we recognize that such grievances are inseparable from the conditions which now exist and that they must be borne with patience. It is our firm belief, however, that fuller knowledge and better understanding on the part of the

American people of our aims and aspirations as residents of the great State of California will tend to disabuse some prejudices and make our condition happier. We would convince the people of California that our presence and our activities are not a menace to the commonwealth, but that its dearest interests are our own. We are happy to be able to count with confidence upon your love of justice and we ask your powerful help in so shaping public thought and opinion that every obstacle to harmony may be removed. It is the earnest desire of the Japanese people in this state to dwell in peace and good will with their American neighbors, and they desire to so direct their energies that the best interests of the state and communities in which they live may be subserved.

If it is our good fortune to impress you with the sincerity of these, our purposes and aims, we shall feel that your visit to the West has been most fortunate and we shall remain gratified and grateful.

We have the honor to remain, Sir,

Most respectfully yours,
The Japanese Association of America.

ᨠ Notes

CHAPTER I

1. Harry Emerson Wildes, "The Kuroshiwo's Toll," Transactions of the Asiatic Society of Japan, Series 2, Vol. 17, pp. 221–233; *see also* Proceedings of the California Academy of Sciences, "Japanese wrecks stranded and picked up adrift in the North Pacific Ocean, ethnologically considered" by Charles Wolcott Brooks, San Francisco, 1876.
2. University of California Publications in Archeology and Ethnology, Vol. 4. "The Earliest Historical Relations between Mexico and Japan," by Zelia Nuttal, pp. 9–15; *see also* James Murdoch, *A History of Japan*, Vol. II, pp. 478–480.
3. R. C. Clark, "Wreck of a Japanese Junk," *The Oregon Historical Quarterly*, XXXVIII (June 1937), pp. 161–163.
4. H. E. Wildes, *op. cit.,* p. 232.
5. The basic source on the life of Manjiro is a biography by his son, Nakahama Toichiro, entitled *Nakahama Manjiro Den*, published in Japanese in Tokyo in 1936 and still untranslated. Two accounts which have relied on this source are by Masuji Ibuse, *John Manjiro, the Castaway* (Tokyo, 1941), and Hisakazu Kaneko, *Manjiro, the Man who Discovered America* (Boston, 1956).
6. Joseph Heco, *The Narrative of a Japanese*, 2 vols., edited by James Murdoch (Tokyo, 1895).
7. *Pacific Citizen*, July 7, 1961.
8. *The Daily Morning Chronicle* (San Francisco), June 17, 1869, p. 2, col. 1.
9. This account of the Wakamatsu Tea and Silk Colony places reliance upon the following reports in newspapers: *Alta California*, June 16 and October 24, 1869; Sacramento *Union*, June 5, 7, 18, 19, 21, and October 24, 1869; March 2, April 5, June 11, September 1 and 3, and December 31, 1870, and April 7, 1871. *See also* Paolo Sioli, *Historical Souvenir of El Dorado County, California* (Oakland, 1888) for recollections of the Schnell venture by the Veerkamp family which took over the property.
10. Forty-first Congress, third session, Ch. 71–74, 1871.

11. The names of the members of the colony are recorded on pages 8 and 9 of the census for Coloma Township, El Dorado County, California, dated July 1 and 2, 1870, and entered by Enoch N. Stout, assistant marshal.

12. The Los Angeles *Times*, March 30, 1970.

13. Ralph S. Kuykendall and A. Grove Day, *Hawaii—A History* (Englewood Cliffs, N.J., 1948, 1961).

14. *Ibid.*, pp. 117–122.

15. Hilary Conroy, *The Japanese Frontier in Hawaii, 1868–1898* (University of California Press, 1953), p. 16. Professor Conroy's study is the most authoritative treatment of the subject.

16. *Ibid.*, p. 24.

17. E. K. Wakukawa, *A History of the Japanese People in Hawaii* (The Toyo Shoiw, Honolulu, 1938), p. 40.

CHAPTER II

1. Yamato Ichihashi, *Japanese in the United States* (Stanford University Press, 1932), p. 8.

2. Inazo Nitobe, *The Intercourse Between the United States and Japan* (Baltimore, 1891), pp. 165–166.

3. This cumulative total for these years is provided in the first issue in 1882 of *Nihon Teikoku Tokei Nenkan* (Imperial Statistical Annals of Japan).

4. The Japanese American Research Project at UCLA was permitted to microfilm all documents in the archives of the Japanese Ministry of Foreign Affairs concerning Japanese immigration to the United States in the Meiji and early Taisho periods. The Foreign Minister's instructions to the new Minister to the United States are found in a document dated May 7, 1888, and contained in Volume I of *Zaibei Hompojin no Jyokyo Narabini Tokosha Torishimari Kankei Zakken* (Miscellaneous Documents Reporting the Conditions of Japanese Residents in the United States and Those Relative to the Control of Their Passage to that Country). There is no pagination in this volume of the Foreign Ministry Records but the document here quoted is listed as Transmittal No. 335.

5. *Ibid.* Mutsu's report is found in the same section cited above but without transmittal number and is listed at "private correspondence" (*Shishin*).

6. Gaimusho, *Nihon Gaiko Bunsho:* January, 1891–December, 1891, Vol. 24. (Ministry of Foreign Affairs, Japanese Diplomatic Documents, Vol. 24.) Tokyo: *Nihon Kokusai Rengo Kyokai*, 1952, p. 460.

7. Document No. 229, dated July 20, 1891, in Volume I of *Zaibei Hompojin no Jyokyo Narabini Tokosha Torishimari Kankei Zakken.*

8. *Ibid.*

9. Compiled by author from the Imperial Statistical Annals for the years concerned. The author's findings are at slight variance with those of Yamato Ichihashi in *Japanese in the United States.*

CHAPTER III

1. Sir G. B. Sansom, *A History of Japan*, 3 vols. (Stanford, 1958–1963). This is the most authoritative general history of Japan in English. See also his *The Western World and Japan*, New York, 1958. In the following brief account of the long centuries of Japanese history, reliance has been placed upon these and other volumes.
2. C. R. Boxer, *The Christian Century in Japan, 1549–1650* (Berkeley, 1967).
3. Hugh Borton, *Japan's Modern Century* (New York, 1955).
4. See Harry H. L. Kitano, *Japanese Americans, The Evolution of a Subculture* for a lengthy and valuable description and analysis of Japanese norms and values as transmitted to the American scene and the ensuing adaptations.

CHAPTER IV

1. E. H. Norman, *Japan's Emergence as a Modern State* (New York, 1940), pp. 157–158.
2. Dispatch from Takahashi Shinkichi, Japanese consul at New York, dated February 13, 1884, specified as Official #14 and addressed to the Japanese Foreign Minister.
3. This point is admittedly speculative. Professor Yamato Ichihashi takes an opposing position. See his *Japanese in the United States*, pp. 87–88.
4. Yoshida Yosaburo, "Sources and Causes of Japanese Emigration," *Annals of the American Academy of Political and Social Science*, Vol. 34, #4, September, 1909, pp. 379–382.
5. *Ibid.*, p. 384.
6. *Ibid.*, p. 380.
7. *Ibid.*, pp. 383–384.
8. See the lengthy report on the activities of the Apton Steamship Company agents in the Fujita Report of Japanese Activities in the Pacific Northwest which the Japanese consul in San Francisco, Chinda Sutemi, forwarded to the Foreign Affairs Office in Tokyo on July 30, 1891.
9. The Law to Protect Emigrants in the amended version of June 1, 1896. Foreign Ministry Archives (*Hokubei Gasshukoku ni okeru Hompojin Toko Seigen Oyobi Haiseki Ichiran*) "Documents Relating to the Restriction of Japanese Passage to the United States and Their Exclusion by the United States." Vol. 3, pp. 1428–1429.
10. *Ibid.* This was provided for in Confidential Instruction No. 44, dated November 13, 1903.
11. Yamato Ichihashi, *op. cit.*, p. 246.
12. *Ibid.*, pp. 247, 294.
13. *Ibid.*, p. 296.

CHAPTER V

1. *Reports of the Immigration Commission* (GPO, 1911). Published in twenty-five volumes, it is Volumes 22–25 that present material on the Japanese in the United States. Hereafter cited as *ICR*.
2. *Ibid.*, p. 197.
3. *Ibid.*, p. 405.
4. See Appendix for full text.
5. H. A. Millis, *The Japanese Problem in the United States* (New York, 1915), p. 161.
6. *ICR*, Vol. 24, p. 635.
7. *Ibid.*, pp. 436–437.
8. Millis, *op. cit.*, pp. 148–149.
9. *Ibid.*, pp. 194–196.
10. State Board of Control, *California and the Oriental*, pp. 204–206. Sacramento, 1920.
11. *Ibid.*, p. 205. Also see Appendix for text.
12. *The Journal of San Diego History*, Vol. XXIII, No. 3, pp. 9–10.
13. Oregon, 2,501; Washington, 5,617.
14. Yamato Ichihashi, *op. cit.*, pp. 153–156.
15. Yakima Nihonjin Kai, *Yakima Heigen Nihonjin Shi* (History of the Japanese in the Yakima Valley) (Japan, 1935), p. 2.
16. *ICR*, Vol. 24, pp. 502–503.
17. *Ibid.*, pp. 521–527.

CHAPTER VI

1. Enclosure #1, Confidential Dispatch No. 22: San Francisco, September 27, 1892, from Chinda Sutemi, Consul at San Francisco, to Mutsu Munemitsu, Minister of Foreign Affairs.
2. ICR, Vol. 24, *passim*.
3. *Ibid.*, Vol. 23, pp. 45–46.
4. *Ibid.*, pp. 37–38.
5. *Ibid.*, p. 42.
6. *Sanchubu to Nihonjin*, p. 96. Salt Lake City, 1925.
7. *ICR*, Vol. 23, p. 54.
8. *Ibid.*, p. 518.
9. *ICR*, Vol. 22, p. 566.
10. *Ibid.*, p. 568.
11. *ICR*, Vol. 22, Chapter VII. The Immigration Commission judged the Japanese in Texas to be sufficiently unique to warrant a separate chapter in the report.
12. The name employed, Yamato, is the ancient name for Japan and is also used for the Japanese people, the Yamato race.
13. We are indebted to Professor T. Scott Miyakawa for information con-

cerning the separate experience of Japanese on the East Coast, who were spared some of the strains of racist prejudice which was the lot of Japanese on the West Coast and in lesser measure in the mountain states.

CHAPTER VII

1. Sociologists have made important contributions to our understanding of Japanese American and Chinese American society. Historians have given much less attention to these two important minorities. There is no satisfactory history of the Chinese in the United States, though fragments of the long story have been well told.
2. Gunther Barth, *Bitter Strength, A History of the Chinese in the United States 1850–1870.* (Harvard University Press, 1964). See pp. 9–31 for a description of the districts from which the Chinese came.
3. Stanford M. Lyman, *Chinese Americans,* pp. 37–46.
4. *Ibid.,* pp. 29–54. Here Lyman presents the various institutions which together made up the Chinese community organization.
5. Barth, *op. cit.,* pp. 195–209.
6. Lyman, *op. cit.,* pp. 119–191. See these pages for an excellent presentation of the changes and changing picture of the Chinese American community since World War II.
7. ICR, *I*, p. 674.
8. Bubonic plague appeared in Honolulu in December, 1899.
9. Yamato Ichihashi, *op. cit.,* p. 224.
10. *Ibid.,* p. 226.
11. Roger Daniels, *The Politics of Prejudice,* p. 26.
12. S. Frank Miyamoto, *Social Solidarity Among the Japanese in Seattle,* p. 118.
13. This statement must be qualified. In Hawaii some *kenjinkai* persist in a relatively healthy condition.

CHAPTER VIII

1. *Coast Seaman's Journal,* July 25, 1888.
2. Roger Daniels, *The Politics of Prejudice,* p. 19.
3. San Francisco *Bulletin,* May 4, 1892.
4. Consular Dispatch, Confidential No. 6, from Consul Chinda to Foreign Minister Aoki Shuzo.
5. *Ibid.*
6. Consular Dispatch, Confidential No. 14, dated May 10, 1892, from Consul Chinda to Minister of Foreign Affairs Enomoto Buyo.
7. Enclosures, Consular Dispatch, Official No. 36, dated July 29, 1893, from Consul Chinda to Vice-Foreign Minister Hayashi.
8. *Ibid.*

9. Dispatch Official, No. 4: Seattle, April 18, 1899, from Eleve-Consul Sometani Nariaki of the Seattle Branch of the Consulate of Japan in Tacoma to Vice-Foreign Affairs Minister Tsuzuki Kaoru.

10. *Ibid.*

11. Shiro Fujioka, *Ayumi no Ato.* The title of this study has been rendered in English as "The Path We Trod" and as "A Trail of Footprints."

12. *The Star*, Seattle, April 24, 1900. The writer was misinformed concerning Niigata which was an old port city on the Sea of Japan located in the old province of Echigo. When prefectures (*ken*) were created during the Meiji Period Niigata Ken, comprised in part of the former Echigo region, came into being. It was a populous district.

13. *The Star*, April 25, 1900.

14. The San Francisco *Chronicle*, May 8, 1900.

15. The San Francisco *Chronicle*, November 22, 1901. Enclosure No. 2 in Dispatch Official No. 136, November 23, 1901, from consul at San Francisco, Ueno Kisaburo, to Foreign Minister Komura Jutaro.

16. San Francisco *Chronicle*, May 8, 1905.

17. *The Politics of Prejudice*, p. 41. This study is the finest presentation of the anti-Japanese campaign in California down to 1924. First published as a University of California Press monograph in the Publications in History Series. It was reprinted in 1966 by Peter Smith, Gloucester, Massachusetts. Pagination above is from the reprint edition.

18. The Los Angeles *Times*, the leading newspaper in Southern California where there was little hostility to the Japanese at this time, responded to a declaration by Mayor Schmitz that he would if necessary lay down his life in battle with the Japanese by saying: "It is a notable fact that His Honor has never laid down anything of value. His promise, however, would almost reconcile anyone to a war with Japan."

19. 34 Stat. 898, c. 1134, par. 1.

20. *Political Science Quarterly, XXXVIII:* 1 (March, 1923), p. 71. Raymond Leslie Buell, "The Development of Anti-Japanese Agitation in the United States II."

CHAPTER IX

1. Dee Brown, *Bury My Heart at Wounded Knee.* A reading of the record of the treatment of the American Indian nations from the beginnings of colonization by Europeans is a painful experience.

2. This pattern held for the Chinese in the nineteenth century and for the Japanese into the twentieth century. In the case of these Orientals, they knew little and cared less about management-labor relations except as it applied to them personally as they sought accumulation as quickly as possible and an early return to China or Japan.

3. Maldwyn Allen Jones, *American Immigration*, pp. 258–259.

4. Madison Grant's influence on authors such as Kenneth Roberts and

Peter B. Kyne led to an extension of his influence to many whom he had not reached with his own publications.

5. Jones, *op. cit.*, p. 262.
6. Roger Daniels, *The Politics of Prejudice*, pp. 68–69.
7. *Ibid.*, p. 70.
8. Control of Japanese immigration had been established by executive agreement. Congress at this time, therefore, made an exception of Japanese immigration in new legislation.

CHAPTER X

1. Hilary Conroy, *The Japanese Frontier in Hawaii, 1868–1898*. This study published in the University of California Publications in History Series in 1953 remains as the best survey of Japanese labor immigration into Hawaii down to annexation. Professor Conroy has reproduced the Treaty of Friendship and Commerce between the kingdom of Hawaii and the Empire of Japan (1871) on pp. 146–147.
2. *Ibid.*, p. 54.
3. *Ibid.*, pp. 54–55.
4. *Ibid.*, p. 55.
5. *Ibid.*, pp. 61–62.
6. *Ibid.*, p. 85.
7. *Ibid.*, p. 86.
8. *Ibid.*, p. 88.
9. *Ibid.*, p. 113.
10. *Ibid.*
11. *Ibid.*, p. 119.
12. Ernest K. Wakukawa, *A History of the Japanese People in Hawaii* (Honolulu, Toyo Shain, 1938), pp. 125–126.
13. *Ibid.*, pp. 112–123.
14. United Japanese Society of Hawaii, *A History of Japanese in Hawaii*, (Honolulu, 1971), pp. 158–159.
15. Alex Ladenson, *The Japanese in Hawaii*, an unpublished doctoral dissertation in history, University of Chicago, 1936, p. 131.
16. Wakukawa, *op. cit.*, pp. 146–156.
17. *Bulletin of the Bureau of Labor, No. 94, May 1911* (Washington Government Printing Office, 1911), p. 744.
18. Wakukawa, *op. cit.*, p. 330.
19. *Ibid.*, p. 186.
20. *Ibid.*, pp. 187–188.
21. Ladenson, *op. cit.*, p. 142.
22. Wakukawa, *op. cit.*, pp. 259–260.
23. Farrington et al. v. T. Tokushige et al., II Fed. (2nd Series) 714.
24. Wakukawa, *op. cit.*, p. 300
25. *Ibid.*, pp. 357–359.

26. *Ibid.,* pp. 372–382.
27. John A. Rademaker, *These Are Americans, The Japanese Americans in Hawaii in World War II* (Palo Alto, 1951), p. 8.
28. Colleen Leahy Johnson, *The Japanese-American Family and Community in Honolulu: Generational Continuities in Ethnic Affiliation,* pp. 359–360. Unpublished doctoral dissertation, Syracuse University, 1972.

CHAPTER XI

1. William Petersen, *Japanese Americans, Oppression and Success.* Random House, 1971. In his concluding chapter, Petersen develops the idea of "subnation" and argues that Japanese Americans fit the various criteria in his definition.
   Harry H. L. Kitano, *Japanese Americans, The Evolution of a Subculture* (Prentice-Hall, 1969).
2. Edward K. Strong, Jr., *The Second-Generation Japanese Problem* (Stanford University Press, 1934), p. 199.
3. *Ibid.,* pp. 20–21.
4. Petersen, *op. cit.,* p. 225.
5. Dorothy Swaine Thomas, *The Salvage* (University of California Press, 1952), p. 19.
6. Yamato Ichihashi, *Japanese in the United States* (Stanford University Press, 1932), p. 350.
7. Kitano, *op. cit.,* pp. 130–131.
8. E. K. Wakukawa, *op. cit.,* pp. 401–404.
9. Bill Hosokawa, *Nisei* (William Morrow and Company, Inc., 1969), p. 201.

CHAPTER XII

1. *Final Report.* Japanese Evacuation from the West Coast, 1942. U.S. Government Printing Office. p. 28.
2. *Ibid.,* p. 26.
3. Washington *Post* and other newspapers, February 15, 1942.
4. Roger Daniels, *The Decision to Relocate the Japanese Americans* (J. B. Lippincott Co., 1975), p. 87.
5. Tolan Committee—Hearings before the Select Committee Investigation National Defense Migration, U.S. Government Printing Office, 1942.
6. Stetson Conn, *Guarding the United States and Its Outposts.* Japanese Evacuation from the West Coast, p. 126.
7. Tolan Report.
8. Daniels, *op. cit.,* p. 80.
9. Roger Daniels, *Concentration Camps USA: Japanese Americans and World War II* (Holt, Rinehart and Winston, Inc., 1971), p. 80.

10. Mike Masaoka had been national secretary and field executive of JACL from September 1, 1941, to June 22, 1943, when he was inducted into the U.S. Army. While training with the 442nd Regimental Combat Team at Camp Shelby, Mississippi, he wrote a 190-page "Final Report" reviewing the discussions of the special JACL meeting in 1942.

CHAPTER XIII

1. *Final Report, Japanese Evacuation from the West Coast, 1942.* U.S. Government Printing Office, pp. 25–26.
2. *The Relocation Program,* War Relocation Authority.
3. *Final Report,* p. 145.
4. Letter from Father Hugh T. Lavery to President Truman, as reported in *Pacific Citizen,* September 24, 1949.
5. *Final Report,* pp. 145–146.
6. *Ibid.,* p. 147.
7. *Ibid.,* p. 15.

CHAPTER XIV

1. Roger Daniels, *Concentration Camps USA: Japanese Americans and World War II* (New York: Holt, Rinehart and Winston, 1971), pp. 102–103.
2. War Relocation Authority, U.S. Department of the Interior, *WRA: A Story of Human Conservation.* p. 82.
3. *Ibid.,* p. 32.
4. Robert W. O'Brien, *The College Nisei* (Palo Alto, Pacific Books, 1949), p. 60 *et. seq.*
5. WRA, *op. cit.,* p. 132.
6. *Ibid.,* p. 85.
7. *Ibid.,* pp. 93–95.
8. *Ibid.,* pp. 46–47.
9. *Ibid.,* pp. 47–49. See also Alexander H. Leighton, *The Governing of Men* (Princeton, Princeton University Press, 1945), pp. 162–210.
10. WRA, *op. cit.,* pp. 49–51.
11. *Ibid.,* pp. 54–55.
12. *Ibid.,* pp. 53–59.
13. Roger Daniels, *op. cit.,* p. 114.
14. *Ibid.,* p. 115.
15. WRA, *op. cit.,* pp. 72–73.

CHAPTER XV

1. U.S. Army Western Defense Command, *Final Report: Japanese Evacuation from the West Coast,* pp. 32–33.

2. Dillon S. Myer, *Uprooted Americans, The Japanese Americans and the War Relocation Authority during World War II*, p. 245.
3. These were Nisei who had not been discharged by the Army. Many others had been released after December 7, 1941, but there appears to have been no general order to do so, thus leaving the question in the hands of individual commanders.
4. We have employed three works as principal resources for the history of the 100th Battalion from Hawaii and the 442nd Regimental Combat Team into which the 100th Battalion was ultimately integrated. In the order of their publication they are Orville C. Shirey, *Americans—The Story of the 442nd Combat Team*, published by the Infantry Journal Press, 1946; John A. Rademaker, *These Are Americans: The Japanese Americans in Hawaii in World War II* (Palo Alto, California, Pacific Books, 1951); and Thomas D. Murphy, *Ambassadors in Arms* (University of Hawaii Press, 1955). The latter work provided us with the most detailed and authoritative treatment.
5. Sidney F. Mashbir, Colonel, Ret., U.S.A., *I Was an American Spy* (Vantage Press, New York, 1953). In what is essentially a personal military history, Mashbir provides us with the record of the Allied Translator and Interpreter Section (ATIS) which was under his command in General MacArthur's headquarters.
6. *Ibid.*, p. 238.
7. *Ibid.*, p. 247.
8. *Ibid.*, p. 242.
9. Roger Daniels, *Concentration Camps USA: Japanese Americans and World War II*, p. 129.

CHAPTER XVI

1. Milton R. Konvitz, *The Alien and the Asiatic in American Law* (Cornell University Press, Ithaca, 1946), pp. 190–200.
2. Frank F. Chuman, *The Bamboo People* (Publishers Inc., 1976), pp. 67–71.
3. John K. Emmerson, *The Japanese Thread* (Holt, Rinehart and Winston, New York, 1978), pp. 125–126.
4. Chuman, *op. cit,* p. 185.
5. Interview with Hirabayashi in Salt Lake City, 1978.
6. Bill Hosokawa, *Nisei* (William Morrow and Company, Inc., 1969), pp. 312–313.
7. Chuman, *op. cit.*, pp. 189–197.
8. Hosokawa, *op. cit.*, pp. 427–431.
9. Minutes, Ninth Biennial Convention, JACL, Denver, Colorado, February 28–March 4, 1946.

CHAPTER XVII

1. Bill Hosokawa, *Nisei* (William Morrow and Company, Inc., 1969), pp. 447–448.
2. Frank Chuman, *Bamboo People* (Publisher's Inc., 1976), pp. 203–204.
3. Minutes, Tenth Biennial National JACL Convention, September 4–8, 1948. Appendix, pp. 33–34. Hereafter cited as Minutes, 1948.
4. Minutes, 1948, p. 21.
5. *Ibid.*, pp. 30–31.
6. *Nisei*, p. 446.
7. Minutes, 1948, pp. 23–24.
8. *Nisei*, pp. 451–454.
9. Taped interview with Harry Takagi, 1978.
10. *The Bamboo People*, 218–221.
11. *Nisei*, p. 449.
12. *The Bamboo People*, pp. 221–223.

CHAPTER XVIII

1. Darrel Montero, *The Japanese American Community: A Study of Generational Changes in Ethnic Affiliation*, p. 13.
2. *The Memoirs of Chief Justice Earl Warren* (Doubleday, 1977), p. 149.
3. Resolution distributed to JACL chapter presidents and national JACL Board by Dr. David Miura, August 12, 1969.
4. Memo from Raymond Uno to Masao Satow, September 3, 1969.
5. S. I. Hayakawa, *Through the Communications Barrier* (Harper and Row, 1979), pp. 139–141.
6. *Iva Toguri: Victim of a Legend*. Japanese American Citizens League, 1975.
7. Montero, *op. cit.*
8. Thomas Sowell, *Commentary* magazine published by the American Jewish Committee, 1979.
9. *Identity Crisis of the Sansei and the Concentration Camp*, a research paper by Nobu Miyoshi, p. 32.
10. *Ibid.*, p. 6.

✿ A Note on Sources

The Imperial Statistical Annals of Japan (Nihon Teikoku Tokei Nenkan) have long been available in the United States. To the resources we have recently added the entire diplomatic and consular records of Japan to 1924 on Japanese immigration into the United States. The Foreign Ministry of Japan graciously permitted the microfilming of this collection, only small fragments of which had previously appeared in print.

This very large collection is composed of ninety-five reels of microfilm, each reel containing about one thousand frames and many frames containing two pages of material. This resource, available for the use of scholars in the UCLA Research Library, also provides much useful material for those who do not read Japanese. Diplomatic and consular officials kept the authorities in Japan informed of the situation in the United States by including in their dispatches copies of U.S. Government pronouncements and Congressional actions and by a continuous clipping service from primarily West Coast newspapers.

In view of the loss and abandonment of historical records at the time of the Relocation, the collection and preservation of what remained have been an important role of the Japanese American Research Project at UCLA. A substantial collection of personal records, newspapers, etc., has been accumulated. Nevertheless, the employment of the Japanese American community as human documents was considered imperative. A three-generational sociological survey was undertaken, employing a random sample of the Issei, their children and grandchildren. The findings of this study have, in part, been published. The raw data are available in interview schedules filed in the Special Collections Section of the UCLA Research where the anonymity of those interviewed has been preserved by the use of numbers rather than names.

The volume of material published about the Japanese Evacuation and Relocation exceeds that published for the rest of the slightly more than a century of the Japanese American story. The data accumulated by the War Relocation Authority on the evacuees have been preserved on magnetic tape and are available at both the Berkeley and Los Angeles campuses of the University of California.

Very special mention should be made of *Years of Infamy*, Michi Weglyn's landmark book, which was of such great value to the authors in connection with almost every reference to the evacuation and internment of 110,000 Japanese Americans. Many of the other published works regarded as useful by the authors appear in the footnotes to this study. The full bibliography has grown to very lengthy proportions.

ꙮ Index